About the Author

Don S. Browning was born in Trenton, Missouri. He received his A.B. from Central Methodist College in Fayette, Missouri, and his B.D., M.A., and Ph.D. from the Divinity School of the University of Chicago. In 1969/70 he was the recipient of a fellowship from the Association of Theological Schools for a special research year in Paris, France. In 1975/76 he was awarded a Guggenheim Fellowship for a year of study at Oxford, England, where *Pluralism and Personality* was completed. Dr. Browning is the author of over thirty articles that have appeared in scholarly publications and of three other books: *Atonement and Psychotherapy, Generative Man,* and *The Moral Context of Pastoral Care. Generative Man* was a finalist for the National Book Award in the area of philosophy and religion in 1974. Dr. Browning is professor of religion and psychological studies at the Divinity School of the University of Chicago. Since 1977 he has been Dean of the Disciples Divinity House of the University of Chicago. Dr. Browning is an associate editor of *Zygon,* a journal on religion and science, and serves on the editorial committees of *The Journal of Religion, Pastoral Psychology,* and *The Journal of Pastoral Care.*

Pluralism and Personality

Also by DON S. BROWNING:

Atonement and Psychotherapy
Generative Man
The Moral Context of Pastoral Care

Pluralism and Personality

William James
and Some Contemporary Cultures
of Psychology

Don S. Browning

Lewisburg
Bucknell University Press
London and Toronto: Associated University Presses

LIBRARY
McCORMICK THEOLOGICAL SEMINARY
1100 EAST 55th STREET
CHICAGO, ILLINOIS 60615

Associated University Presses, Inc.
Cranbury, New Jersey 08512

Associated University Presses Ltd.
69 Fleet Street
London EC4Y 1EU, England

Associated University Presses
Toronto, Ontario, Canada M5E 1A7

Printed in the United States of America

Library of Congress Cataloging in Publication Data

Browning, Don S
Pluralism and personality.

Bibliography: p.
Includes index.
1. Psychology—Philosophy.   2. James, William,
1842-1010.   3. Pluralism (Social sciences)
4. Personality and culture.   I. Title.
BF38.B73   150.19   78-75196
ISBN 0-8387-2265-2

To Jerald Brauer *and* Joseph Kitagawa, *my deans at the Divinity School of the University of Chicago*

Contents

7

Contents

List of Abbreviations

PP William James, *Principles of Psychology,* 2 vols. (New York: Dover Publications, 1950).

WB *The Will to Believe and Other Essays in Popular Philosophy and Human Immortality* (New York: Dover Publications, 1956).

TTP *Talks to Teachers on Psychology and to Students on Some of Life's Ideals* (New York: Dover Publications, 1962).

VRE William James, *The Varieties of Religious Experience* (New York: Mentor Books, 1958).

P William James, *Pragmatism* (New York: Meridian Books, 1955).

ERE and *PU* William James, *Radical Empiricism and A Pluralistic Universe* (New York: E.P. Dutton & Co., 1971).

MT William James, *The Meaning of Truth* (Ann Arbor: University of Michigan Press, 1970).

MEW and *SSP* William James, *The Moral Equivalent of War and Other Essays* and *Selections from Some Problems in Philosophy,* ed. John K. Roth (New York: Harper and Row, 1971).

MS William James, *Memories and Studies,* ed. Henry James (New York: Longmans, Green and Co., 1911).

CER William James, *Collected Essays and Reviews,* ed. R.B. Perry (New York: Longmans, Green and Co., 1911).

LWJ William James, *The Letters of William James,* 2 vols., ed. Henry James (Boston: Atlantic Monthly Press, 1920).

TCWJ Ralph Barton Perry, *The Thought and Character of William James,* 2 vols. (Boston: Little, Brown, and Co., 1935).

WJ Gay Wilson Allen, *William James* (New York: Viking Press, 1967).

Preface

In the recent past, widespread concern has appeared about what some commentators have called "the new narcissism." This phrase refers to a new attitude which may be emerging among people in Western societies. It refers to a tendency on the part of many people to meet the tensions, conflicts, and transitions of modern life by turning inward, becoming preoccupied with one's own internal well-being, and searching for ways to avoid or transcend the shocks of living in a pluralistic and changing technological society. William James, the founder of academic psychology in the United States, sensed most of the main characteristics of modern life. Yet he developed a view of life and a psychology to support it which avoided the cul-de-sacs down which modern psychology has gone since his death. Although he was interested in self-knowledge and insight as is psychoanalysis, the control of human behavior as is contemporary behaviorism, and self-actualization as is the human potential movement, his final view of human nature and fulfilment was considerably different from any of these major contemporary options. His normative image of the good life is captured by the phrase "the strenuous mood." It celebrated the virtues of an ethical view of life nurtured by religious and mystical sensibilities. It was a view of life vastly different from the "new narcissism" which may be descending upon us. Although both psychologically and philosophically incomplete, its scope was so broad and its balance so unique that it is worth a second look before we irreversibly commit ourselves to one of the more glamorous contemporary options about the nature of the good life in the context of modernity.

Acknowledgments

I would like to acknowledge with deep appreciation the grant I received from the John Simon Guggenheim Foundation for the year 1975–76, the period during which I wrote the major portion of this book. This made it possible for me to locate myself at Oxford, England, for the year as a Fellow of the Senior Commons Room of Mansfield College. I would also like to thank the Divinity School of the University of Chicago for assistance and a leave of absence during this period. I gratefully thank the following for permission to include quotations: Dover Publications for those from William James, *Principles of Psychology,* volumes 1 and 2, 1950, and William James, *The Will to Believe,* 1956; E. P. Dutton and Co., William James, *Essays in Radical Empiricism,* 1971. Finally, I want to express my deep gratitude to two deans who have generously supported and encouraged my work throughout my tenure as a member of the faculty of the Divinity School of the University of Chicago. Without the friendship and good will of Dean Jerald Brauer and Dean Joseph Kitagawa, this effort, as well as many others, would have gone uncompleted.

Chicago
Spring, 1979

Pluralism and Personality

1

Pluralism, Change, and the Strenuous Life

What is the nature of human beings? More than any other question that people ask, this is the most important. The answer which they accept dictates their final view of themselves—of who they are and what they are capable of doing. Like radar guiding a ship through the fog, a community's understanding of human nature gives it a sense of direction and a belief that its journey is safe and meaningful.

All societies have held up normative images for their citizens to emulate. This is equally true for advanced industrial countries in the Western world. But in these societies the situation becomes vastly more complex. There is no single image of the good man or woman that society dangles before us. It spreads before our eyes a veritable banquet of images and models. As frequently happens at a feast, we try to sample everything. But then sometimes our mental and spiritual digestion turns sour from the rich mixture of incompatible elements

In advanced, highly complex societies, it is difficult to find a meaningful scale of values by which to live. This is due to the great plethora of patterns held out for us to emulate. As modern societies grow more complex, various subgroups become more autonomous from any single dominating system of symbols which might define who they are.[1] In such societies, it is difficult for individuals to select the images and symbols which should be uppermost in their lives.

The question of the nature of man is so large, so all-encompassing that it is difficult to answer. In simpler societies, religious myths give the answer. But in sophisticated societies, many sources compete to provide an answer. "Official" religion, popular culture, political ideologies, and the cultural and scientific disciplines are some of the more prominent.

In the twentieth century, the disciplines of psychology—both academic and clinical—have had increasing influence on our images of the human. Man "the machine," man "the maker," and man "the pleasure seeker" were highly influential images put forth by popular interpretations of early behaviorism, functionalism, and psychoanalysis. More recently, a great bevy of new words and phrases has been concocted to represent the distinctively human. "Dionysian man," "productive man," "generative man," "radical man," or man "the decision maker," "information processor," or "responder" have all been advocated vigorously in recent years.

Modern psychology has avoided explicit consideration of general questions about the nature of man. Progress in science is thought to come by asking small, easily controllable questions and pushing for limited but definitive answers. Nonetheless, both by accident and by necessity, the psychological disciplines hold before the wider society more or less global images about human beings which are both descriptive and normative. By *descriptive* and *normative,* I mean that these images hold implications for both what humans *are* and for what they *should become.*

Psychology as Culture

In other words, psychology can become culture. Even those psychologies which present themselves as objective and scientific can become culture. Cautious scientific psychologists can, in ways that they do not perceive, gradually elevate their objective findings into more general statements which often have clear and even shocking cultural implications. Scientific findings seldom remain as simply cold, neutral, and impersonal facts. They get interpreted. Someone, maybe the scientist himself or herself, may attempt to tell us what they mean. When this happens, scientific findings can become culture and cautiously stated scientific propositions can easily become inflated and take on wider meanings. If psychologists themselves do not create culture out of their findings—and some do not—the wider public may. Some psychological data and theories are so stimulating to the human imagination that the general population reworks them and assigns them a broader meaning.

Of course, some psychologies have very little that is scientific in them at all. They consist of observations unsystematically if not casually collected and theories which are unproven and fit only loosely the data they are thought to explain. Such psychological theories are culture through and through; they are intuitively created alternative approaches to life. Just because they are bad science, however, does not mean they are bad culture. Some poorly validated psychological perspectives have made timely and profound contributions to the broader cultural scene. By the same token, magnificently validated psychological principles can have unhealthy cultural implications if wrongly interpreted by either the psychologist who developed them or the wider public.

But what is culture and what, more precisely, is meant when I say that psychology can become culture? Culture is a system of symbols and norms that defines and guides a society and the individuals within it. These symbols hold forth diffuse but generally recognizable maps and patterns. These maps convey a society's goals, purposes, or projects and some of the preferred means or strategies for accomplishing these ends. These symbols convey a general interpretation of life. They tell us the meaning of life, point to the good, suggest why life goes wrong, and depict the final destinies which life holds forth. When culture takes on the characteristics of ultimate seriousness, when certain symbols become objects of ultimate concern, then culture takes on the features of religion. Culture can become religion in two ways. People can claim for their preferred symbols the backing of supernatural powers, and can, in this way, claim explicit ultimacy for them. Or people can, through their attitudes, take their symbols with final and ultimate seriousness, and put all their faith in them. Either way, culture becomes religion. Of course, not all culture has the seriousness of religion, but some does.

The sources of culture are multiple: official religion, formal philosophies, art, and popular movements in music, journalism, and literature. But the sciences, especially the social sciences, are also prominent sources of culture. This book is primarily about one aspect of modern psychology, namely clinical or psychotherapeutic psychology. It will deal with the implicit cultural horizons or fringes of these disciplines, especially those parts which deal with their understanding of the nature of humans and the nature of modern society. Global images about the nature of man and modern society are often not explicit in particular psychologies but they are often implicit—a matter of the fringe or horizon of meaning that surrounds the psychology.

In addition to the psychology of James, we will review four contemporary cultures of psychology. I call them the culture of detachment, the culture of joy, the culture of control, and the culture of care. The culture of detachment is strongly associated with Freud and orthodox psychoanalysis. The culture of joy is best exemplified by humanistic psychology. The culture of control can be illustrated with the psychology of B. F. Skinner. And the culture of care can be found in the writings of a variety of psychologists; for our purposes, we will turn to the thought of Erik Erikson, Erich Fromm, and Rollo May.

Normality and Utopia

It is among the clinical or psychotherapeutic disciplines that psychology gives birth to its most important general images of human nature. To help someone overcome a neurosis, depression, work disability, or marital problem, the working psychiatrist, psychologist, or social worker must have some standard for measuring what is normal or healthy living.

It should be quite simple to define the meaning of normality or health. But experience has shown otherwise. The definition of the normal or healthy is one of the gravest problems facing psychology today. Because it is a problem for psychology, it is also a problem for the wider society. The definition of these terms is a general cultural problem in which both society and the psychological disciplines participate. The clinical psychological disciplines are in a privileged cultural position. Society has been highly responsive to their pronouncements about the nature of the "normal," the "healthy," and even the "good" in human behavior. Philip Rieff, Paul Halmos, Robert White, and Brewster Smith are just a few of the more eloquent commentators who have written about the cultural influence of the psychotherapeutic psychologies on our normative images of man.[2] Robert White has expressed it well when he writes,

> There is no escaping the conclusion that the mental health professions have been deeply involved in the value business. We have steadily, forcefully communicated to our clients our conceptions of how to live, and we have played a part in a contemporary change of values that is called a revolution. . . . Freud did not achieve his monumental position in contemporary culture because he invented a new way of treating neurosis. He is there because he symbolized, and almost certainly helped to produce, a value revolution—an ideal of a better way to live.[3]

Of course, Freud is not the only psychologist whom White could have mentioned as having enormous cultural influence on our images of human nature. Jung, Rogers, Maslow, Erikson, Skinner are just a few who have gained considerable professional influence as well as public visibility.

In this book, I want to nominate another psychologist whose vision of man is worthy of serious consideration by both professional psychology and the wider society. Known to almost every literate person as the popularizer of philosophical pragmatism, the founder of academic psychology in the United States, and the author of a great book entitled *The Varieties of Religious Experience,* William James and what he stood for still has a very vague profile even among the so-called educated classes. Yet he has a great deal to tell us about many subjects— *especially about the kinds of people we must be to live in a modern society.* We can characterize James's contribution to this issue more clearly if we review some current categories applied to the question of health and normality.

Daniel Offer and Melvin Sabshin have identified four distinct styles in psychological literature defining health or narmality. There is normality as "absence of disease," normality as "utopia," normality as "average," and normality as "transactional systems."[4] Normality as absence of disease is that traditional medical-psychiatric approach which assumes that behavior is within normal limits "when no manifest pathology is present."[5] Normality as average is a research measure used to standardize psychological tests and refers to that great statistical "middle range" of behaviors, attitudes, and emotional responses which one would find in a particular population.[6]

But these two necessary though overused measures for determining normality are not my primary interests. Such measures by themselves can never provide a civilization with the images of human nature which it needs to give its members a positive sense of direction. Rather, it is normality as utopia and normality as transactional systems which require more immediate attention. William James had an image of man that brought together both of these approaches, and his legacy is uncannily relevant during this last quarter of the twentieth century.

Normality as utopia refers to the truth that many psychologies hold images of normality which are acutally ideal goals about what men and women *should be like* but may never actually attain.[7] Offer and Sabshin believe that both psychoanalysis and most humanistic psychologies project these kinds of understandings. The psychoanalytic image of the completely "psychoanalyzed person," Maslow's understanding of "self-actualization," Rogers's ideal of the "fully functioning person" are all excellent examples of this way of thinking.

Normality as "transactional systems" is an increasingly fashionable way of looking at normal human functioning. It is associated with a systems-theory approach to the behavioral sciences. It believes that what is normal and healthy is relative to the specific contexts and particular points in time with which individuals and groups are trying to cope and adapt.[8] What is normal and adaptive for a primitive caveman, a twelfth-century European peasant, a pioneer on the American frontier, or a twentieth-century suburban teenager from Chicago will be considerably different. Or even within a single society such as the United States, what is normal and adaptive for an upper-middle-class executive, a farmer's wife from the Midwest, or a black man from the inner-city slum may entail highly significant differences. This view of normality is influenced strongly by evolutionary theory which sees all systems, including human systems, as changing and adapting over time. Although this point of view is not antithetical to a utopian view of normality, clearly no single image of the ideal man or woman can serve all of the various adaptive needs for the great variety of human communities at different times and places. William James could have agreed with this point of view. He had a great appreciation for the rich diversity of ecological niches with which human beings must deal in their efforts to survive and flourish. Yet he was also willing to talk about a general image of man that must guide us in a modern environment which is becoming increasingly more pluralistic and rapidly changing.

We can grasp the contemporary importance of James if we ponder some recent words penned by the highly respected social psychologist, Brewster Smith. In his *Humanizing Social Psychology,* Smith advances the startling thesis that psychologists cannot define mental health or normality—at least not by themselves. Defining mental health is more appropriately a task for the political scientist, the ethicist, or maybe even the theologian—someone trained in the methods of normative thinking. Smith acknowledges the usefulness of utopian thinking about normality; but he also values the transactional systems approach. Psychologists, he believes, can help us determine how to develop the kind of people society needs. But the psychologist *qua* scientist cannot dictate what utopian images a civilization should aspire for in the first place.[9]

Having said these things, Smith now removes his hat as a scientific social psychologist and dons the hat of a social philosopher and ethicist. This is a switch in professional identity that William James frequently, quite self-consciously made when the questions he pursued demanded it. However, few academicians are willing to try it today—at least not directly, consciously, and publicly. As a social philosopher, Smith surveys the broad trends developing in the environments of all modern civilizations. He concludes that ever-accelerating social and cultural change will mark everyone's environment in the world of the future, no matter where their particular social niche is located. In the future, Smith predicts we will need people who can become socially and politically responsible for the direction and control of these changes. He writes, "In the current fast-moving and changing social and cultural world, . . . how can individuals organized in society gain control over the stresses?"[10] In other words, what kind of human being can accomplish this control and help direct society in a responsible fashion? This, of course, is a utopian vision but one arrived at, in part, from a systems analysis of the kind of environment people will inhabit in the future.

Smith is suggesting that the very ideas of health and normality are too narrow to provide the positive images of humans needed both by society and the behavioral sciences. But the eminent Harvard professor of psychology, Robert White, goes even further. Although the polarity of health and illness are adequate to cover some mental difficulties such as brain damage and biochemically caused schizophrenia, on the whole it is inadequate, he believes, as a guide for both psychotherapy and the general task of living. Nor is it satisfactory to go in the direction of Marie Jahoda in her highly influential attempt to extend the metaphor of health into the idea of "positive mental health."[11] Such a procedure only results in adding one value-laden characteristic next to another until we come up with an abstract image of the well-rounded person. White makes his point with arresting simplicity when he writes,

> But the picture that resulted of the ideally healthy person always struck me as being the portrait of a lightweight. This character appeared to me incapable of sacrifice—that would mean he was depressed. He appeared incapable of worrying about world problems—that would mean he was neurotic. He seemed to be denied inner life, privacy, imagination—that would signify schizophrenia. So the personal values that were first advocated under the banner of mental health seemed to me better suited to a Caribbean vacation than the serious aspects of living.[12]

Modernity and the Strenuous Life

Although this issue can be viewed from the perspective of the behavioral sciences, it goes far beyond the professional concerns of these disciplines. These disciplines have implicitly influenced our general image of human nature and have done so since the turn of the century. But the issue is explicitly an ethical, cultural, and civilizational one. What kind of human beings do we need and want? How do we go about determining our ideal images? How do we keep our ideals from becoming dictatorial, overdemanding, unrealistic, and oppressive? And finally, how does psychology relate to this task of clarifying our positive images of the human? Is it psychology's task to develop these images or must it collaborate with other cultural disciplines?

William James had a style of thinking and a general vision which was relevant to these questions. Five years after the publication of his great *Principles of Psychology,* when he was still basking in the glory of having written the greatest introduction to the subject which had ever appeared, he set down these words on the subject of health.

> Now, health is a term of subjective appreciation, not of objective description, . . . it is a teleological term. There is no purely objective standard of sound health. Any peculiarity that is of use to a man is a point of soundness in him, and what makes a man sound for one function may make him unsound for another. Moreover, we are all instruments for social use; and if sensibilities, obsessions, and other psychopathic peculiarities can so combine with the rest of our constitution as to make us the more useful to our kind, why then we should not call them in that context points of unhealthiness, but rather the reverse.[13]

It may be shocking to hear James, the reputed great apostle of individual freedom and creativity, say flatly that "we are all instruments for social use" and that neurotic disturbances should be tolerated if they prove "useful to our kind." Furthermore, this concern with the social whole is a clue to the meaning of his idea of health as a term of "subjective appreciation." It is not something which each human being can determine for himself on the basis of arbitrary tastes and preferences. Instead, "health" is a term which takes on meaning only when placed in the context of broader concepts about the meaning of the good in ethical terms.

It is possible to read James in light of a central theme which pervades his psychology, philosophy, ethics, informal essays, and letters. This was his concern to develop an image of the kind of human needed to live in the modern world. This optimal image of the human James called the "strenuous life" or the "strenuous mood." The idea of life as strenuous will doubtless grate on the ears of a generation nourished by utopian images of free-flowing self-actualization, unconflicted Dionysian release, or smoothly engineered humans who live in efficiently reinforced environments. But these harsh sounds are mitigated when we realize that James saw his image of the strenuous life as the upper level of an ideal whose lower depths entailed an almost romantic appreciation for the passional and instinctual foundations of human life. Furthermore, although the idea of the strenuous life conveyed distinctively ethical and self-sacrificial overtones, James had a nearly equal appreciation for the mystical and passional depths of life. The person living in the strenuous mood was for James an individual who was simultaneously mystical, ethical, and heroic. But what is such a person like and why might such an individual be particularly adapted for modern life?

As soon as one asserts that James had a normative image of the human, it must be added that he was the greatest of the twentieth-century pluralists. He was the last person to believe that a single rigid image of a man could suffice for all people, with all their different temperaments, living in all the greatly varying environments which this world displays. Against the commonly held assumption that "there can be one intrisically ideal type of human character," James asserted that "ideals are matters of relation."[14]

"Ideality in conduct," he once wrote, "is altogether a matter of adaptation."[15] Nonetheless, James did discern some generic traits more or less present in all environments, and these common features constituted broad trends calling forth the adaptive patterns he associated with the strenuous mood. This is why the idea of "mood" is so compatible with James' way of thinking. A great variety of different types of people with varying styles of life occupying dissimilar environments can still have in common a strenuous mood in dealing with the vicissitudes of life.

James saw pluralism and change as common features of all

environments. All environments are composed of relatively independent and conflicting centers of energy. In addition, all environments undergo constant change as do the individuals within these environments.

All of this is highly relevant to an understanding of modern societies. James never fully applied his metaphysics of pluralism and change to the dynamics of highly advanced technological societies. Yet he was more than dimly aware that modern societies were an extreme, and possibly lethal, manifestation of the general pluralism and change which run through every level of reality. But at the level of modern societies, it was clear to James that only the person capable of the strenuous life could deal with the dynamisms which they unleash. He was fully aware of the great increase of technological advancement that the twentieth century was witnessing. He once observed that the rate of technological increase "accelerates so that no one can trace the limit."[16] But lest we think that James was overjoyed by this relentless increase in technologically induced change, we should note his deep concern when he wrote,

> One may even fear that the being of man may be crushed by his own powers, that his fixed nature as an organism may not prove adequate to stand the strain of the ever increasingly tremendous functions, almost divine creative functions, which his intellect will more and more enable him to wield. He may drown in his wealth like a child in a bath-tub, who has turned on the water and who can not turn it off.[17]

James was aware, in his own way, of what we now call "future shock"—the disintegrating effects to our spiritual and psychological integrity of living in a world of endless and unpredictable change.[18] But it was this understanding of the modern world that led James to emphasize both an ethical and a mystical response to life. The ethical response makes it possible to control with some sense of responsibility the multifarious changes which beset human beings in modern societies. The mystical response makes it possible to gain some detachment from these changes, find some transcendent ground upon which to base one's security, and open the self to a deeper sense of oneness with both humanity and the wider cosmos. In the end, the ethical was for James the measure of the mystical, but he was prophetic in his vision that they need not be in contradiction.

James Reconsidered

An enormous amount of scholarly activity has been exerted during the last fifteen years in reevaluating William James. As a consequence, several new dimensions have been added to our understanding of him. We have known him always as the father of academic psychology in the United States, the co-founder, along with Charles Peirce, of pragmatism, and the propagator of a philosophical attitude called "radical empiricism." But he was much more. His massive two-volume *Principles of Psychology* was one of the most important treatises in philosophical psychology ever written. Both his psychology and his philosophy take on increased significance when read in the light of one another, something that interpreters have done with care only recently. His remarkable introspective descriptions in his *Principles* we now know had a profound influence on Edmund Husserl, the founder of European phenomenology, and through him on the entire existential-phenomenological movement that includes such giants as Martin Heidegger, Jean-Paul Sartre, and Maurice Merleau-Ponty. He was one of the early great protectors and stimulators of research into "psychic phenomenon"—that illusive but promising study of such things as mediumship, mental telepathy, and clairvoyance. With the publication of his correspondence and several important biographical studies, he is now being assessed as one of the great human beings in American history.[19] He projected such warmth, charm, and wit in both his professional writings and his personal correspondence that it is widely agreed there were few equals and probably no superiors in his capacity to convey a deep humanity and broad sympathy to almost everyone who knew him.

As one of the early originators of pragmatism, James's influence was so pervasive that it is almost immeasurable. When James's pragmatism was supplemented by that of John

Dewey, this style of philosophy and psychology was considered as prototypical of the America intellectual spirit. In spite of this general influence, James today has only a small number of followers in the usual sense of that word. There are few philosophers who follow James as some do Husserl, Wittgenstein, A. J. Ayer, or Heidegger. In the field of psychology there are no Jamesians as there are Freudians, Jungians, Rogerians, or Skinnerians. It is not the point of this book to make Jamesians out of anyone, but it is my goal to suggest we have a great deal to learn from James, especially on the subject of the optimal image of man in the context of modern life—a theme that was pervasive throughout his writings.

In spite of the fact that there are no easily identifiable Jamesian psychologists and philosophers, important new studies reevaluating James have emerged recently from both of these disciplines. The seventy-fifth anniversary of the American Psychological Association was celebrated by a symposium published under the title of *William James: Unfinished Business.*[20] The preface of the book makes the remarkable claim that his two-volume *Principles of Psychology* "is without question the most literate, the most provocative, and at the same time the most intelligible book on psychology that has ever appeared in English or in any other language."[21] Among other topics, James's contribution to existential phenomenology is touched on in his symposium. Robert MacLeod makes the bold assertion "that Heidegger and Sartre have made no significant contributions to the understanding of human experience that were not anticipated by James."[22]

Alfred Schutz, Aron Gurwitsch, and Herbert Spiegelberg were among the first to call attention to the phenomenological themes in James's psychology.[23] Since then several first-rate book-length studies have appeared, by Linschoten,[24] Wild,[25] Wilshire,[26] and Stevens.[27] All of these have investigated various phenomenological themes in James. In addition, a large number of important shorter studies has appeared, by James, Edie, Ash Gobar, and Andrew Reck.[28]

These studies demonstrate that James had a healthy respect for the role of description as a fundamental first step in the study of the human mind. This simple truth is the basic theme of all phenomenological philosophers and psychologists. According to them, to study the human mind one should first study human consciousness. The first step in studying human consciousness is to describe it, or more specifically, to describe the various objects which appear to consciousness. Phenomenologists believe that consciousness is always "conscious of" something. To study consciousness means to study the various modes of appearance of these objects in consciousness. This is also true if one is studying such phenomena as emotions, will, motivation, needs, or attention. The first task for the phenomenologist is to make a highly disciplined description of the phenomenon just as it appears, and only as it appears, in consciousness.

There is ample evidence that James gave description this kind of first step priority—most of the time. His understanding of the stream of consciousness, his groundbreaking descriptions of the self, his view of attention and will were all based primarily upon fundamental descriptions of a phenomenological kind. But James was full of what Gordon Allport called "productive paradoxes."[29] One of these was James's simultaneous appreciation for both descriptive and explanatory approaches to psychology. Yet description and explanation are different things. Description seeks to understand with a minimum of preconceptions the basic "meanings" of consciousness; explanation searches after the causes behind a phenomenon of consciousness.

The heart of James's creativity was his attempt to hold together a descriptive *and* an explanatory approach to the study of human nature. He unwittingly synthesized a vision of psychology as a natural science with a phenomenological psychology of the kind suggested by Husserl, Heidegger, Sartre, Merleau-Ponty, Medard Boss, and Rollo May. James's scientific and explanatory psychology was built around a so-called functionalist view of mind—a view of mind which sees it basically in the service of the body's efforts to adapt to the surrounding environment. Yet in his psychology, James brought together the best aspects of both a functional and a phenomenological psychology. Rather than charge him with inconsistency, one should agree with Hans Linschoten that "we ought to consider whether this inner conflict is not at the root of the fruitfulness of James' psychological thought."[30] James could never decide which of these points of view should dominate his formal psychological writings. Of course, as a philosopher and ethicist, James was clear that the world of meanings (which only description can discern) is prior to the scientific search for casual determinants of our lives. But he held firmly to the idea that our understanding of both of these levels should be extended. During a period of deep depression in his early manhood, he expressed this conviction with almost poetic force when he wrote,

> I'm swamped in an empirical philosophy. I feel that we are Nature through and through, and that we are wholly conditioned, that not a wiggle of our will happens save as the result of physical laws; and yet, not withstanding, we are *en rapport* with reason. — How to conceive it? Who knows? . . . It is not that we are all nature *but* some point which is reason, but that all is nature *and* all is reason too. We shall see, damn it, we shall see![31]

Here we can see the exciting and fruitful possibilities of James's approach to the study of man. The brilliant phenomenological studies of Husserl, Heidegger, and Sartre make hardly any systematic contact with the world of scientific explanation. There is little effort in their phenomenological psychologies to make use of scientific explanations of the natural regularities of human life. Merleau-Ponty and Paul Ricoeur are phenomenologists who are exceptions to this rule, but even here they have little of the professional grasp of the total field of psychology that James possessed. James may be more of a paradigm than one might first think of a fully rounded and multifaceted approach to the study of human beings.

Romanticism and Asceticism

Gordon Allport once said that William James "wanted psychologists to confront the fundamental moral fact that by their own theories of human nature they have the power of elevating or degrading this same human nature. Debasing assumptions debase the mind; generous assumptions exalt the mind."[32] Much of James's career was an attempt to counteract the debasing assumptions about human nature associated with certain forms of the Enlightenment and certain expressions of Puritan Calvinism. But James was an innovator, not a revolutionary. He transmuted but did not totally reject these traditions. He accepted the Enlightenment respect for science but rejected its mechanical view of man. He affirmed the ethical seriousness of his Calvinistic heritage, but rejected its oppressive moralism.

His vision of the strenuous life shares with Puritan inner-worldly asceticism an accent on the active, committed life which pursues a socially meaningful vocation. He once spoke of himself in the French language, which he commanded so well, as "the most Protestant of Protestants" *(le plus protestant des protestants).*[33] But James's moralism is built on top of what William Clebsch has called his "aesthetic spirituality."[34] In addition, James's moral seriousness was based on a nonrepressive and almost romantic appreciation for the "passional" dimensions of man. And finally, it assumes a view of God vastly different from the austere Puritan God of total sovereignity and arbitrary divine election. James's view of the strenuous life combined with his theory of the will to produce a uniquely melioristic understanding of history which believed an individual could combine his efforts with his fellowman and God to make a difference in the direction and quality of human life.

James was equally in tension with various forms of Enlightenment rationalism. Whether it was the mechanistic images of Descartes or Newton; the atomistic empiricism and associationism of Berkeley, Hume, or Herbart; the social Darwinism and environmental determinism of Spencer and Fiske; or the ubiquitous monistic rationalism of Hegel, Royce, Green, and MacTaggart, James opposed them with a new emphasis upon the agency, spontaneity, and subjectivity of the inner person. He also developed a fresh understanding of the dynamic and transactional character of thought. As David Marcell has argued, this permitted James to make some decisive contributions to the newly developing revolt against formalism which was being led by such men as Charles Pierce, Chauncey Wright, Oliver Wendell Holmes, Charles Beard, and John Dewey. These men argued that the "arbitrary, abstract, *a priori,* and artificially mechanistic" categories of the nineteenth century could no longer be adequate to control and guide the chaos of forces and dynamisms of the modern world.[35] Deeply disturbed by the dislocations in American society brought about by industrialization and urbanization and the unchecked power of party bosses and cliques of wealthy men, James and other antiformalists "looked to different areas of scholarship to support what were *essentially democratic* modifications of American education, law, the laissez-fair political economy, and the practices of politics."[36]

James believed in the possibility, but not the inevitability of progress. Inspired by the evolutionary theories of Darwin, he interpreted them in a vastly different way than did the great protagonists of social Darwinism such as Herbert Spencer, John Fiske, and Graham Sumner. For them, progress was the inevitable unfolding of the evolutionary process itself and would come about as an automatic consequence, if left alone, of the processes of natural selection.[37] Such formalist visions of progress left no place for the "human will as an agent of historical improvement."[38] And on the other side, James was equally resistant to deterministic and quasi-physicalistic doctrines such as his friend Henry Adams's application of the second law of thermodynamics to human history. James once wrote, "The 'second law' is wholly irrelevant to 'history'—save that it sets a terminus—for history is the course of things before the terminus."[39] Between the beginning and the end, human activity rather than levels of physical energy "is the most important rill we know of."[40] But even though James believed that human action could reduce modestly the level of suffering and improve moderately the quality of life, he was not a starry-eyed utopian. He sought for optimal images of the future, but he never believed that we would arrive at the perfect state or ever completely rid human life of its ambiguity, suffering, and evil.

James and Contemporary Cultures of Psychology

James believed that life must be lived in alternating rhythms of ethical action and relaxation, strenuous moral effort and mystical contemplation. We must be ethical creatures not because we *should be* but because we *must be* to survive in the kind of world in which we find ourselves. James found the strenuous life and the moral way personally and psychologically exhilarating. In fact, it was through his insights into the nature of the moral will that the malaise and depression which marred his early life were lifted. Moral purpose was his cure. The realization that humans have the freedom and the need to contribute to present and future society was the royal road to his own therapy and rehabilitation.

In spite of this, James knew that humans could not live in the active mode all of the time. In addition, he had no great love for change for the sake of change. In contrast to the judgment of Charles Morris, James was no simple proponent of the Promethean path of life.[41] There are prominent conservative dimensions in James which have been neglected. John Dewey, not James, was the instrumentalist and the patron saint of Amerca's new culture of power. James, on the other hand, saw change as an inevitable dimension of any environment; the issue was how to handle it rather than how to create it. James saw very clearly that human beings can tolerate only moderate amounts of change and that continuity with the past was as important as adaptation to the future.

But even if the reader is tantalized sufficiently to give James a protracted hearing, why should we assume that he has anything important to say to contemporary psychology? Psychology, as Philip Rieff has demonstrated,[42] can easily become culture, but how does James help us see the contemporary cultures of psychology more clearly and more profoundly? The answer is this: James's psychology and philosophy were so complex that, when we understand them, we discover an excellent analytic tool for deciphering the cultural implications of certain contemporary trends in psychology. As a psychologist, James was also a reasonably good scientist. But his psychology was also philosophically and ethically self-conscious. Furthermore, he had a keen sense for the cultural "cash value" of his psychological and philosophical ideas. Analyzing James helps expose some of the basic decisions that any modern psychology has to face, should face, but, unfortunately, does not always face. Reviewing James's psychology gives us a better idea of the relation of scientific data to theoretical constructs, of data and theory to philosophical presuppositions, and of data, theory, and philosophical presuppositions to ethical and cultural implications.

We will examine the data and theories of James's psychology as well as the data and theories of several other trends in contemporary psychology. But we will do this with a special eye toward their cultural implications and involvements. To use James's terms, we are interested in the "fringe" or, as Husserl called it, the "horizon" of cultural meaning that surrounds a reputedly scientific psychology. We are interested in psychological data and theory, but primarily for the way they feed or inspire broader cultural meanings. In fact, James provided a useful set of terms to guide an analysis of the relation of scientific data and theory to culture. In chapter 3, we will review in detail James's theory of meaning and his distinction between the "topic" and the "object" of thought. To convey his meaning, James used the analogy of a sentence. In the sentence, "Columbus discovered America in 1492," the topic of the sentence might be Columbus or America. But the object, the full meaning of the sentence, is the whole sentence. In general, then, the topic of meaning is the discrete and definite thing referred to by an utterance. The object of meaning is the entire fringe, horizon, or context in which the definite thing referred to is explicitly or implicitly placed.

Psychological data and theories can be viewed as analogous to what James meant by his concept of the topic of meaning. But they almost invariably have a larger context, fringe, horizon, or object of meaning. This larger object or fringe of meaning might be called the "culture" of the psychology in question. The topic of a psychological system might be the facts and theories which pertain to its ideas about instincts, consciousness, emotions, reasoning, memory, or attention. The object or culture of the psychological system might consist of the wider fringe of philosophical presupposition and inherited social meanings in which the scientific data and theories are placed. For instance, in chapter 7, we will learn that James and Skinner have a very similar understanding of the role in human life of habit and positive reinforcement. Yet James places his concept of habit and positive reinforcement within a different set of philosophical presuppositions and a different understanding of modern culture than does Skinner. This radically shifts the overall meaning of James's understanding of habit and reinforcement.

In general, the relation between topic and object, scientific concept to wider cultural implications, appears indeterminate and unpredictable. James's theory of habit and reinforcement does not lead him to a thoroughgoing culture of control of the kind espoused by Skinner, although he does in fact greatly appreciate the place of environmental control in human life. In contrast to Skinner, scientific methodology does not directly control James's wider metaphysical presuppositions. James's general metaphysical position on the nature of freedom, ethics, knowledge, and God was never dictated by the requirements of a narrowly conceived scientific methodology. This is why he was critical of all forms of modern determinism, whether in the form of British empiricism and associationism or German philosophical monism. All determinisms render the human mind bereft of agency and responsibility and portray it as passive and basically reactive. Such a view of mind might make it easier for certain forms of scientific inquiry to study better the ways mind is determined, but it is an inadequate metaphysical assumption for the direction of everyday moral behavior. There is great continuity between the passive view of mind found in British empiricism and the views of both the culture of detachment and the culture of control. On the other hand, the romantic determinism found in German idealism has its own strange continuity with romanticism of the culture of joy.

Let us review in broad strokes some of the affinities and points of tension between James and the various cultures of psychology that we will be studying.

The culture of detachment, psychoanalysis, converges at points with the strenuous mood and democratic pluralism of James, but on the whole, it is vastly different. Both James and

Freud, as Stuart Hughes would say, were in different ways "loyal critics" of the Enlightenment. They wittingly or unwittingly gave us images of man which went beyond the logical and mechanistic paradigms of the eighteenth and nineteenth centuries,[43] although, as was mentioned above, Freud never completely escaped this ethos. But Freud's normative vision of man and his interpretation of the modern world varied significantly from James's. Freud believed in an inherent antagonism between an individual's chaotic instinctuality and the frustrations of social institutions. He ended by advocating a retreat into self-conscious and prudential husbandry of one's pleasures in a basically inhospitable world. James gave birth to an image of life as active engagement; Freud helped found a vision of life as civil yet hedonic *detachment*. Freud saw modernity as the control of life through science; James saw it as an acceleration of competing forces which could be guided only by the unifying powers of practical moral activity. Freud substitutes the ordering power of the rational ego for the law and superego of his Jewish heritage; James, no Jew by birth, substituted for the dead archaisms of irrelevant moralities a living *midrash* of practical moral inquiry. The strenuous life was, for James, primarily a life of inquiry, a practical moral inquiry designed to develop new moral traditions and new cultural syntheses to guide man through the transitions of modernity. Freud had a great nostalgia for Moses but felt condemned to live without him. James had little or no regret over Moses' demise but hit on a method of practical moral investigation designed to give us ethical principles which could be living and forever revised to fit the changing circumstances of life.

But other modern traditions of psychology have given birth not to cultures of detachment, but to cultures of *joy*. Some of the so-called humanistic psychologies—the psychologies of Abraham Maslow, Carl Rogers, Fritz Perls, and William Shutz—are examples of such psychologies. Self-actualization and self-fulfilment, rather than the strenuous life, are the goals for living of these psychologies. Although James shares with the psychologies of joy a fierce appreciation for the integrity and initiative of the individual, he is different from them in seeing the meaning of the individual not only in his feelings and fantasies but in his actual behavior. Feelings and imagination must be measured against the consequences of actual behavior; their value, in part, rests upon their actual contribution to the larger society. For James, life can never be simply a matter of unfolding potentialities and spontaneous joy; it must entail sacrifice and suffering. James also could have shared with the culture of joy an antipathy toward the large, oppressive institutions of modern society which crush the creativity of individuals and small groups. But a generalized anti-institutionalism is difficult to find in James, although rather easy to find in the representatives of the culture of joy, with the possible exception of Maslow. But in a variety of ways not fully appreciated by James's interpreters, he knew that individuals at various times in their lives needed protective environments, direction, supportive and regulating institutions, culture, and tradition. The necessity of these things is not always admitted by the culture of joy.

James has surprising affinities with another important culture of modern psychology—what we will call the "culture of control," best represented by the psychology of B. F. Skinner. James, as does Skinner, knew the value of environmental reinforcements. He frequently saw himself primarily as a psychologist of behavior and the consequences of behavior. It is one of the great paradoxes of the history of psychology that the same man who influenced phenomenology as James is also credited with having had a significant influence on modern behaviorism.[44] James was a Darwinist, but one who emphasized both the mysterious spontaneities of nature which Darwin named "free variation" and the enormous selective powers of the environment which Darwin called "natural selection."[45] James's great emphasis upon behavior and the *consequences* of one's acts stems from his respect for the selective power of the environment. This insight was the foundation of his pragmatism and his insistence on the importance of "fruits of action" as a measure of the value of human deeds. James would have known what Skinner was about and would have respected it— up to a point. But James's behaviorism was subordinate to his phenomenology of attention and will; his emphasis upon the importance of habits and reinforcement takes its place within a broader theory about the way free choices direct the more automatic processes of life.

James has the most affinity with a loose and unorganized group of contemporary psychologists who, in their own ways and without communication with one another, are groping to establish a culture of care. By culture of care, I mean a normative view of man which holds out as vital a human quality which is both *possible* to develop and *necessary* in the context of modernity. This is a view which sees human nature as capable of being oriented to the future in active care and concern. It is a concern for the future not only of oneself and one's progeny but the wider human community. This is exactly what is involved in the idea of the strenuous life. The strenuous mood is the opposite of the "easygoing mood" and the attitude of "I don't care."[46] It is a positive attitude of care—care for oneself, one's family, the wider community, and possible future communities which may extend beyond the limits of one's individual life. The strenuous mood entails a personal identification of one's self with a wider range of people and communities, both present and future. It involves heightening one's sympathies and overcoming what James called that "certain blindness" in human beings which makes it difficult for us to appreciate and respect the inner meaning of another's experience.[47]

James's concept of the strenuous life has the most similarity with Erik Erikson's vision of "generativity," Erich Fromm's concept of "productivity," and Rollo May's unique interpretation of "intentionality." All these psychologists and their respective "utopian" visions were trying to develop an ethical definition of the human which emphasizes responsibility and care for both present and future generations.

James resonates with the view of modern life which is to be found in the culture of care. The culture of control tends to see modern life as too chaotic, too loose, free, unplanned, and unengineered. On the other hand, the culture of joys sees modern life as too controlled, too much dominated and conditioned by home, institutions, church, government, and the culture of the past. The culture of care has very much caught the spirit of James in seeing pluralism and rapid social change as the main features of the modern world. It understands that

these forces can produce alternating pockets of arbitrary control and chaotic freedom and may eventually destroy us unless
human beings can respond with an individual and collective
sense of responsibility and care for the present and for the
future.

It is not the purpose of this book to say that James is the
greatest psychologist of the modern world and the potential
savior of us all. It is my goal to show that although neglected he
is important. I compare him with other modern psychologists
not to show where they are wrong, but to illustrate the issues at
stake in the positions which James took. In addition, it is hoped
that this new interpretation of James will make him more
available to the general public so that along with thinking
Freudian, Rogerian, Jungian, or Skinnerian, more people—
without turning him into a popular guru or forming around him
a dogmatic school—will occasionally catch themselves thinking
Jamesian.

Notes

1. Peter Berger and Thomas Luckmann, *The Social Construction of Reality* (New York: Anchor Books, 1967), pp. 138–45.

2. Philip Rieff, *The Triumph of the Therapeutic* (New York: Harper and Row, 1966); Paul Halmos, *The Faith of the Counselors* (New York: Schocken Books, 1970); Robert White, "The Concept of Healthy Personality," *The Counseling Psychologist* 4 (1973): 3–12; M. Brewster Smith, *Humanizing Social Psychology* (San Francisco: Jossey-Bass, 1974).

3. White, "The Concept of Healthy Personality," p. 4.

4. Daniel Offer and Melvin Sabshin, *Normality* (New York: Basic Books, 1974), pp. 97–112.

5. Ibid., p. 99.

6. Ibid., p. 105.

7. Ibid., pp. 102–5.

8. Ibid., pp. 108–9.

9. Smith, *Humanizing Social Psychology*, p. 151.

10. Ibid., p. 151.

11. White, "The Concept of Healthy Personality," p. 5; see also Marie Jahoda, *Current Concepts of Positive Mental Health* (New York: Basic Books, 1958).

12. White, "The Concept of the Healthy Personality," p. 6.

13. *CER*, p. 404.

14. *VRE*, p. 288.

15. Ibid., p. 289.

16. *P*, p. 123.

17. Ibid.

18. Alvin Toffler, *Future Shock* (New York: Random House, 1970).

19. Henry James, ed., *The Letters of William James* (Boston: Atlantic Monthly Press, 1969); Ralph Barton Perry, *TCWJ*; Gay Wilson Allen, *WJ*.

20. Robert MacLeod, *William James: Unfinished Business* (Washington, D.C.: American Psychological Association, 1969).

21. Ibid., p. iii.

22. Ibid., p. vii.

23. Alfred Schutz, "William James' Concept of the Stream of Thought Phenomenologically Interpreted," *Alfred Schutz: Collected Papers* (Hague: Martin Nijhoff, 1966), 3:1-14 and "On Multiple Realities," *Collected Papers*, 1:207-59; Aron Gurwitsch, "William James' Theory of the 'Transitive Parts' of the Stream of Consciousness", *Studies in Phenomenology and Psychology* (Evanston, Ill.: Northwestern University Press, 1966), pp. 301-31; Herbert Spiegelberg, *The Phenomenological Movement* (Hague: Martin Nijhoff, 1960), 1:66-69.

24. Hans Linschoten, *On the Way Towards a Phenomenological Psychology* (Pittsburgh: Duquesne University Press, 1968). First published as *Auf dem Wege zu einer Phänomenologischen Psychologie* (Berlin: Gruyter, 1961).

25. John Wild, *The Radical Empiricism of William James* (New York: Anchor Books, 1970).

26. Bruce Wilshire, *William James and Phenomenology* (Bloomington, Ind.: University of Indiana Press, 1968).

27. Richard Stevens, *James and Husserl: The Foundations of Meaning* (The Hague: Martinus Nijhoff, 1974).

28. James Edie, "Notes on the Philosophical Anthropology of William James" *An Invitation to Phenomenology* (Chicago: Quadrangle Books, 1965), pp. 110-33, "William James and the Phenomenology of Religious Experience," *American Philosophy and the Future*, ed. Michael Novak (New York: Charles Scribner's and Sons, 1968), pp. 247-69, "Necessary Truth and Perception: William James on the Structure of Experience," *New Essays in Phenomenology*, ed. James Edie (Chicago Quadrangle Books, 1969), pp. 234-55, "Critical Studies: William James and Phenomenology," *The Review of Metaphysics* 23 (March 1970): 481-526 and "The Genesis of a Phenomenological Theory of the Experience of Personal Identity," *Man and World* 6 (September 1973): 322-40; Ash Gobar, "The Phenomenology of William James," *Proceedings of the American Philosophical Society* 114 (August 1970): 294-309; Andrew J. Reck, "The Philosophical Psychology of William James" *Southern Journal of Philosophy* 9 (Fall 1971): 293-312, "Dualisms in William James' *Principles of Psychology,*" *Tulane Studies in Philosophy* 21 (1972): 23-38, "Epistemology in William James's *Principles of Psychology.*" *Tulane Studies in Philosophy* 22 (1973): 79-115. Reck is willing to concede that there are phenomenological themes in James, but he is far more reluctant than the other commentators to make a great deal out of this.

29. Gordon Allport, "The Productive Paradoxes of William James," *Psychological Review* 50 (January 1943): 95-120.

30. Linschoten, *On the Way Towards a Phenomenological Psychology*, p. 23.

31. *LWJ*, 1:153.

32. Allport, "The Productive Paradoxes of William James," p. 117.

33. Horace M. Kallen, "The Modern World, The Intellectual, and William James," *The Wesleyan Political Quarterly* 13 (December 1960): 876.

34. William Clebsch, *American Religious Thought: A History* (Chicago: The University of Chicago Press, 1973), p. xvi.

35. David Marcell, *Progress and Pragmatism* (Westport, Conn.: Greenwood Press, 1974), p. 37.

36. Ibid., p. 38.

37. Ibid., p. 47: Richard Hofstadter, *Social Darwinism in American Thought* (Boston: Beacon Press, 1971), pp. 31–84.

38. Marcell, *Progress and Pragmatism*, p. 47.

39. *LWJ*, 2:345.

40. Ibid.

41. Charles Morris, *Paths of Life* (Chicago: University of Chicago Press, 1972), p. 100.

42. Rieff, *The Triumph of the Therapeutic*, p. 246–49.

43. H. Stuart Hughes, *Consciousness and Society* (New York: Vintage Books, 1961) Paladin, p. 29.

44. Linschoten, *On the Way Towards a Phenomenological Psychology*, p. 31.

45. *WB*, p. 221.

46. Ibid., p. 212.

47. *TTP*, pp. 113–29.

2

Ways of Knowing Man

How did William James study human beings? And what can we learn from him for our contemporary efforts to know the nature of man?

To answer these questions, we must distinguish between William James the psychologist and William James the philosopher. There was a difference between the James who once aspired to establish psychology as an independent natural science and the James who also wanted to develop a comprehensive understanding of man broad enough to include his ethical, religious, and aesthetic expressions. James sometimes tried to set firm boundaries between his psychological and philosophical inquiries; many of his interpreters rightly believe that he was unable to maintain these boundaries successfully. Disciplines which later were to become almost completely isolated from one another in different parts of our universities were understood and practiced by this single individual known as William James. James was successively, and at times simultaneously, a physiologist, anatomist, psychologist, epistemologist, moral philosopher, and philosopher of religion. Much of the debate about how to interpret James is about questions of boundaries. Did James truly want to separate psychology from philosophy and epistemology? Did ethical and religious commitments dominate and distort his philosophical understandings of meaning and truth?

Our concern in this chapter will be with the methods and presuppositions which controlled the early development of James's philosophy of the human. From the beginning, his image of man was a philosophical-psychological view which combined insights from the more naturalistically oriented physiological and psychological sciences with certain philosophical arguments. Our concern, then, is how James envisioned the subject matter and boundaries of his psychology and how he related it to broader philosophical inquiry into man.

Preliminary Definitions of Psychology

Let us begin with the way he defined psychology in the first volume of his *The Principles of Psychology* (1890). The first line of the book sets out the scope of psychology in one bold sentence: "Psychology is the Science of Mental Life, both of its phenomena and their conditions."[1] To say that psychology deals with both the "phenomena" and the "conditions" of mental life is to announce that psychology must be both a *descriptive* and an *explanatory* endeavor. On the one hand, it must describe the phenomena of the mind—"such things we call feelings, desires, cognitions, reasonings, decisions, and the like."[2] On the other hand, it must search for the *causes* or conditions of these phenomena, especially those which are anchored in the physiological makeup of the human brain.

In this broad definition of the scope of psychology, James is straddling the full range of methodological options which psychologists are now discussing so heatedly. Such a definition throws into the same kettle the hard-nosed seekers after causes such as the physiological psychologists, experimentalists, and behaviorists right along with the more descriptively oriented introspectionists and phenomenologists. This is exactly the mixture which James intended. But unfortunately, he did not always answer certain relevant questions so clearly and consistently as one would like. For instance, which has the logical priority, the causal conditions or the phenomena? Should the psychologist first try to describe the phenomena of mental life and then search for causes, or should the reverse be the case? How are causes and phenomena related to one another? And finally, how are the phenomena of the mind related to things outside the mind? There is little doubt that the answers which

James gave to these questions were not entirely consistent with what he actually did, both as a psychologist and as a philosopher. On the surface, he tried to answer them in such a way as to establish psychology as a natural science very analogous to physics and almost completely dedicated to the search for causal explanations for the workings of the mind. In practice, however, as both a psychologist and a philosopher, he tended to give both methodological and logical priority to the phenomena of mind and the meanings which related it to an environment and world.

James's definition of psychology as a natural science would make it a discipline following very much the procedures and goals of physics, chemistry, and physiology. To make psychology a natural science was to make it an objective discipline in the search of causal explanations of mental life. "To the Psychologist," James once wrote, "the minds he studies are *objects*, in a world of other objects."[3] For the moment, James appears to be saying that the psychologist studies the human mind as an *object or a thing,* just like any other object or thing. Objects and things are, of course, lifeless entities without purposes, meanings, and intentions. As we will see, however, James never stuck with this definition of mind nor did he, in the end, confine scientific psychology totally to this narrow definition of its task.

James's effort to establish psychology as a natural science was *not* done out of the conviction that only controlled scientific inquiry can tell us what we need to know about man. In fact, just the contrary was true. James believed that scientific psychology could only provide a very small and humble part of what we really needed to know about human beings.[4] He once said in an address before the psychology club at Harvard, "When a student of psychology, I always regarded it as but a part of the larger science of living beings. . . . Official psychology is a very *small* part." His efforts to establish psychology as a natural science was done as a gentlemanly gesture; it grew out of James's *recognition* of the need for a division of labor between the psychologist and the philosopher. The psychologist could not be expected to solve all of the relevant philosophical questions prior to the beginning of his philosophical work. The psychologist cannot be asked to bother his head about such questions as the nature of knowledge, the relation of mind to external reality, and how states of mind can exist at all.[5] James believed that these were questions "of the kind for which general philosophy, not natural science, is held responsible."[6]

Nonetheless, they were important questions for psychology. Whether or not scientific psychology should attend to these questions, someone needs to do so. Furthermore, if this task—which James called a "metaphysical" task—was to be done by the general philosopher, James assumed that the philosopher and the scientific psychologist necessarily would stay in communication with each other. His desire to separate philosophy and psychology was primarily a practical consideration, not a hardened theoretical dogma; it was primarily designed to "distribute the labor" and get the most "efficient results."[7] James thought that some of the most creative insights into psychology had come from the biologists and medical doctors who had taken a very commonsense approach to these weighty philosophical questions. He believed it was a dangerous thing to "thwart" their productive insights by pressing epistemological matters upon them.

Yet, however magnanimous James was in wanting to liberate scientific psychology from the tyranny of metaphysical questions, it is clear that James could not liberate himself. Time and time again his two-volume *Principles of Psychology* is interrupted by metaphysical discussions. In the last chapter of his *Psychology: The Briefer Course,* a condensation of the massive *Principles,* James writes that psychology as a natural science cannot stand by itself and be "on solid ground." In the end, psychology as a natural science means "a psychology particularly fragile, and into which the waters of metaphysical criticism leak at every point, a psychology all of whose elementary assumptions and data must be reconsidered in wider connection and translated into other terms."[8] What James meant by the ominous word "metaphysics" was simply an "unusually obstinate attempt to think clearly and consistently."[9] However much James was willing to free individual psychologists from the burden of metaphysics, he knew that psychology as a discipline must get its metaphysical principles straight and have a close and enriching contact with philosophical inquiry. As Andrew Reck has suggested so appropriately,[10] James's great *Principles of Psychology* should be read as an essay in philosophical psychology—a philosophical psychology in which a single man has done both the philosophy and psychology involved.

Multiple Methods

James derived most of his methods for the study of man from the field of psychology. But as we have seen he also used the methods of the philosopher; that is, he attempted to think "clearly and consistently" about the larger problems of the nature of humans. Psychology, however, had a privileged place in James's approach to the study of human existence. For a good portion of his academic career, James was a professor of psychology. James's first position at Harvard began in 1872 and was in anatomy and physiology. But even then his real loves were psychology and philosophy. He almost refused an appointment for a second year with the conviction that the "line of mental science" was where he really wanted to invest his energies.[11] Even though he continued his teaching in the general areas of biology, students report huge portions of his lectures dealt with the interface between biology and psychology.[12] But it also must be remembered that very early in his teaching career (1879) James actually began offering courses in philosophy. James was beginning to understand the methods of several fields—biology, psychology, and philosophy—from the very beginning of his academic career.

In chapter 7 of his *Principles,* James discusses the chief methods of psychology. *Introspection, experimentation,* and *comparison*—these are the major methods which the science of psychology should use. James was certainly not unique in using these methods, but he was unique in the way he developed them and brought them together. I intend to discuss James's understanding of introspection more in the next chapter. I will say this about it now. Introspection generally was thought to be a process of *describing* the contents of consciousness. James made it more than this, although he may not have realized fully the great importance of his amplification of the method of introspection. It is his extension of the method of introspection which has led to the remarkable revival of interest in James by the phenomenological school of philosophy. Introspection was for James a fallible but necessary *first* step in doing psychology. James could write, "Introspective Observation is what we have to rely on first and foremost and always."[13] Although he was not consistent in applying this maxim, part of his great strength as a psychologist and a philosopher of human nature was due to his belief in and practice of this truth.

About the experimental method, James does precious little actually to define it, but a great deal to characterize it as a style of human activity. The experimental method was beginning to flourish in Germany under the leadership of Weber, Fechner, Vierordt, and Wundt. It used controlled procedures and statistical methods to check out the insights of introspective data. James respected the method, but saw it as boring and tedious. It submits the mind to a "regular *siege*" and gains truth by "starving out," "harassing," "spying and scraping," and by applying deadly tenacity and almost diabolic cunning."[14] The method of experimentation had not yielded a great deal of theoretical insight, but James felt that it was very important— the wave of the future—and vast sections of the *Principles* are given over to recording and assessing the results of its application.

The method of comparison was far more important for James than its short definition in the *Principles* would lead one to think. For it is actually out of the comparative method that James's so-called functional understanding of mind arose. It was out of James's studies in biology, anatomy, and physiology that he became familiar with the comparative method in evolutionary studies. It was Darwin's own comparative analysis of the adaptive patterns of different species which led to his discovery of the theory of evolution. James himself was grounded thoroughly in evolutionary theory and the methods of research which accompanied it. He took his own *Beagle*-like zoological expedition to Brazil to collect specimens of fish with Professor Louis Agassiz during the years of 1865–66. James's most creative contribution to psychology was his attempt to work out the implications of evolutionary theory for man's emotional and intellectual life. Part of this involved using the fruits of the comparative method, especially on such topics as the meaning of the instincts, the emotions, and the general understanding of the meaning and function of the mind.

James believed, however, that the comparative method was subordinate to the method of introspection. He wrote, "This method presupposes a normal psychology of introspection to be established in its main features."[15] But where the nature of features of our psychological life cannot be discerned through introspection, "then it is of the utmost importance to trace the phenomenon considered through all its possible variations of type and combination."[16] We look at the instincts of animals to throw light on our own. We examine the reasoning abilities of bees, ants, savages, and infants to gain some idea of the larger context of biological capacities out of which our own intelligence may have arisen.

Like the method of introspection, the comparative method is also susceptible to errors. Differences between species can be obscured; prejudices can be projected upon our view of savages, infants, and animals; hypotheses can be poorly conceived and inadequately tested. But it is out of James's acquaintance with this method that his most groundbreaking insights into psychology came. If there has been any single violence done to our understanding of William James by the phenomenologists, it is the intendency to play down the importance of this method and its fruits for his understanding of man. James may have discovered much that has similarities to the existentialists and the phenomenologists. But the long-term power of his contributions comes from the fact that he combined his incipient existentialism and phenomenology with an enlightened functionalism which took seriously evolutionary theory and comparative biology. But here the phenomenological interpreters of James are in part correct. Taken as a whole, his writings testify to the supreme importance of locating our functional views of human nature within the context of broader phenomenological descriptions and philosophical meditations on the nature of human existence. With this truth in mind, let us look for a moment at just what James did do with his reflections on evolution. What kind of vision of humans did his early comparative studies engender?

Evolution and the Individual

James's intellectual career during the 1870s was preoccupied with two topics—an evolutionary theory of mind *and* a phenomenology and philosophy of the will. It was in the spring of the first year of that decade, April of 1870, that James was grasped so profoundly by Renouvier's definition of free will as "the sustaining of a thought *because I choose* to when I might have other thoughts."[17] This concept helped turn the tide of his downward drift into depression and moral impotence. But there were other influences on James during this period. Of decisive importance were the evolutionary theory of Charles Darwin and the evolutionary philosophy of the energetic Herbert Spencer. Some of James's earliest writings reflect the depth of these influences. The theme of an evolutionary theory of mind and the individual was carried on in three exceptionally important papers—"Remarks on Spencer's Definition of Mind as Correspondence" (1878), "Great Men and Their Environment" (1880), and "The Importance of Individuals." The last paper was written shortly after the first two but not published until several years later (1890). James's systematic concern with the philosophy of the will appeared during this same period in an article entitled "The Feeling of Effort" (1880), which served as the basis for his later famous chapter on the "Will" in his *Principles.*

When James wrote about the nature of the will, he conceived it as a will which could take its place within his broader evolutionary and functional psychology. At the same time, James tried to develop an evolutionary theory of mind large enough to include his emerging concept of will. It gets to the very heart of what is fruitful and exciting in William James's understanding of man that he wrestled to bring these two dimensions together within a single vision of human nature.

But for the remainder of the chapter, I want to examine James's evolutionary theory of the mind and the individual.

Between Darwin and Spencer, Darwin was for James the hero and Spencer, the villain. In spite of his criticisms of Spencer, the phenomenologist Bruce Wilshire is in error when he implies that evolutionary theory was unimportant for James.[18] James believed that Spencer's definition of mind had done "real service" for psychology.[19] At the same time, Spencer constituted a punching bag for James—a foil used to reflect his own brand of evolutionary thinking. He once wrote that Spencer's "one virtue is his belief in the universality of evolution—the 1000 crimes are his 5000 pages of absolute incompetence to work it out in detail."[20] James used both Spencer's *Principles of Psychology* and his *First Principles* in classes at Harvard. In the margin of the latter, James scribbled such responses as "absurd," "the ass," "damned scholastic quibble," "good God," and other similar exclamations. Spencer had a great talent for obscure and nearly meaningless definitions which James relished in ridiculing. He once defined evolution as "an integration of matter and concomitant dissipation of motion, during which the matter passes from an indefinite, incoherent homogeneity to a definite, coherent heterogeneity; and during which the retained motion undergoes a parallel transformation." James paraphrased this remarkable specimen of unintelligibility with the following statement: "Evolution is a change from a no-howish untalkaboutable all-alikeness to a somehowish and general talkaboutable not-all-alikeness by continuous stick-togetherations and something elseifications."[21] With regard to Spencer's understanding of God as the "Unknowable," James believed that the only thing that the invincible English philosopher had demonstrated was that "self-contradictory nonsense does not exist."[22]

But James's reflections on Spencer were far more than occasions to display his wit. His 1878 article entitled "Remarks on Spencer's Definition of Mind as Correspondence" sets forth most of the major themes which dominate the rest of James's philosophical development. Here James reflects on Spencer's contention that mind must be compared with the evolution of life in general and that the best possible definition of mentality is the "adjustment of inner to outer relations."[23] By the word "adjustment" Spencer meant "correspondence." It is the task of the mind to make inner biological life correspond to or fit external environmental conditions. James's objection is that this definition is entirely too "cognitive" and far too deterministic to fit the actual facts. Correspondence, in the end, clearly meant for Spencer "survival." The moth which flies into the candle rather than away from it has a failure of intelligent mental action and does not "correspond" to the environment. James believes that such a definition makes mind entirely too passive and far too subordinate to and determined by the environment. It overlooks the active, spontaneous nature of mind and obscures the fact that all creatures have internal subjective needs and interests which lead them actively to search and shape the environment. These desires, needs, and interests—some of which include the need for survival—are a priori aspects of every creature's life which are brought to the environment and not created by the environment. In other words, Spencer's definition leaves out the obvious "teleological" nature of mind,[24] the fact that mind both serves the subjective interests of creatures *and* guides these interests to fit with environmental conditions.

In addition to asserting the active character of mind in its quest to satisfy subjective interests, this essay makes other important points which James refines throughout his writings. First, James asserts a reinterpreted Darwinism over against Spencer's environmental determinism. Spencer, James believes, put too much emphasis upon what Darwin called "natural selection"—the capacity of the environment either to blindly crush what does not fit or to reinforce and preserve those adaptations which luckily do correspond to its provisions. Natural selection is that capricious tendency for the environment to favor certain adaptive capacities over others. For instance, natural selection is that tendency for the environment to favor those animals which are luckily born with slightly longer necks in order to feed off fruits on trees which others of their species cannot reach. These other poor creatures will go hungry, starve, and perish along with all the other short-necked beings which someday might have issued as their progency. Natural selection was the *major,* but not the only, factor in evolutionary change according to Darwin. This was the difference between the two famous theorists of evolution, Darwin and Spencer. Certainly Darwin emphasized natural selection. In fact, it was his studies of the way domestic animals were bred selectively by their owners to reproduce those strains with desirable traits which led to the most scientifically convincing articulation of the concept.

But James loved to point out that this was not *all* that Darwin emphasized in his theory of evolution; he also emphasized, although probably not so much as James, the phenomenon of "free variation." Free variation was for Darwin a random and mysterious process whereby the organism generated accidental variations in its own structure. Darwin was not certain how these accidental variations occurred. Subsequent scientific research, however, has demonstrated that Darwin's model was essentially correct. Accidental variations do occur, although the exact causes are still under debate. Failure in genetic transmission or genetic alteration resulting from radiation are two of the more prominent explanations for these changes. James states his case very succinctly in the article entitled "Great Men and Their Environments." He writes,

> If we look at an animal or a human being, distinguished from the rest of his kind by the possession of some extraordinary peculiarity, good or bad, we shall be able to discriminate between the causes which originally *produced* the peculiarity in him and the causes that *maintain* it after it is produced; and we shall see, if the peculiarity be one that he was born with, that these two sets of causes belong to two such irrelevant cycles. It was the triumphant originality of Darwin to see this, and to act accordingly. Separating the causes of production under the title of "tendencies to spontaneous variation." and relegating them to a physiological cycle which he forthwith agreed to ignore altogether, he confined his attention to the causes of preservation, and under the names of natural selection and sexual selection studied them exclusively as functions of the cycle of the environment.[25]

Spencer's mistake was that he overemphasized natural selection and failed to realize that the causal cycles of natural selection and spontaneous variation are relatively independent of each other. Changes are *produced* spontaneously, but they are *preserved* by the environment. The environment is not causally omnipotent.

As we will see more clearly later, this passage suggests why James could have partially affirmed much of the environmental determinism associated with present-day behaviorism. But the uniqueness of James's position is his belief that spontaneous variation gave each creature a rich supply of subjective interests which were a priori and which were not the result of environmental determinations.

Furthermore, James believed that many creatures had a priori subjective interests which go beyond the simple urge for survival, although he conceded that survival was a central concern of every animal. But in the case of man, survival is clearly not the only interest. Here James mixes with his scientific pursuit of causal cycles and explanations a phenomenological point of view. He observes and describes how human beings have additional interests.

> What are these interests? Most men would reply that they are all that makes survival worth securing. The social affections, all the vaious forms of play, the thrilling intimations of art, the delights of philosophic contemplation, the rest of religious emotion, the joy of moral self-approbation, the charm of fancy and of wit—some or all of these are absolutely required to make the notion of mere existence tolerable.[26]

In chapter 7 we will learn how James enriched this observation with an explanatory model of the instincts. All of this suggests that James's functionalism is complex and rich, a fact which his imitators and interpreters have not always appreciated. For James, mind is not just an organ which conforms a creature to the brute realities of the external environment. Rather, mind is an organ for *realizing* subjective interests and ideals *in the context* of particular environments and what in fact they will select and permit. The difference is subtle but important.

In this early response to Spencer, James certainly does not do away with the importance of the environment and its selective powers. The principle of natural selection found in both Darwin and Spencer is affirmed although to some extent qualified. Lamarck's idea that evolutionary change occurs through the hereditary transmission of acquired characteristics was a principle which James repudiated as not fitting the available evidence.[27] He rejected, and modern biology has continued to reject, the idea that giraffes develop and then communicate to their offspring long necks because they first stretched them while reaching for food or that anteaters develop and then reproduce long noses because they used them so much while poking into little holes for those tiny black insects which sustain their lives.

The principle of natural selection retains a permanent place in James's psychology and later philosophy. The entire scaffold of his pragmatic theory of truth and meaning is built loosely on this aspect of evolutionary theory. But a subtle shift occurs in the way the idea of environmental selection is interpreted. It is not just the stark demands of the environment—not just the environment as naked Freudian "reality principle"—which is emphasized. Rather, James begins to talk about what "works best."[28] And what "works best," although not well defined, refers to those acts which promote for oneself and for others the fullest realization of subjective interests in the context of what is possible in given environments. This can be known only with reference to the future, i.e., with reference to what is durable and satisfying over a period of time. Furthermore, what "works best" is discerned most clearly when it is also recognized that our own acts have a self-validating influence and help create the conditions which lead to their verification. James writes,

> The knower is an actor, and co-efficient of truth on one side, whilst on the other he registers the truth which he helps to create. Mental interests, hypotheses, postulates, so far as they are bases for human action—which to a great extent transforms the world—help to *make* the truth which they declare. In other words, there belongs to mind, from its birth upward, a spontaneity, a vote. It is in the game, and not a mere looker-on.[29]

Most existentialists could agree with this statement. Certainly Sartre could accept it. Man the actor helps to create the conditions which select and test the workability of his deeds. Of course, cyberneticists could also applaud most of these words; when James is speaking about the mind as registering "the truth which [it] helps to create," James is saying that the mind is a subtle feedback mechanism which constantly seeks to evaluate the consequences of its acts in the context of the selective powers of particular environments.

The Philosophy of the Individual and the Philosophy of History

James's view of the nature of mind is related directly to his philosophy of history. James's philosophy of the individual—his understanding of the place of the individual in history and social change—is still substantially informed by his evolutionary vision and the comparative method which is so important to it. But his tendency to compare man with other animals was never permitted to obscure what was distinctive about man. His philosophy of the individual was built out of wide observation of the human scene just as much as it was out of the direct comparison of man with other earthly creatures.

The essay entitled "Great Men and Their Environment" may be the single most important writing for revealing the broader social and cultural significance of James's psychology and philosophy. It shows a variety of things about James—that although interested in the individual, he also was interested vitally in such topics as the meaning of community, the causes of social change, and the nature of moral and religious leadership. This essay more than any other which James ever wrote sets forth the proper context in which to interpret his so-called individualism.

The question which motivates this article is one which few commentators have recognized as important for James: "What are the causes that make communities change from generation to generation?[30] James's firm reply to this question is this: "The difference is due to the accumulated influences of individuals, of their examples, their initiatives, and their decisions."[31] In this essay James's opponent is a member of the Spencerian school, a Mr. Grant Allen, who had written recently some articles insisting that social change occurs irrespective of individuals and their acts; it is completely a matter of environmental forces such as geography, war, and catastrophe. James admits that these are real forces producing social change. But they should be understood more as challenges to which a community and its leaders can respond in a variety of ways.

James is almost as explicit as Max Weber in his appreciation for the role of strong individuals and men and women of genius in social evolution. Great individuals make the final difference in which direction a community will turn when coping with environmental pressures. The great person is not just a product of environmental conditioning. He or she is a mysterious creation of forces which can best be spoken about under the rubric of Darwin's "spontaneous variations." Once again, James follows Darwin's famous division of evolutionary forces into spontaneous variation and natural selection. The genius is a product of the former but in the end is forced to test himself or herself against the latter. James writes that the social philosopher

> must simply accept geniuses as data, just as Darwin accepts his spontaneous variations. For him as for Darwin, the only problem is, these data being given, how does the environment affect them, and how do they affect the environment? Now, I affirm that the relation of the visible environment to the great man is in the main exactly what it is to the "variation" in the Darwinian philosophy. It chiefly adopts or rejects, preserves or destroys, in short selects him. And whenever it adopts and preserves the great man. it becomes modified by his influence in an entirely original and peculiar way. He acts as a ferment, and changes its constitution, just as the advent of a new zoological species changes the faunal and floral equilibrium of the region in which it appears.[32]

For James, the two factors of spontaneous variation and natural selection, although devised to explain physical evolution, provide an illuminating analogy for understanding social evolution as well. But James is not just concerned with the so-called great leaders—the charismatic individual and the religious prophet or such universally acknowledged giants as Jesus, Alexander the Great, Cromwell, Gandhi, or Churchill. James was interested also in the contribution to social evolution of the average individual. In this same essay he wrote, "We see this power of individual initiative exemplified on a small scale all about us, and on a large scale in the case of the leaders of history."[33]

In Mr. Allen's response to James, he continued to deny that individuals, be they great leaders or common human beings, made anything more than the smallest of differences. In the "Importance of Individuals" James replies that it is exactly these "small differences" which he is interested in and which are worthy of serious attention by any philosopher and student of history.[34] It is in fact just these little differences, these small variations and exceptions, which elicit our most lively interest and sometimes our deepest admiration. In that flickering moment of transition from the present to the future, in that split second of open possibility when things have still not fallen into that dump heap of the frozen and unchangeable past, these small variations of individual response and initiative can make momentous differences in both the short and long course of history.

Therefore introspection, experimentation, and comparison are the major methods used by James to open up the empirical givens of human nature. Of these, the comparative method had a privileged role to play in developing his functionalist view of mind. This must never be overlooked even though, as the reader will see in the next chapter, I can affirm along with the phenomenologists, as James did himself, the logical priority of the descriptive (introspective or phenomenological) point of departure.

James's functionalsim was rich and complex. Mind was not just a servant of the environment which registered upon a passive organism the inexorable demands of the external world. Nor does James's functionalism see the mind as totally in the service of the basic creaturely drives of food, thirst, and survival. Certainly mind serves these subjective interests, but it serves others as well. That there are other interests dealing with morality, art, humor, play, and religion is something James has affirmed only on descriptive grounds. Human beings everywhere seem to have these interests and they seldom reduce them simply to the brute struggle for survival. But as we will see later, in James's discussion of the instincts,[35] in his theory of the roots of morality,[36] and in his understanding of the rise of our intellectual capacities for classification,[37] he believes that many of these so-called higher interests can be *explained* only by seeing them as autonomous and innate capacities of man due to the fortune of spontaneous variation in evolutionary history. Which is to say, they cannot be explained as derivable from our lower bodily needs nor are they simply products of learning.

Even though James believed that these higher subjective interests of man do not have as their purpose survival as such, James never went so far as to say that they are irrelevant to survival or can ever afford to become oblivious to issues of survival. In this, James is somewhat different than the late Abraham Maslow. Maslow also posited higher subjective interests; he called them "the tendency towards self-actualization," in order to distinguish them from lower drives involved in the maintenance and preservation of the organism. But Maslow disconnects the tendency toward self-actualization from issues of survival more than is necessary and more than did James. Self-actualization never becomes an end in itself for James as it does for Maslow and for other members of the culture of joy. The selective power of the environment and the demands of survival are never too far out of the picture for James. But then for him, survival refers to the survival of the community as well as the individual and to survival in the remote future as well as in the present. James's individualism is not a negative individualism, an individualism which says that the rights, satisfactions, and survival of the solitary person take precedence over the good of the community. Rather, it is just the reverse. James's individualism is a positive one which says that individual action *can make a difference,* both on the small and the grand scale, for the good of the community—its collective satisfactions, its health, strength, and capacity to cope with the inevitable vicissitudes of existence.

The methods of phenomenological description, experimentation, and comparison follow James into his later studies of religion. But even then—even in studying the religious behavior of humans—James is developing his philosophical anthropology and his vision of the strenuous life. Phenomenological description of religious experience is used to gain new data relevant to the nature of man. But for the purposes of explanation and evaluation, the comparative and evolutionary concerns which we have reviewed in this chapter also make their appearance.

But now we must turn to other questions. If James was an early phenomenologist, what does this mean? And if it is best to understand James's *Principles* as a philosophical psychology, what more precisely does this indicate?

Notes

1. *PP,* 1:1.
2. Ibid.
3. *PP,* 1:183.
4. Perry, *TCWJ,* 2:121.
5. *PP,* 1:184: *CER,* p. 318.
6. *CER,* p. 318.
7. Ibid., p. 320.
8. *Psychology: The Briefer Course* (New York: Harper Torchbooks, 1961), pp. 334–35.
9. Ibid., p. 328.
10. Andrew Reck, "The Philosophical Psychology of William James," *Southern Journal of Philosophy* 9 (Fall 1971): 295.
11. Allen, *WJ,* p. 181.
12. Perry, *TCWJ.*
13. *PP,* 1:185.
14. Ibid., p. 192–93.
15. Ibid., p. 194.
16. Ibid.
17. Perry, *TCWJ,* 1:323: Allen, *WJ,* p. 168.
18. Bruce Wilshire, *William James and Phenomenology* (Bloomington, Ind.: Indiana University Press, 1968), p. 141.
19. *PP,* 1:6.
20. Perry, *TCWJ,* p. 475.
21. Ibid., p. 482.
22. Ibid., p. 484.
23. *CER,* p. 44.
24. Ibid., p. 50.
25. *WB,* pp. 221–22.
26. *CER,* pp. 52–53.
27. *WB,* p. 223; *PP,* 2:678.
28. *CER,* p. 66.
29. Ibid, p. 67.
30. *WB,* p. 218.

31. Ibid.
32. Ibid., p. 226.
33. Ibid., p. 227.
34. *WB*, p. 256.
35. *PP*, 2:383–439.
36. Ibid., 2:617–83; *WB*, p. 189.
37. *PP*, 2:617–83.

3

Meaning and Mind: Phenomenology and Functionalism

A small but discernible ripple of excitement recently has streamed through the generally unperturbable waters of philosophic inquiry. It can be detected especially among those philosophers who are Americans but who have drunk deeply from the mysterious wells of Continental phenomenology. The discovery that there is indigenous style of phenomenology flowing right down the mainstream of American philosophy—right in the psychology and philosophy of William James—has given many scholars in the United States a renewed interest in their own philosophic heritage.

Thanks to the insights from a number of important books and articles, it is now possible to say two things: (1) that James anticipated some of the major themes of European phenomenology and phenomenological psychology, and (2) that he actually influenced some of the directions which this school of thinking was to take.

These discoveries, although of material interest to philosophers and psychologists, should be of great interest to theologians. The vision of human nature found in such diverse theologians as Paul Tillich, Karl Barth, Reinhold Niebuhr, Martin Buber,[1] Rudolph Bultmann, and John MacGuarrie have all been influenced by European phenomenology. Especially American theologians, who have tended to orient themselves toward the European intellectual scene, should take note of the synthesis of phenomenological and functional themes in that distinctively American thinker, William James.

But what does it mean to say that James was a phenomenologist? James was committed to the study of man at several different levels. Moreover, he tried to put these various levels together. One of the steps he took to integrate them was to give priority to the level of description. But no matter which perspective he took, a very similar overall image of human nature emerged. *It was a vision of humans as active and purposive creatures who are oriented toward the future in an effort to realize subjective interests and shape their environments into a richer and more hospitable place to live.*

Was this a view to which James was committed prior to his systematic studies? After all, this was the image of human nature which effected his own recovery from depression and psychosomatic incapacity and which gave him the courage to venture forth and act once again. To acknowledge such personal roots to thinking would correspond completely with James's own view of the origins of philosophic reflection. Philosophic positions are "accidents more or less of personal vision." But from the standpoint of the task of the philosopher, neither the vision nor conclusion is sufficient in itself. "What distinguishes a philosopher's truth is that it is *reasoned.*"[2] James would say the same for his own view of mind as active and purposeful. His obligation does not end with asserting this view of human life; it is the data, descriptions, and reasons which he sets forth that make the critical difference.

Recent efforts to demonstrate the phenomenological dimensions of James's thought have been largely successful. In this chapter, I will illustrate briefly a few of the phenomenological themes found in James's psychology and philosophy. But it is important not to overstate the phenomenological character of James's thought. It is not fair to suggest, as Hans Linschoten does in the title of his seminal book, that James was *On the Way Toward a Phenomenological Psychology.*[3] It is more accurate to agree with Andrew Reck; James was not so much developing a "proto-phenomenological psychology" as he was moving toward a "philosophical psychology critical yet appreciative of the possibilities of metaphysics."[4] Although more than a phenomenologist, James does believe that the fundamental starting point in any study of man is the task of *describing* the inner experience of living in a world of *meanings*.

The Aims of Phenomenology

Phenomenology as a self-conscious philosophic movement was founded by Edmund Husserl (1859-1938). Yet it builds on the insights of many other philosophers such as Descartes, Kant, Brentano, and even James. Husserl saw in the phenomenological method a way of providing philosophy with truly scientific foundations, a program for saving psychology from the corrupting influences of naturalistic philosophies, and an approach to knowledge which would give Western civilization the rational grounds it so desperately needed.

Phenomenology's bête noire is naturalism. This is the conviction that everything in nature can be explained as caused by prior physical forces which can be measured quantitatively and located precisely in mathematically conceived time and space.[5] These are the assumptions which led to the miraculous achievements of the physical sciences and which many scientists believed would establish psychology as a truly scientific study of the mind. But when naturalism is applied to psychology, an inevitable "naturalizing of consciousness" occurs.[6] This means that consciousness is now viewed in analogy with the rigorous causal system of physical nature. Everything which we generally associate with consciousness such as intentions, ideas, ideals, purposes, and norms are either disregarded or treated as "facts." To treat something as a "fact" is, according to the phenomenological perspective, to treat it as explainable by physical causes and laws.

It was Husserl's conviction that to naturalize consciousness is both self-contradictory and unscientific. It is self-contradictory because scientists themselves have intentions, ideas, ideals, and purposes which they act on and assume are not just the result of causal laws. Furthermore, a naturalizing psychology is itself completely unscientific; it attempts to create a mental science without taking the given structure of consciousness as the basic phenomenon to be studied. These criticisms were directed primarily toward the scientific psychology of Husserl's day— the psychophysiology of Wundt, Weber, Fechner, and Vierodt, with which James himself was well acquainted. To Husserl, it was absurd to hope that the brand of experimental psychophysiology would provide the foundations for the cultural disciplines of logic, epistemology, and ethics upon which the direction of Western civilization depends.[7]

Husserl wanted to subordinate experimental psychology and place it within the larger context of a truly foundational phenomenological science of the basic structures of human consciousness. The position which he developed, which was first published in his *Ideen I* (1913), was a radical attempt to find total objectivity through a description of the completely immanent and subjective ways which the objects of our experience appear to consciousness.

Certainly a proposal which claims to find objectivity totally within subjectivity seems paradoxical. But closer consideration reveals that his program is indeed thinkable and, more than that, commands powerful reasons in its defense.

Husserl believed that both philosophy and psychology must be built on a method which first describes how objects and events of experience reveal themselves to consciousness. Husserl rejected the view of consciousness which saw it as a mere receptacle full of brute facts related like causally determined electrons and neutrons within an atom. Rather, consciousness consists of "meanings." Meanings are vastly different things than causally related facts. Meanings have, according to Husserl, an intentional structure. Following the insights of his former teacher Franz Brentano, Husserl believed that consciousness was always "a more or less complex consciousness of."[8] Consciousness is not just an empty and aimless light which shines on nothing. Our consciousness is always a conscious *of* something—a consciousness *of* a tree, a person, a memory, a hope, the images of a dream, the personages of a myth, or the numbers of a mathematical formula. It is because consciousness is made up of intentions which are always *of* something that Husserl asserts it has an objective correlate as a part of its very structure. Our subjectivity contains objectivity within it, and when we get back to absolute subjectivity, we also discover absolute objectivity.

Phenomenologists are aware that our everyday consciousness is full of cultural assumptions, personal biases and tribal prejudices. Husserl fully acknowledged that there are enormous differences between people and groups in the ways that they interpret their experiences. The meaning of buffaloes to the Sioux Indian was vastly different than it was to the hunter-entrepreneurs who nearly wiped this precious animal off the face of the earth. Certainly the flag of the United States meant something very much different to an American soldier during World War II than it did to a member of the German military. Therefore, if subjectivity is the royal road to objectivity, some method of ridding consciousness of those prejudices must be established. And this is what the phenomenological movement is all about. Phenomenology is primarily a series of methodological procedures for removing assumptions and prejudices so that the pure and undistorted meanings of consciousness can come to light.

The full theoretical elaboration of this method did not appear until his *Ideen I*. It consisted of three main steps. First, there was a step called the *epoche,* which was designed to remove from consideration any concern whatsoever about the *existence* of the object of consciousness under study. In our everyday consciousness of "natural attitude," we tend to be very concerned about whether the objects of our perception actually exist or not. But in the phenomenological mode, we suspend this concern. Instead, one is interested only in the object's appearance in consciousness. This frees the phenomenologist to take everything seriously just as it is given. Material objects, human communities, mathematical concepts, dreams, hallucinations, myths, and memories can be viewed exactly as they are given in consciousness without regard to their actual existence in the "real" world. The second step is a more positive technique of "reduction" whereby this "appearance" or phenomenal residue is attended to with great care and rendered more and more present to consciousness. The final step is called "ideation" or the "eidetic reduction" and consists of varying the point of view in an effort to extract the ideal essence of the appearance which is common to the different perspectives. In a far less methodical and self-conscious manner, James shared many of the assumptions and some of the methods of the phenomenological attitude.

It has been of great historical interest to uncover the depth of influence which James had on Husserl. Husserl acknowledges having read James's *Principles* for a course taught in 1891–92.[9] In his diary he acknowledged having read James, said that he had received some "lightning flashes," and called James a "courageous and original man."[10] In his *Logische Untersuchungen,* he credits James with teaching him how to overcome psychologism, and in a writing toward the end of his career he stated that James was the first to notice the horizonal character of experience with his idea of the "fringe of consciousness"—a concept which we will soon consider in some detail.[11]

Yet, for every similarity between James and Husserl one also can show a genuine divergence. James had nothing like Husserl's drive to establish an absolutely certain fund of rational knowledge which would provide the foundation for all the cultural disciplines. Although James was interested in knowledge that is certain, he was far more interested in knowledge that is relevant to the changing circumstances of man. Nevertheless, it is to the credit of James that he understood the need for something like a phenomenological point of departure for the study of man.

Consciousness and Meaning

At the beginning of his *Principles,* James is dedicated to assumptions which are anything but phenomenological. Yet he gradually reverses his position in the process of writing the book. Throughout the first seven chapters of his great book, he advocates both a psychophysical dualism and an epistemological dualism. They both are highly antiphenomenological assumptions. When James later carefully analyzed his experience, as he did in his *Essays in Radical Empiricism,* he found that these dualisms do not actually exist at all. By psychophysical dualism, I mean that James held that there is distinction between consciousness and the body or between mind and brain. Although he was never willing to say that consciousness is a simple epiphenomenon of the brain,[12] he did at this early stage insist that there is a correspondence between brain states and conscious states. For every conscious state there must be a corresponding brain state.[13] James believed that the psychology of brain functions must assume this correspondence theory for its own work. But he denied that psychology as a whole must go further and accept the "unwarrantable" metaphysical assumption that consciousness is just an "automaton" of deeper physiological determinisms.[14] James clearly recognizes that the entire question is a metaphysical issue, but he proposes that psychology follow the metaphysical assumptions of commonsense and accept an "interactionist" theory which says that sometimes the brain causes mental states and sometimes mental states directly influence the brain. Here James clearly is advocating a kind of psychophysical dualism. But it is certainly not a Cartesian dualism which sees mind and body (brain) as *entirely* different substances, the former being material and extended and the later being immaterial and unextended. In accordance with James's general functionalism, mind and body —even in this early formulation—are related intimately but distinguishable by their functions.

In these early chapters of the *Principles,* James also commits himself to another form of dualism. This is an epistemological dualism which sees the mind in its knowing activity as related to totally separate objects in the outside world. Questions about the philosophical possibility of knowledge of these outside objects are "ultimate puzzles" about which the psychologist need not bother himself.[15] The psychologist's attitude toward cognition, writes James,

> is a throughgoing dualism. It supposes two elements, mind knowing and thing known, and treats them as irreducible. Neither gets out of itself or into the other, neither in any way *is* the other, neither *makes* the other.[16]

But then James adds a prophetic afterthought as if he almost sensed the direction of his thought. For the purposes of psychology as a natural science, the psychologist must assume a commonsense dualism of subject and object regardless of "whatever ulterior monistic philosophy he may, as an individual who has the right also to be a metaphysician, have in reserve."[17] James would capitalize very soon on this proviso, even before finishing the very book that he was writing. And by the years 1904–5, when the essays on his radical empiricism were first being published, he was busily tackling the job of explicitly rejecting these dualisms. He developed a theory which reduced them to working hypotheses that gain their meaning from the specific contexts in which they are used.

In an early chapter of the *Principles,* James had written that "Introspective Observation is what we have to rely on first and foremost and always."[18] But James never quite followed his own advice. If he had, his great chapter on the "Stream of Thought" would have come earlier in the *Principles* than it did. Only after eight chapters, several of which were devoted to the psychophysiology of the brain, does he turn to the descriptive approach and announce that he is now beginning "the study of the mind from within."[19] In this famous chapter, James turns to a remarkable description of the very texture of consciousness. When looked at descriptively, consciousness seems to be on the move, going somewhere, aiming toward known and unknown goals. In short, James's description of the stream of consciousness reveals it as purposeful through and through. This chapter, possibly more than anything else that James ever wrote, influenced the art and philosophy of his day. Not only was it read, and absorbed by Husserl and through him greatly influenced Sartre, Heidegger, and Merleau-Ponty, but it also immeasurably inspired such literary giants as Gertrude Stein and James Joyce.

In this chapter, James describes consciousness as a "stream." "A 'river' or a 'stream' are the metaphors by which it is most naturally described."[20] The full significance of this metaphor cannot be appreciated without realizing that James is opposing other metaphors which liken consciousness to a "train" or a "chain." The latter set of metaphors depicts consciousness as discrete elements or separate units—perhaps small individual ideas or sensations—which somehow get combined into larger clusters of experience. But who believed such a thing as that? And what did James hope to accomplish by opposing this belief with the metaphor of stream?

Actually there was a famous school of British philosophy associated with the names of Hume, Locke, and Berkeley and a German school associated with Herbart who believed the very thing that James felt compelled to refute. And they were influential. As James wrote, the idea of consciousness as a stream "makes it impossible for us to follow obediently in the footprints of either the Lockean or the Herbartian school, schools which have had almost unlimited influence in Germany and among ourselves."[21] The British school had in fact provided most of the philosophical underpinnings of the German school of physiological psychology pioneered by Weber, Fechner, and Wundt. The more recent stimulus-response psychologies in America and to some extent the operant-conditioning theories of Skinner and his followers also assume that consciousness is nothing more than discrete sense impressions from the outside. The starting point of James's approach to psychology is different from any of these traditions. He writes, "Most books start with sensations, as the simplest mental facts, and proceed synthetically, constructing each higher stage from those below it."[22] But James believes that this method clearly abandons the empirical method of investigation.

> No one ever had a simple sensation by itself. Consciousness, from our natal day, is of a teeming multiplicity of subjects and relations, and what we call simple sensations are results of discriminative attention, pushed often to a very high degree.[23]

This statement contains the nucleus of James's incipient phenomenology and the promise of an emerging radical empiricism. *Objects* and *relations,* not simple sensations—these are the basic stuff of consciousness.

James lists five characteristics of the stream of consciousness. These five characteristics are discussed in considerable detail in almost every book on James. Our treatment will be far more brief. Consciousness always presents itself as *personal, changing, continuous, related to objects independent of itself,* and *selective.*

To say that the thoughts of consciousness are part of a *personal* consciousness means that the contents of consciousness are always attached to a "self." The "universal conscious fact is not 'feeling and thoughts exist,' but 'I think' and 'I feel.' No psychology, at any rate, can question the existence of personal selves."[24] Of course, some psychologies have tried to and the psychology of B. F. Skinner is a contemporary example of one which has. But according to James, when they do this, they are being unscientific. Thoughts attached to personal selves are a fundamental data of consciousness. Or at least, this is what James says in the *Principles.* In his *Essays on Radical Empiricism,* James himself places a qualification on this principle, which we will review at a later time.[25]

Consciousness is always *changing.* Using the words of his friend Shadworth Hodgson, James contends that it is always a "sequence of different feelings."[26] Once again, the enemy is primarily popular interpretations of the Lockean doctrine that experience is made up of "simple ideas" or elements which always remain the same. On the basis of his description of immediate experience, James denies that we ever get the same idea *or* sensation twice. The concept of a permanently existing idea "which makes its appearance before the footlights of consciousness at periodical intervals, is as mythological an entity as the Jack of Spades."

In these first two generalizations, James is building a picture of consciousness as purposeful and directional no matter how vague this directionality may seem for people in different mental states or at different levels of mental development. Consciousness is not just a cold and unrelated group of distinct elements rattling around like little potatoes in an empty basket which accidentally organize themselves into interesting shapes and hues. Consciousness is warm, changing, and above all, *continuous.*

Continuity and Context

Under the topic of the *continuity* of consciousness, James makes some of his most striking phenomenological descriptions. Throughout the rest of chapter 9, James primarily is doing philosophical psychology; he is discussing basic metaphysical assumptions about how the mind is related to the world. He is, although he hardly knew it, laying the foundations for his radical empiricism—his full-blown doctrine of pure experience, the reality of relations, and the unity of conscious-

ness and its objects. Here, too, we see the psychological foundations for his vision of the strenuous life, for in these pages there
emerges as a view of consciousness as ambiguous, oriented to
meanings, purposeful, interested, selective, and condemned to
decision and commitment.

James uses his introspective descriptions to defeat the dog-
mas of previous superficial introspective psychologies. The
British and German empiricists were also introspectionists. But
their brand of introspection led them to grasp only the discrete,
stable, and definite components of consciousness and to neglect
the transitions and continuities. This is the reason they could
not rid themselves of the erroneous view that consciousness was
a group of *discontinuous* elements which prance before our
mind's eye more or less one at a time. Nothing shows the affinity
of James with the aims of phenomenology more than his
resistance to this degraded introspectionism. James could see,
as did Husserl, that this was no description of consciousness at
all; it was an imposition upon consciousness of a model borrowed from physics about how the material particles of nature
are related. Husserl called it the "natural attitude." But in
reality it is not natural at all, for neither consciousness nor
nature "naturally" reveal themselves as disconnected atomic
particles. This is a construct of science, not a given of experience. If one pays careful attention to experience, if one truly
describes it accurately, one can see that there are vague transitions, continuities, and overlappings which are a part of the
very fabric of consciousness and just as real as the distinct ideas.

Although consciousness changes, James believes that these
changes are never "absolutely abrupt." There are indeed
"breaks" and "contrasts" in experience but careful description
reveals that they are connected and overlap. To illustrate his
point, James gives his famous example of a clap of thunder;
certainly thunder interrupts our consciousness and in this sense
is separate and disconnected. Interrupt our consciousness it
most certainly does, but James denies complete abruptness. We
do not just hear thunder; we hear "thunder-breaking-upon-
silence-and-contrasting-with-it."[28] The silence which precedes
the thunder overlaps and penetrates the thunder. Experience is
made up of "resting places" and movements or "flights." James

wants to call the resting places the "substantive parts" of consciousness and the movements or flights the "transitive parts."[29] James admits that consciousness likes the security of the resting places; it generally means that we have attained some goal, realized some ambition, or found something for which we have been searching. But the transitions are as much a part of our experience as the substantive parts; they are also as much a part of our language. In our language we find these transitions in our conjunctions and prepositions—our "ands" and "buts" and "bys."[30] These prepositions and conjunctions refer to real feelings in experience and are just as real as those feelings which refer to nouns such as cold, hot, blue, or red.

James's point may be unclear until we remember that he is describing the phenomenal fact that consciousness is composed of meanings which have a direction and which seem to be going some place. This becomes more obvious when he describes a slightly more sophisticated transitive experience, what James calls a "tendency." Throughout his discussion of the experience of tendency, James is demonstrating that there is directionality to thought and a context of meaning which surrounds every distinct idea or word in our consciousness. He illustrates this with the example of a sentence. The meaning of a sentence is more than the distinct and separate words within it. James writes "that large tracts of human speech are nothing but *signs of direction* in thought, of which direction we nevertheless have an acutely discriminative sense, though no definite sensorial image plays any part in it whatsoever."[31] Or again, "All of us have this permanent consciousness of whether our thought is going. It is a feeling like any other, a feeling of what thoughts are next to arise, before they have arisen."[32]

Sometimes this feeling of meaning, the "intention of saying a thing before" we have actually said it, comes to us even when the words themselves do not follow. We have in consciousness only a sense of "gap" or "absence," or we sense looking for something like a name that we have forgotten or a problem which we want solved. But even here we have a sense of meaning about what we are looking for; when we finally find it, we recognize it as the thing that was missing. This sense of tendency, direction, and movement is the large part of consciousness and forms a meaning context—a "halo," "penumbra," "horizon," or "fringe"—around the definite words or discrete images which are the only things in consciousness that British and German empiricism have been able to see.

James makes two more sets of distinction in his discussion of the continuity of consciousness which are important for our understanding of the phenomenological themes in his psychology. There is the distinction between the "topic" and the "object" of thought and the distinction between "knowledge by acquaintance" and "knowledge about." The two sets of distinctions are related.

In most of our thinking, especially voluntary thinking, there is some "topic subject about which all the members of the thought revolve."[33] This topic or subject may be a gap which we want to fill or an interest which we want to satisfy. There is an important relation between the topic of a thought and its fringe, and the meaning of the topic is controlled by its relation to the wider fringe or horizon. The relation between topic and fringe can either be a matter of "harmony" or "discord," of either "furtherance or hindrance of the topic."[34] Making a point which will have great implications for his controversial psychology of rationality, James says, "When the sense of furtherance is there, we are 'all right;' with the sense of hindrance we are dissatisfied and perplexed."[35] The fringe of meaning which surrounds the topic is either an impediment or an asset to the fulfilment of the topic.

It is of crucial importance to understand James's distinction between the "topic" and the "object" of thought. Using the typical "sentence" as an illustration, the object of "Columbus discovered America in 1492" is the entire thought, the entire sentence.[36] Most people, James supposes, would see some specific part such as "Columbus" or "America" as the object of the sentence, but James says these more specific portions are really the "topic." The following points are so important for James's thought that I must quote in full:

> But the *Object* of your thought is really its entire content or deliverance, neither more nor less. It is a vicious use of speech to take out a substantive kernel from its content and call that its object; and it is an equally vicious use of speech to add a substantive

kernel not articulately in its content and call that its object. Yet either one of these two sins we commit, whenever we content ourselves with saying that a given thought is simply "about" a certain topic, or that that topic is its "object." The object of my thought in the previous sentence, for example, is strictly speaking neither Columbus, nor America, nor its discovery. It is nothing short of the entire sentence, "Columbus-discovered-America-in-1492." And if we wish to speak of it substantively, we must make a substantive of it by writing it out thus with hyphens between all its words. Nothing but this can possibly name its delicate idiosyncrasy. And if we wish to *feel* that idiosyncracy we must reproduce the thought as if it was uttered, with every word fringed and the whole sentence bathed in that original halo of obscure relations, which, like an horizon, then spread about its meaning.[37]

At the end of the previous chapter, entitled "The Relations of Minds to Other Things,"[38] and throughout these sections in chapter 9, James makes an important distinction between two types of knowledge—knowledge by "acquaintance" and "knowledge about." Knowledge by acquaintance is the knowledge of the brute "presence" or "bare impression" of something such as our knowledge of how an apple tastes or feels, knowledge of the color blue when I see it, or the sense for a second of time when I feel it pass.[39] In knowledge by acquaintance our sense for the relations or fringes surrounding a thing is small and we are "aware only in the penumbral nascent way of a 'fringe' of unarticulated affinities about it."[40] In knowledge about, however, our awareness of the fringe of relations surrounding a thing is far more articulate and explicit. Although knowledge by acquaintance and knowledge about are relative to one another, referring primarily to degrees of simplicity and complexity of our knowledge of a particular thing, on the whole acquaintance refers to our bare "sensations" or "feelings" of something, while knowledge about refers to our "thoughts" and "concepts" about a thing.[41]

The discrimination between *topic* and *object* and knowledge by *acquaintance* and knowledge *about* are fundamental descriptive distinctions which James draws on time and time again throughout this massive two-volume *Principles*. It touches his discussion of the meaning of sensation, perception, conception, discrimination, and many others. They constitute the backbone of his radical empiricism and are given their most advanced theoretical statement in the *Essays on Radical Empiricism*. By and large, grasping the topic of a thought is a matter of knowledge by acquaintance; this is because our explicit awareness of the relations surrounding it is minimal. Our knowledge of the wider object of a thought or sentence—the fringe or horizon—is derived from our knowledge about.[42] Of course the differences are only relative. Certainly some sense of a fringe is known even at the most rudimentary level of knowledge by acquaintance. In addition, knowledge by acquaintance is the origin of all knowledge, the basic raw experience out of which every later and more abstract stage of knowledge is derived. Knowledge by acquaintance becomes the pure experience of the *Essays on Radical Empiricism* and plays an important part in James's later theory of truth.

Hans Linschoten[43] and Alan Gurwitch[44] are correct in their judgment that James's distinction between object and topic corresponds to similar distinctions made by Husserl. Linschoten says it well when he writes,

> Already in the *Logishe Untersuchungen,* we find that a distinction is made between the "Gegenstand, so wie er intendiert ist" (the thing or object in the way it is intended) and the "Gegenstand, welcher intendiert ist" (the object or thing that is intended). It is evident that this is identical with James' distinction between "object" and "topic."[45]

But whether or not it corresponds to descriptions actually made by Husserl, the overall outlines of James's descriptions are basically correct and give us a commanding understanding of the purposeful, directional, meaningful, and prospective nature of consciousness.

We have already discussed certain aspects of James's fourth characteristic of consciousness when we reviewed his understanding of the *object* of thought. His fourth point was this: "Human thought appears to deal with objects independent of itself; that is, it is cognitive, or possesses the function of knowing."[46] In this principle, James begins to overcome the epistemological dualism of his earlier chapters. James has already broken down the epistemological dualism of British empiricism with its belief that consciousness exists and is somehow filled with distinct ideas which are thrown into consciousness as various odds and ends might be tossed into an empty closet.

But James takes a step further in qualifying his original epistemological dualism. At the level of knowledge by acquaintance, one really doesn't know whether the thing experienced is mental or physical. For instance, take the experience of heartburn; we don't ask the question whether it is mental or something outside of our mental life. It is something that is simply "there" as "that taste." Only later when the doctor says that we have heartburn does it become a quality with an independent existence. "The first spaces, times, things, qualities, experienced by the child," James writes, "probably appear . . . as simple *beings,* neither in nor out of thought."[47] It is only by having repeated experiences of sameness with these objects that the child gradually builds up a sense of an external world which exists independently of consciousness.

In asserting that the dualism of consciousness and object is not primitive and that originally consciousness is always a consciousness *of* something, he is moving remarkably close to a phenomenological concept of intentionality. James had read Brentano on the unity of consciousness and here we see evidence of the latter's view of consciousness as intentional. This vision of the unity of thought and object was later sharpened into the cornerstone of James's radical empiricism. Many years later, in his *Essays* he wrote the following words about the commonsense separation of subject and object: "Experience, I believe, has no such inner duplicity; and the separation of it into consciousness and content comes, not by way of subtraction, but by way of addition."[48] This "addition" is the special contexts into which this basic stuff of experience is placed by later stages of reflection. In some contexts a given experience of a thing—perhaps a room or a tree—seems mental; in other contexts it might seem physical. It all depends upon the purposes to which we are putting the original experience. Yes, the dualism of subject and object completely collapses in the *Essays;* but long before that it begins crumbling in the *Principles.*

But in James's last generalization about the stream of consciousness, he may have gone beyond the weak and passive view of intentionality found in Brentano.[49] Both James and Brentano agree that consciousness is inextricably related to objects, but James goes further and sees consciousness actively forming and shaping the objects to which it is necessarily related. Consciousness is "always interested more in one part of its object than in another, and welcomes and rejects, or chooses, all the while it thinks."[50] Consciousness is constantly selecting and rejecting, emphasizing and ignoring various aspects of its experience. This is true to some extent at every level of consciousness, although, as we will see when mysticism is discussed, it is far less true for this kind of experience. But in the *Principles* James develops a hierarchial view of the mind and argues that selectivity and choice of some kind functions at each of these levels.

He first starts at the highest level. He writes, "The phenomena of selective attention and of deliberative will are of course patent examples of this choosing activity."[51] Here James is starting at the top of the hierarchy of examples, pointing first to those examples of selectivity which are most obvious and most available to phenomenological description. He adds the further point that these purposes, goals, directions, and tendencies are varied, multiple, and sometimes in conflict. This means that choice must be made between them. The most productive results of James's phenomenology of consciousness can be found when he writes,

> We see that the mind is at every stage a theatre of simultaneous possibilities. Consciousness consists in the comparison of these with each other, the selection of some, and the suppression of the rest by the reinforcing and inhibiting agency of attention.[52]

To say that mind is a "theatre of simultaneous possibility" is the same as saying it is inherently ambiguous. Our subjective interests can be realized in a variety of ways with different objects. Conflict and tension between the diverse possibilities is of the essence of life. For James, insecurity and incompleteness are pervasive ingredients of our mental life. In this sense for the ambiguity of consciousness, James places himself in the company of a long line of existentially oriented writers such as

Kierkegaard, Heidegger, Sartre, Ricoeur, and Fromm, who have made this insight a fundamental element of their philosophical anthropologies. Consciousness has its pluralisms and multiplicities for James just as it did for the British empiricists. But it is not a pluralism of atomic sensations and ideas; *it is a pluralism of meaningful possibilities.* Humans are condemned to a life of decision and commitment because it is only through these modalities that they can find a higher sense of unity between the ambiguous and contending possibilities which beset their existence. The unity of consciousness about which James has spoken is the unity of thought and object—the fact that thought can never be conceived without an object. The continuity of consciousness has been the continuity which places discrete topics within a larger fringe of meaning. But all of this has only led up to James's understanding of a higher kind of discontinuity and fragmentation, and this is the divisiveness which comes from diverse and competing meanings.

But James is more complex than many existentialists in their understanding of the ambiguous and decisional character of consciousness. James is aware that decision goes on at the higher levels of deliberative will and reasoning, but this level rests on several hierarchically organized levels of sensation, perception, and attention which are selective as well. Selectivity goes on at the most primitive levels of sensory reception; the very structure of our sense organs constitutes limitations on the magnitude and kind of sensory experience which we can receive and digest.[53] Out of all the sensations which bombard and register on our senses, our conscious perception pays attention to only a small number which actually *interest* us.[54] Futhermore, perception, James admits, is conditioned and guided in its selectivity by habit and custom. After all of these earlier selective processes the final role for deliberative will is relatively limited. But as we will see more fully later, these relatively circumscribed acts of free choice make all the difference in the world. They establish the broad contexts, the overarching directions, the encompassing fringes and horizons of our lives. This is the sphere of ethics. James writes, "The ethical energy par excellence has to . . . choose which *interest* out of several, equally coercive, shall become supreme. The issue here is of utmost pregnancy, for it decides a man's entire career."[55]

In this and other sections of the *Principles,* a phenomenological tone begins to emerge. In fact, something very close to
Husserl's *epoché* appears. James suggests that the primary
obligation of the psychologist is to capture the object of consciousness (the meaning or fringe) just as it appears to consciousness. In one place he explicitly states that we can have
knowledge of something as it reveals itself in consciousness
without also assuming that it must actually exist outside of us in
the real world.[56] He criticizes those psychologists who are guilty
of the "psychologist's fallacy." They assume that they "know
the object to be one thing and the thought another; and they
forthwith foist their own knowledge into that of the thought of
which they pretend to give a true account. . . . *Thought may, but
need not, in knowing, discriminate between its object and
itself.*"[57] In his highly important chapter entitled "The Perception of Reality" he makes a clear distinction between knowing
something as it reveals itself in experience and actually "believing" in it. Taking a cue from Brentano, he contends that there is
a difference between the "object of thought" and the "belief in
its reality."[58] This is certainly close to the distinction Husserl
makes between the natural attitude which believes in the existence of the objects of the world and *epoché,* which brackets, for
the purposes of phenomenological description, the question of
the object's existence. And finally, in the *Essays on Radical
Empiricism,* James boldly writes that the first obligation in
grasping the conjunctive meanings of consciousness is to hold
fast to it and "take it at its face value, neither less nor more,"
which means "to take it just as we feel it and not to confuse
ourselves with abstract talk *about* it."[59]

But James's move to what we would today call "phenomenology" was unsteady. It was his great strength that he never
excluded experimental or comparative approaches, but he
frequently got confused about which method had logical priority. For example once, after a beautiful description of the
continuity of experience and the idea of fringe, he takes re-
course to brain physiology to explain the "causes" of these
characteristics of consciousness. He suggests that maybe these
continuities and transitions of consciousness are due to the fact

"that no state of the brain can be supposed instantly to die away."[60] James seems unaware that to suggest such a thing flies in the face of the logic of his own position. It obscures the point that to search for brain states which seem to correlate with consciousness, one first of all must describe consciousness—its meanings, tendencies, transitions, and objects—in order even to begin to know what brain processes to look for. In addition, these brain processes indeed may correlate in some way with the meanings of consciousness, but one cannot imply by this that they directly *cause* them. If one did this, one would be reducing the meanings of consciousness to mere natural processes and things. Of course, this is just what James is criticizing British and German empiricists for doing.

With regard to the other dualism discussed earlier—the relation of mind and body—James more and more saw mind or consciousness as a dimension of the "felt" and "lived" body in contrast to the dead and mechnical body of physiology and anatomy. The body was first of all for James "my body"—a lived and felt body. In addition, consciousness more and more became consciousness which belonged to the lived and felt body. Even in chapter 9, James writes,

> We think; and as we think we feel our bodily selves as the seat of the thinking. If the thinking be *our* thinking, it must be suffused through all its parts with that peculiar warmth and intimacy that make it come as ours. Whether the warmth and intimacy be anything more than the feeling of the same old body always there, is a matter for the next chapter to decide.[61]

As Wild, Wilshire, and James Edie have pointed out, it is because James holds this view of consciousness as an "embodied consciousness" rather than a completely "pure, disembodied ego" that his incipient phenomenological orientation was closer to the existential phenomenology of Sartre, Merleau-Ponty, and Ricoeur than the more strictly "transcendental" phenomenology of Husserl himself.[62]

James is working toward what Hans Linschoten calls a "complementary"[63] or Paul Ricoeur calls a "diagnostic"[64] understanding of the relation between mind and body. This is the view which sees mind and body as joined in the concrete experience of living. James's later dictum that there is no "thought stuff" different than a "thing stuff" but just "the same identical piece of pure experience" applies equally well to the relation of mind and body.[65] Whether at later stages of reflection something appears as an object of consciousness or as a physical thing such as the mechanical workings of the brain depends upon the context of thought and inquiry into which the experience is placed. The question is, then, what is the relation between felt experience and scientific abstractions? James never fully settled this question. But the answer which is entirely compatible with James is that the relation is a "complementary" or "diagnostic" one. He can never accept that consciousness as experienced or brain as examined by empirical science are related in a simple causal fashion or that there are exact parallel occurrences between them. Rather, the relationship between these two perspectives should be seen as a diagnostic relation. What science may observe from the third-person observation of the brain or body may be diagnostic of what consciousness is experiencing. On the other hand, what consciousness is experiencing may in some way be diagnostic of processes in the body or brain viewed from the objectifying stance of scientific observation. But these two perspectives say nothing about the fundamental relation between mind and body or consciousness and brain. And in the end, the two perspectives must be seen as joined in the consciousness of the lived, intimate, warm "feeling of the same old body always there."

In the chapters that follow, I will try to keep the phenomenological starting point, which James flirted with but never consistently employed, in the forefront. But then, having done this, we will go further than most phenomenological interpreters of James in retrieving and ordering the entire vision of the human which James possessed. After the descriptive viewpoint is established, then the full range of James's methodological pluralism—his functionalism, his experimentalism, his comparative analyses—will find their place. And the full force of his vision of the strenuous life should take on increased power and persuasiveness.

Notes

1. *WB*, pp. 33–34; *PU* p. 127.
2. *PU*, p. 128.
3. Hans Linschoten, *On the Way Towards a Phenomenological Psychology* (Pittsburgh: Duquesne University Press, 1968).
4. Andrew Reck, "The Philosophical Psychology of William James," *Southern Journal of Philosophy* 9 (Fall 1971):311.
5. Edmund Husserl, *Phenomenology and the Crisis of Philosophy* (New York: Harper and Row, 1965), p. 79.
6. Ibid., p. 80.
7. Ibid., p. 84.
8. Ibid.
9. James Edie, "Critical Studies: William James and Phenomenology," *The Review of Metaphysics* 23 (March 1970): 487.
10. Linschoten, *On the Way Toward a Phenomenological Psychology*, p. 17.
11. Edie, "Critical Studies," p. 489.
12. *PP* 2:129.
13. Ibid., p. 63.
14. Ibid., p. 138.
15. Ibid., p. 184.
16. Ibid., p. 218.
17. Ibid., p. 220.
18. Ibid., p. 185.
19. Ibid., p. 224.
20. Ibid., p. 239.
21. Ibid., p. 236.
22. Ibid., p. 224.
23. Ibid.
24. Ibid., p. 226.
25. *ERE*, p. 10.
26. Ibid., p. 230.
27. Ibid., p. 236.
28. Ibid., p. 240.
29. Ibid., p. 243.
30. Ibid., pp. 245–46.
31. Ibid., pp. 252–53.
32. Ibid., pp. 255–56.
33. Ibid., p. 259.
34. Ibid.
35. Ibid.
36. Ibid., p. 275.
37. Ibid., pp. 275–76.
38. Ibid., pp. 221–23.
39. Ibid., pp. 221, 222, 259.
40. Ibid., p. 259.
41. Ibid., pp. 222, 459–82; *PP*, 2:3–9.

86   PLURALISM AND PERSONALITY

42. *PP,* 1:222.
43. Linschoten, *On the Way Toward a Phenomenological Psychology,* p. 194.
44. A. Gurwitsch, *The Field of Consciousness* (Pittsburgh: Duquesne University Press, 1964), pp. 185 ff.
45. Linschoten, *On the Way Toward a Phenomenological Psychology,* pp. 194-95.
46. *PP,* 1:271.
47. Ibid., p. 272.
48. *ERE,* p. 7.
49. Edie, "Critical Studies," p. 493.
50. *PP,* 1:284.
51. Ibid.
52. Ibid., p. 288.
53. *PP,* 1:284.
54. Ibid., p. 285.
55. Ibid., p. 288.
56. Ibid., p. 274.
57. Ibid., pp. 274-75.
58. *PP,* 2:286.
59. *ERE,* p. 28.
60. *PP,* 1:242.
61. Ibid., p. 242.
62. John Wild, *The Radical Empiricism of William James* (New York: Anchor Books, 1970), pp. 143, 151, 159, 396; Bruce Wilshire, *William James and Phenomenology,* (Bloomington, Ind.: Indiana University Press, 1968) p. 200; Edie, "Critical Studies," pp. 509-10.
63. Linschoten, *On the Way toward a Phenomenological Psychology,* pp. 244-48.
64. Paul Ricoeur, *The Voluntary and the Involuntary* (Evanston, Ill.: Northwestern University Press, 1966), pp. xv-xvii, 13, 15, 87-88, 421-24.
65. *ERE,* p. 72.

4

Triumph of the Empirical Self

Human nature must be understood in relation to its environment, not as passively conditioned by it, but as actively and creatively responding to its challenges. Yet to speak of human beings in relation to their environments is to take the external and comparative approach. From the inner, phenomenological perspective one can point to an analogous truth by speaking of the relation of consciousness to its objects. James believed that both perspectives present a view of human nature as being inextricably related to the world which surrounds it. In the one view, it is man influenced by and influencing his environment, his particular ecological niche; in the other view, it is consciousness defined in part by the nature of the objects which compose it. It is because James maintains these two perspectives in close proximity throughout his writings that he has so much in common with the "transactional systems" point of view discussed in chapter 1.

Let us look more closely at James's highly important contribution to a theory of the "self." Much of the psychological background to James's image of the strenuous life can be found here. New dimensions are added to his vision of an active and purposeful human nature. James sees the self as a more or less unified pluralism of roles and subselves, contending with a variety of competing historical and social forces, living with a real openness to possibilities, growing and declining as fortune and inner resources work together for good or ill, and existing in a world where real gains and irretrievable losses are the lot of every human being. James's vision of a changing and evolving self was probably the most powerful refutation ever written of those views which saw the self as an imperishable and unchanging substance or soul that did not grow or decline and was never essentially altered by experience.

Better than in most of James's writings, his famous chapter in his *Principles* entitled "The Consciousness of the Self" maintains the relation we have advocated between the phenomenological and the naturalistic approaches to the study of the human. In this chapter, James presents some remarkable phenomenological descriptions of the human self. But he also gives some explanatory hints about the functional and adaptive foundations of the self. Furthermore, here James is rather consistent in maintaining the priority of the descriptive point of view.

James's theory of the self goes through several stages. There is more continuity in the different manifestations of his theory than certain Jamesian interpreters have been willing to admit. The self as active and selective was an implication of the early chapters of the *Principles*, especially the chapters on "The Automation Theory" and "The Mind-Stuff Theory," where consciousness as efficacious was argued for so effectively. And then there is the stage of his important chapters on the stream of thought and the consciousness of the self. Here the efficacious and choosing self is still affirmed, and physiological and environmental determinism are still denied. But in the chapter on the self, James does move dangerously close to undermining his position and adopting an almost classically behavioristic view of the self. And then there is the self of the *Essays* in his well-known chapter entitled "The Experience of Activity." This self has great continuity with the theory of the self found in the *Principles*, but here the tone is even more radically phenomenological; the vision of an efficacious and active self is asserted on the basis of the Berkleyan principle of *esse est percipere,* which meant, in effect, that we should take our experience of a free and causally effective self at face value and affirm it for "just what we feel it to be."[1] And then there is the subliminal self of his *Varieties of Religious Experience* (1902) and *A Pluralistic Exercise* (1909) which was so fundamental for his view of mysticism and which provided a context of meaning for his understanding of the ethical mode of life. We will not attempt to pull all of these various facets of James's concept of the self together in this chapter, but we will do it eventually. Now we will see how the phenomenological distinctions between the object and the topic of thought, or between the fringe and the focus of thought, will order the relation between what James called the "subliminal" and "empirical" selves.

The Self as "Me"

The main point of James's formal theory of the self was his distinction between the "empirical self" and the "pure ego." The way he defined both aspects of the self was revolutionary and had a profound influence on subsequent philosophical and psychological concepts of selfhood. The empirical self was boldly defined as everything a person is tempted to call "me." The empirical self is an "object" just as the pronoun "me" can be an accusative and therefore the object of a verb. James writes, *"In its widest possible sense . . . a man's self is the sum-total of all that he can call his,* not only his body and his psychic powers, but his clothes and his house, his wife and his children, his ancestors and friends, his reputation and works, his lands and house, and yacht and bank account."[2] When James speaks of the pure ego, he does not have in mind the traditional Platonic and Aristotelian substantial soul or the Kantian transcendental ego. Rather, he refers to it simply as "the passing thought"—a difficult concept designed to save the best of both Kantian and Humean concepts of the self as knower.

James's theory of the empirical self profoundly influenced the psychologies of John Dewey and George Herbert Mead. It forms the basis of Mead's own distinction between the "I" and the "me" and through Mead has shaped the major direction of modern social scientific theories of the self. Harry Stack Sullivan's theory of the "self-system,"[3] Carl Rogers's understanding of the "self-concept,"[4] Heinz Hartmann's concept of "self-representation,"[5] and Erik Erikson's seminal theory of "ego-identity"[6] must all admit indebtedness not only to Mead but to James as well.

James identifies three constituents of the empirical self—the material self, the social self, and the spiritual self.[7] In each of these three constituents the self emerges in James's vision as not just something "inside" the personality, but as a phenomenon stretched out upon the world, an object in the world right along with other objects, but one toward which we feel a special "warmth" and "intimacy." This can be seen most vividly in James's portrait of the "material" self. The material self is not just our body, although the body certainly forms its "innermost part."[8] The material self includes our clothes, our homes, and our property. Our parents, wife, and children "are bone of our bone and flesh of our flesh." If they become ill or die, a part of our own selves dies as well. Objects which are brought forth by our own labor—things we have become involved with and have invested with energy and hope—are also a part of our material selves. The statue wrought by the sculptor or the painting created by the artist are almost as dear to their creators as the very hands, muscles, and tendons which labored to bring them into existence. Over and above the immediate way these objects give us pleasure or meet our need, their loss brings a sense of "shrinkage of our personality, a partial conversion of ourselves to nothingness, which is a psychological phenomenon by itself."[9]

It is generally acknowledged that James's understanding of the empirical self anticipated certain aspects of Sartre's understanding of the self.[10] Although their overall philosophies have a considerably different tone, their respective theories of the self have much in common. A disciple of Husserl, Sartre broke with the master over the question of the transcendental ego or "I." Sartre denies that it exists. There is no personal ego or I behind consciousness. There is only a self which is an *object* of consciousness.[11] As we will soon see, James can agree with Sartre in viewing both the "I" and the "me" as objects of consciousness. Sartre especially sounds like James when he writes that the "me which hates or which loves" is an object in the world. That me and its various emotional states—its affections, commitments, and aversions—is not just something which can be located in the "interior" of consciousness; rather, the "me" is "an existent, strictly contemporaneous with the world, where existence has the same essential characteristics as the world."[12]

There is an important result for psychology in this tendency of both James and Sartre to see the self as a me spread out before the world with certain public and observable dimensions to it. It means the self is accessible from two perspectives. I can observe myself through introspection, and myself, as it functions in the external world, can be observed by other people. Sartre writes, "External observation and the introspective method have the same rights and can mutually assist each other."[13]

John Wild suggests that in these passages of the *Principles* James is developing a "field conception of the human self."[14] James himself uses the idea of "field" to describe the activities of the self in his *Essays on Radical Empiricism.*[15] To say the self is a field is to assert that the self is experienced as extended over time and space and identified with a variety of objects, tasks, pursuits, and endeavors in the objective world. This can be seen even more clearly in James's description of the *social self.*

A person's social self is the "recognition" which one receives from other human beings. In saying this, James is anticipating George Herbert Mead's famous theory that one's self is composed of internalizations of the way other people view us.[16] But this is where the plot thickens and James becomes relevant to the entire situation in which persons find themselves in modern societies. "Properly speaking," James writes, *"a man has as many social selves as there are individuals who recognize him* and carry on the image of him in their mind. To wound any one of these, his images is to wound him."[17] One could just as easily say that to wound one's self-system (Sullivan), one's self-concept (Rogers), one's self-representation (Hartmann), or one's self-identity (Erikson) is to wound the person himself.

But in all societies (even the most primitive and homogeneous) we respond to the images that more than one person holds of us. In modern societies, the situation is far more complex and there are many different individuals and groups who carry perceptions of us. James seems to have the complexity of modern societies in mind when he writes, "But as the individuals who carry the images fall naturally into classes, we may practically say that he has as many different social selves as these distinct *groups* of persons about whose opinion *he cares."* [18] The savage in a homogeneous and culturally unified tribe may have a few such different selves, but the person in a pluralistic and socially differentiated Western society will undoubtedly have many such selves. There may be the tender self he shows to his wife, the authoritative self he reveals to his children, the obsequious self he expresses to his boss, the romantic and fun-loving self he presents before his mistress, and the faithful and self-sacrificing self he demonstrates to his church. Of course, in modern societies this is only the beginning of the list. From this state of affairs, James believes "there results what practically is a division of the man into several selves."[19] This division may be a "perfectly harmonious division of labor" such as when the various selves and the roles they play, although dramatically different, still somehow fit each other with only a minimum of tension. On the other hand, these various selves and their respective identities can be "discordant" with one another. In pointing to the phenomenon, James is referring to the experience of "identity confusion" which Erik Erikson and others would hold up more than a half century later as one of the pervasive characteristics of people in complex and rapidly changing societies.[20]

People value some of their selves more than others. This is because they value some of the individuals and groups by which they measure themselves more than they do others. A person's sense of honor—his sense of self-value—varies with his "image in the eyes" of the "set" he esteems the highest.[21] The word "set" is James's quaint way of speaking about what sociologists today would refer to with the august title of "reference group." The opinion of valued individuals and groups is, according to James, "one of the very strongest forces in life."[22]

The most startling aspect of James's theory of the self is his analysis of the spiritual self. James writes, "By the spiritual self, so far as it belongs to the Empirical Me, I mean a man's inner or subjective being."[23] This spiritual self—this inner subjective being—is still a part of the "me", that self stretched out upon the world and identified with objects in the world. But the spiritual self is the "innermost centre" of our stream of consciousness— the part which we experience as the "active element" of our consciousness.[24] It has to do with our "ability to argue and discriminate . . . our moral sensibility and conscience, [and] our indomitable will."[25] Phenomenologically, this active element is experienced as something which seems to "*go out* and meet" incoming events and perceptions.[26] It is that within our experience which "welcomes or rejects" and the source of our "attention" and "effort."[27] In his essay entitled "The Experience of Activity," James points out, as he did in chapter 9 of the *Principles,* that the stream of consciousness in general is experienced as a kind of "bare activity"—a kind of simple "going on."[28] But the special activity of the spiritual self is more specific than that; it is an activity "with a definite direction . . . with desire and sense of goal . . . complicated with resistances which it overcomes or succumbs to, and with the efforts which the feeling of resistance so often provokes."[29]

But in the *Principles,* James presses further his effort to describe the feeling of activity connected with the spiritual self. But it is at this point that one of the most perplexing and hotly debated ideas of James's entire philosophy appears. James admits that, when he pushes his introspection of the activity of the spiritual self as far as possible, he discovers only the activity of the body. Acts of "attending, assenting, negating, making an effort, are felt as movements of something in the head."[30] The experience of "consenting and negating" are experienced primarily as the "opening and closing of the glottis."[31] The feeling of "effort of any sort" seems largely to be "contractions of the jaw-muscles and of those of respiration."[32]

How are we to take these remarks? Are we to assume that James had suddenly reversed himself and repudiated almost everything he has said so far about the efficacious and active character of consciousness? Has he now reduced consciousness to the mechanical body? Has he become, in effect, a behaviorist and a psychologist who studies only the movements of the body? Has he in fact repudiated the existence of consciousness? At least one important interpreter of James—his great disciple John Dewey—once thought that James had indeed done all of these things.[33]

It is better, however, to follow the phenomenological interpretations of these passages presented by John Wild and James Edie. Rather than seeing consciousness reduced to the mechanical body, James is, on the one hand, showing that the body is first of all apprehended as a body-self and, on the other hand, demonstrating that the self is never given in experience independent of the body. Using the insights of Merleau-Ponty in his *Phenomenologie de la Perception,* Wild asserts that the body about which James speaks is not the body of "traditional dualistic thought, the mere mass of matter extended in space. It is the moving, living, conscious body which expresses our emotions and is the non-objective centre of my world."[34] Edie also states it well when he writes that for James "consciousness is not given in experience as something independent of the body."[35] In addition, this body is not "just the physical body . . . but a *self* which exhibits feelings, moods, interests, states of mind, disposition."[36] In a selection included in his *Essays on Radical Empiricism,* James in effect confirms this interpretation when he writes,

> The world experienced (otherwise called the "field of consciousness") comes at all times with our body as its center, center of vision, center of action, center of interest. . . . So far as "thoughts" and "feelings" can be active, their activity terminates in the activity of the body, and only through first arousing its activities can they begin to change those of the rest of the world. . . . The body is the storm center, the origin of coordinates, the constant place of stress in all that experience-train. Everything circles around it, and is felt from its point of view.[37]

It may be that the psychologies of Erik Erikson and Jean Piaget are even more satisfactory perspectives from which to understand James's view of the relation between the spiritual self and the lived body. Both Erikson and Piaget see the conscious self as recapitulating the formal properties of bodily action. Erikson calls these formal properties "bodily modes," such as the incorporative modes of the mouth or the eliminative and rejective modes of mouth, hands, and anus.[38] Piaget speaks of these patterns of bodily activity as "schemas" and believes that the most elementary structures of consciousness are composed of memory representations of these basic forms of action.[39] But whether we follow Wild and Edie or use the models from Erikson and Piaget, it is safe to conclude that James was never taking a behaviorist's position in his description of the spiritual self.

Adaptation and the Self

Phenomenological commentators tend to overlook that James does not remain solely on the descriptive level in his theory of the self. As would be expected, James frequently inserts remarks which attempt to explain the functional and adaptational role of the various selves in man's effort to respond creatively to the challenges of his environment. For James, of course, this means returning to his broadly evolutionary point of view.

The material, social, and spiritual selves, according to James, have their instinctual foundations. This, however, does not mean that they are simple and direct expressions of instinctual impulses. The constituents of the empirical self should be understood as "synergistic structures" very much along the lines refined by William Barrett and Daniel Yankelovich in their stimulating book entitled *Ego and Instinct.*[40] Our various selves are not simply the result of "antecedent" biological causes; rather, they are new emergent structures which grow out of complex interactions between the organism and its environment but which transcend the causal factors which helped create them. One first of all knows these selves through a phenomenological description of their structure as given in experience and not by positing simple instinctual origins.

Nonetheless, James believes that, although the empirical self is not an instinct, it builds on instinctive tendencies. A full discussion of James's radical but newly appreciated theory of the instincts must wait for a later chapter, but we can say this much now. Each of the constituents of the empirical self manifests self-seeking and self-preservative behaviors. Tendencies related to the "hunting, acquisitive, the home-constructing and the tool-constructing instincts" must lay behind our material self.[41] The social self must be rooted in an "innate propensity to get ourselves noticed."[42] Even the spiritual self may have its instinctive roots. James speaks of "impulses towards psychic progress," which just may be his dated but suggestive way of speaking about what Abraham Maslow called "growth motivation" or Robert White called "effectance."[43] In these suggestions, James has resorted to his comparative point of view. Starting first with a phenomenological description of the various kinds of initiatives detectable in the empirical self, James then argues that they have some grounding in instinctual regularities widely found throughout the animal kingdom. These remarks assume his theory of instinctual pluralism which we will analyze more carefully at a later time.

The Pluralism, Finitude, and the Conflict of the Selves

The full adaptive significance of the selves can be seen best in light of the pluralism and rivalry of the selves. The values connected with the material, social, and spiritual selves can conflict with one another. One of the major problems of life is that we cannot actualize all the values which adhere to our various selves. This has been a pervasive problem down through the ages. James seems here and elsewhere to be aware that it is a special problem for individuals in modern societies. In addition, human beings have always been and are now quite finite. They cannot become all things, go in all directions, or actualize all values simultaneously. "With most objects of desire, physical nature restricts our choice to but one of many represented goods. . . . I am often confronted by the necessity of standing by one of my empirical selves and relinquishing the rest."[44]

James had an unusually perceptive sense for the myriad of choices which are stretched out before the individual beckoning his or her commitment. We would, if we could, be at the same time handsome, a gourmet, a great athlete, a millionaire, a wit, a lady-killer, a philosopher, a philanthropist, statesman, warrior, explorer, and saint. But, as James writes, "the thing is simply impossible." And then James follows with what may be his most powerful statement about the predicament of human beings at all times and especially in modern societies; it also gives us one of his most profound arguments for the necessity of the ethical and strenuous mood of life.

The millionaire's work would run counter to the saints; the *bon-vivant* and the philanthropist would trip each other up; the philosopher and the lady-killer would not well keep house in the same tenement of clay. Such different characters may conceivably at the outset of life be alike *possible* to a man. But to make any one of them actual, the rest must more or less be suppressed. So the seeker of his truest, strongest, deepest self must review the list carefully, and pick out the one on which to stake his salvation. All other selves thereupon become unreal, but the fortunes of this self are real. Its failures are real failures, its triumphs, real triumphs, carrying shame and gladness with them. This is as strong an example as there is of that selective industry of the mind on which I insisted some pages back (p. 284 ff.). Our thought, incessantly deciding, among many things of a kind, which ones for it shall be realities, here chooses one of many possible selves or characters, and forthwith reckons it no shame to fail in any of those not adapted expressly as its own.[45]

This multiplicity of selves partakes of the same structure as the multiplicity of meanings which we described in the preceding chapter; the selves are meaning structures which are inextricably bound up with their objects. Consciousness is a multiplicity—a pluralism—not of discrete atomic particles and sensations but of meanings, many of which are closely associated with the empirical self.

But how can we coordinate, organize, and choose among our various selves? How can we hierarchically arrange them so that we are not in a perpetual state of hesitation, immobility, and what Erikson has so appropriately called "identity confusion"? How do we keep from becoming what Robert Lifton calls "Protean" selves, changing our self-definitions depending on loved is not the transcendental ego of Kant or the self as ourselves?[46]

In the middle sections of his chapter on "The Consciousness of the Self," James seems to develop two principles for discerning which of the various selves should be uppermost. One is, in effect, a *developmental* principle and the other, an *ethical* principle.

The *developmental* principle values the constituents of the empirical self from the perspective of what they contribute to a particular individual's capacity to survive and grow. It is especially relevant to the growth and development of children. For instance, James believes that human beings love themselves, and James, as does psychoanalysis later, acknowledges self-love as a positive asset to development. But the self that is loved is not the transcendental ego of Kant or the self as substance of Greek and medieval philosophy. The self that the developing human loves in "self-love" is the empirical self—the objective self spread out upon the world and intertwined with the objects of the world.[47] The self that we love is not some abstract principle of our individual existence; it is a self related to a field of objects which we *love* and *care* for. "To have a self that I can *care for*," James writes, "nature must first present me with some object interesting enough to make me instinctively wish to appropriate it for its own sake, and out of it to manufacture one of those material, social, or spiritual selves, which we have already passed in review."[48] We love and care for these objects not because they are mine and we identify with them; rather, we identify with this field of objects and make them ours because we love and care for them for their own sakes.[49] Self-love is really a matter of loving and caring for an entire field of experience which seems valuable in itself. To be a self is to be stretched out upon the world *caring* for that world.

From a developmental perspective, the first acts of self-love by the growing child will be aimed toward his or her own body and its associated objects. Our bodies and their loved objects such as food, clothes, parents, and toys "fascinate by their intrinsic power to do so; they are *cared for* for their own sakes."[50] After this comes our love for our social selves—our fondness for those images of ourselves which "other men have framed."[51] And finally must come our love for our spiritual selves, our relatively perishable and variable powers to know, will, and choose. James concludes this developmental valuation of the various selves with the words—"Its own body, then, first of all, its friends next, and finally its spiritual dispositions, MUST be the supremely interesting OBJECTS for each human mind."[52]

From an adaptive and developmental point of view, it is clear why the vulnerable and fragile infant child must be permitted to love his or her material self first and then the social self. But James does not leave the story here as much as contemporary psychology has been tempted to do. At a certain point in human development, James believes these priorities must be subsumed to a communal and ethical point of view. From this perspective the social and spiritual selves must be given higher value than the material self. James can argue with psychoanalysis that narcissistic appreciation for the material self is a developmental foundation for the health of the other selves. But from an ethical perspective, the social and spiritual selves must be considered higher. "We must *care more* for our honor, our friends, our human ties, than for a sound skin or wealth."[53] And since the spiritual self is the presupposition of the very possibility of the ethical life, it must be considered "so supremely precious that, rather than lose it, a man ought to be willing to give up friends and good fame, and property, and life itself."[54] In James, the developmental insights established by psychoanalysis were present but they were organized into a larger ethical perspective which is visible in the *Principles* but amplified in his other writings. Once again, in this sense James is close to Erikson, who subsumes the early developmental stages of Freud to the later ethical stages of "generativity" and "wisdom."

These two value frameworks give us a clue as to the implicit value theory in James, a problem of considerable perplexity in interpreting James. James in general can give a positive evaluation to the more primitive end of the continuum of our instinctual and passional life. The kind of subjective interests which they empower may be fundamental to the capacity of the developing individual to survive. Hence, the various passions and subjective interests connected with our bodily and material selves play an important adaptive-evolutionary role in the life of every person and must be appreciated as such. James can speak almost rapturously about what he sometimes calls the "passional" dimensions of our lives. In the *Will to Believe* he calls this the "third department" of our mental life and distinguishes it from its cognitive and perceptive aspects.[55] By our passional nature, James meant any aspect of mental life which is at least partially empowered by our instinctive tendencies. By saying that our passional natures must be taken seriously, must be given a positive evaluation, and in fact must be seen as the very fountainhead of our mental activity, James was fully aware that he was placing upon our instinctual life a far more positive interpretation than could be found in the Calvinist and Victorian cultural ethos which dominated the time in which he wrote. What James failed to do was to systematize this implicitly developmental theory of value. This is all the more lamentable since, as we will see later, James had in his concept of the "transitoriness of instincts" important theoretical equipment to do this.[56]

The other value framework is communal and even ethical in character, although it is still evolutionary and adaptive in orientation. Our various selves are valued for what they contribute to the adaptive strength of the larger community, and not just for what they contribute to the adaptive capacities of the individual. Indeed, James has a romantic and quasi-Dionysian appreciation for the grosser levels of our passional and instinctual lives, but at the same time these dimensions of our personalities are finally subordinated to Apollonian and even ascetic requirements of communal need and higher ethical visions. Most of our passional life is needed to live the full range of human possibilities, but not all of our passional life is relevant for particular circumstances and special communal projects and challenges. To this extent, James is different in his sensibilities from Freud. Freud built his appreciation for Apollonian ego controls and restraint on top of a general distrust of the id or our more primitive passional needs. James builds his asceticism—his understanding of the role of self-denial and restraint—on top of a positive and almost romantic assessment of our so-called lower natures. James spoke less freely about both sex and aggression, but had a positive regard for both in their proper contexts. Freud spoke openly and freely about these basic instincts, but was on the whole scandalized by them both. On the other hand, James can be distinguished from the value commitments of most contemporary humanistic psychologists, especially the ones we will review in later chapters. Most of them have a romantic and maybe even Dionysian appreciation for man's passional life without taking the further step of placing it within a larger framework which emphasizes self-denial and sacrifice for wider communal and ethical goals.

Pluralism and the Inclusive Identity

But the social self, as we have learned, does not receive the highest evaluation from James. The spiritual self—our capacity for independent judgment and action—is even higher. But, as we shall see, even the thoughts and actions of the spiritual self are judged by wider communal standards—standards which go beyond local, tribal, or even national goals and needs.

We may rise above some of our social selves. We may repudiate and move beyond these social selves. The spiritual self can assert itself, disentangle itself from one of its social encasements, and set it aside. But James believes it generally does this in the name of and with the symbolic support of another, more "ideal" social self. When I relinquish one of my social selves, "I am always inwardly strengthened in my course and steeled against the loss of my actual social self by the thought of other and better *possible* social judges then those whose verdict goes against me now."[57] In some cases, this capacity to remove ourselves from the influence of one of our social selves comes from "the pursuit of an ideal social self, of a self that is at least worthy of approving recognition by the highest possible judging companion, if such companion there be."[58] This higher self may be "God, the Absolute Mind, the 'Great Companion.'"[59] Here James is outlining his basic theory of religion, which was essentially a social theory with surprising affinities to Durkheim. With his self theory and implicit reference theory, James was stating from the perspective of the experiencing individual a theory of religion which could have easily complemented those theories which emphasize the socially integrative functions of religion. James believes that our mental life is such—the drive for recognition so important—that our moral life must always be supported by higher tribunals of social support, whether they be actual living people, remote historical personages or simple imaginative representations. For this reason James believed that prayer would be a never-ending practice among humans. "The impulse to pray is a necessary consequence of the fact that whilst the innermost of the empirical selves of man is a Self of the *social* sort, it yet can find its only adequate *Socius* in an ideal world."[60] For in the final analysis, all progress of the "social Self is the substitution of higher tribunals for lower." The independence and initiative of the spiritual self is a momentary flicker of decision as it chooses between one social self or another—choosing, in fact, with the help and support of one of these social selves. "Probably no one can make sacrifices for 'right,'" James writes, "without to some degree personifying the principle of right for which the sacrifice is made. . . . *Complete* social unselfishness . . . can hardly exist."[61] This implicit social psychology of religion will have profound influence on James's ethical and religious writings.

James is building here one of the first and most powerful cases for the role of social identity in the life of man—a theme which was not to be pursued vigorously by psychoanalysis until Erik Erikson was to pick it up again more than sixty years later. James, in effect, is giving a defense of the role of cultural and historical images and prototypes in human affairs. James's appreciation for the individual did not mean that he believed individuals could live alone in splendid isolation from ideal cultural and historical symbols and images. The content of the self, even the content of the spiritual self, is shaped greatly by these images. More than has been generally understood, James was deeply aware of the role of culture in human life and was fully convinced that we cannot live without it.

Identity and the Way of Sympathy

James discusses the problem of finding an appropriate unity and hierarchy for the self on several different levels. We have just seen how at the top of James's methods for unifying the self was the ethical or strenuous mode. For James the ethical mode was an *inclusive* and *sympathetic* orientation to life in contrast to an orientation of exclusion. James calls the way of exclusion the Stoic way, although he could just as easily have called it the Buddhistic way. This is the way of renunciation, of breaking our identification with and concern for our various selves and the field of objects from which they are composed.[62] But James repudiates this mode of existence as only possible for individuals of "narrow and unsympathetic characters."[63]

James's method was more hazardous, more likely to fail, but far more attuned to the realities of the modern world. His was the method of sympathy—the way of "expansion and inclusion."[64] True enough, the outline of one's "self often gets uncertain enough, but for this the spread of its content more than atones."[65] This is the way which says *"Nil humani a me alienum"*—nothing human is alien to me. But it is also true that the way of sympathy, the way of opening oneself to a wide range of experiences and possible selves, can only be a teleological ideal which is never fully realized. In all societies—but especially modern societies with their wide range of styles, prototypes, and ideals—the way of expansion and inclusion can soon lead to total disintegration and confusion. Even the way of sympathy finally requires a guiding ethic. James is fighting to establish a style of life which opens us to wide ranges of experience while, at the same time, teaching us to *choose* for ourselves only that which survives the test of practical action.

James amplifies what he means by the way of sympathy in his engaging essay entitled "On a Certain Blindness in Human Beings."[66] Here James laments our general inability to appreciate and sympathize with "feelings of creatures and people different from ourselves."[67] This is humanity's fundamental "blindness" and the very center of James's theory of evil. But there is an understandable reason for this blindness; it follows from the fact that all human beings, because of their finitude and the adaptational requirements of individual and social existence, must live more or less "specialized" lives. This specialization is necessary; in fact, we could not exist without it. On the other hand, this specialization becomes a source of shortsightedness. The very structure of our consciousness becomes more or less rigidly fixed around our own subjective interests and the situations which call them forth. In the parlance of contemporary ego psychology, our specializations give us our "reality principle" and form the patterns of our everyday consciousness.

To sympathize with the experiences of others and broaden one's sense of self, this habituated and specialized self must be destructured and relativized. As important as our inherited cultures, our practical interests, and our habitual patterns of consciousness are for human adaptive strength, there are times when they must be shaken loose and opened up to wider spheres of experience. This, as we will see in chapter 11, is one of the potential contributions of the mystical experience; it can sometimes relativize our everyday consciousness and give us a sense for the "inner significance" and "hidden meaning" of other experiences.[68] In fact, James here is toying with an incipient theory of "liminality" not too different from that most recently put forth by Victor Turner.[69] It is those experiences which put us in a state of transition ("liminality" as Turner would call it) and relativize our everyday consciousness that also open us up to more egalitarian appreciation for other experiences. He writes, "Only the mystic, your dreamer, or your insolvent tramp or loafer, can afford so sympathetic an occupation, an occupation which will change the usual standards of human value . . . and laying low in a minute the distinctions which it takes a hard-working conventional man a lifetime to build up."[70] But however much James appreciated the function in human life of these relativizing experiences and the saints and poets who bring them about, in the end he had even a higher regard for the dominant mode of consciousness he described in the *Principles* which is also the mode in which we must make our ethical choices. This is the mode in which we must assume the ethical and strenuous life and decide what in all of our expanded horizons we will commit ourselves to most completely in our limited and finite lives.

The "I" and the "Me"

A final note is needed on James's theory of the "I." James did away with all concepts such as the soul, the self as substance, or the idea of a transcendental ego. It was primarily the scientist in James which led him to take this position. These concepts explained nothing and brought all inquiry to a dead end. Even the wider religious functions could be handled better by other concepts.

But in doing away with these concepts, James was left with explaining on entirely new grounds our experience of having or being an "I"—an "I" which is finally different than all of our empirical "me's," even the spiritual self. The spiritual self must be understood as the *content* of the experiences and objects which "I" have chosen or are in some way the result of my initiative. But who does the choosing? And if one must believe that some "I" distinguishable from my "me's" does the choosing, how are we to conceive of such an idea?

James's answer to this question is radical, but may stand the test of time. The pure "I" can be nothing more than the present "passing thought." The "I" is no self-identical and transcendent personal knower which stands above or behind the stream of experience. The "I" is the "present judging Thought"—in fact a fresh "pulse" of consciousness—which is not identical to past thoughts but which has continuity with them because it inherits their content.[71] The heart of James's position is found in the following quote:

> It is a patent fact of consciousness that a transmission like this actually occurs. Each pulse of cognitive consciousness, each Thought, dies away and is replaced by another. The other, among the things it knows, knows its own predecessor, and finding it "warm" in the way we have described, it greets it, saying "Thou are *mine*, and part of the same self with me." Each later Thought, knowing and including thus the Thoughts which went before, is the final receptacle—and appropriating them is the final owner—of all that they contain and own. Each thought is thus born an owner, and dies owned, transmitting whatever it realized as its Self to its own later proprietor. As Kant says, it is as if elastic balls were to have not only motion but knowledge of it, and a first ball were to transmit both its motion and its consciousness to a second, which took both up into its consciousness and passed them to a third, until the last ball held all that the other balls had held, and realized it as its own. It is this trick which the nascent thought has of immediately taking up the expiring thought and "adapting" it, which is the foundation of the appropriation of most of the remoter constituents of the self. Who owns the last self owns the self before the last, for what possesses the possessor possesses the possessed.[72]

Hence, the present passing thought, born with each new pulse of consciousness, recognizes its preceding thoughts as its own because of the shared warmth which relates them to its own body. The "inner nucleus" of our personal identity is based on a shared sense of sameness (a shared bodily warmth) which relates all of our past "me's" to the "I" of the present passing thought.

This novel way of speaking about the "I," later considerably refined by Whitehead, is important for what it suggests about the ethical mode of life. This shared bodily warmth which accompanies the present "I" as well as my past "me" indeed make it possible for the "I" to recognize these past selves as its own. But what is recognized is not always what is finally chosen. What is "felt" as "mine" may not always be chosen as that which should be central to my personality. James was fully aware that these choices must be made and this is why the very center of his philosophical psychology deals with the nature of will and freedom. The present "I" at all times and in all places has had to choose between many past empirical selves. This is the very heart of the ethical, the strenuous mood. But this is even more the case in the context of modern societies with their plethora of subcommunities, ideal images, symbols, and potential identities. This leads us then to look more carefully at James's implicit view of modern life.

Notes

1. *ERE,* p. 98.

2. *PP,* 1:291.

3. Harrey Stack Sullivan, *The Interpersonal Theory of Psychology* (New York: W. W. Norton, 1953), pp. 164–68.

4. Carl Rogers, *Client-Centered Therapy* (Boston: Houghton Mifflin Co., 1951), pp. 497–98.

5. Heinz Hartmann, *Essays on Ego Psychology* (New York: International Universities Press, 1964), pp. 226, 231.

6. Erik Erikson, *Identity: Youth and Crises* (New York: W. W. Norton 1968), pp. 49–50.

7. *PP,* 1:292.

8. Ibid.

9. Ibid., p. 293.

10. James Edie, "The Genesis of a Phenomenological Theory of Experience of Personal Identity: William James on Consciousness and the Self," *Man and World* (September 1973): 329.

11. Jean Paul Sartre, *The Transcendence of the Ego* (New York: Farrar, Strauss, and Giroux, 1957), p. 95.

12. Ibid., p. 105.

13. Ibid., p. 96.

14. John Wild, *The Radical Empiricism of William* (New York: Anchor Books, 1970), p. 83.

15. *ERE,* p. 98.

16. George Herbert Mead, *Mind, Self, and Society* (Chicago: University of Chicago Press, 1934), p. 164.

17. *PP,* 1:294.

18. Ibid. The second set of italics is mine.

19. Ibid.

20. Erik Erikson, "Autobiographic Notes on the Identity Crisis," *Daedalus* 99 (Fall 1970): 742.

21. *PP,* 1:294.

22. Ibid., p. 295.

23. Ibid., p. 296.

24. Ibid., p. 297.

25. Ibid., p. 296.

26. Ibid., p. 297.

27. Ibid., pp. 297–98.

28. *ERE,* p. 84.

29. Ibid., p. 85.

30. *PP,* 1:300.

31. Ibid., 301.

32. Ibid.

33. John Dewey, "The Vanishing Subject in the Psychology of William James," *Journal of Philosophy, Psychology and Scientific Method* 37 (1940):589–99.

34. Wild, *The Radical Empiricism of William James,* p. 87.

35. Edie, "The Genesis of a Phenomenological Theory of Experience of Personal Identity," p. 331.

36. Ibid., p. 332.

37. *ERE,* p. 90–91.

38. Erik Erikson, *Childhood and Society* (New York: W. W. Norton, 1963), p. 74.

39. For an interesting comparison with Piaget on "modes" and "schemas," see Peter H. Wolff, "Cognitive Considerations for a psychoanalytic Theory of Language Acquisition," *Motives and Thought* (New York: International Universities Press, 1967), pp. 299–343.

40. William Barrett and Daniel Yankelovich, *Ego and Instinct* (New York: Random House, 1970), p. 372.

41. *PP,* 1:308.

42. Ibid., p. 293.

43. Abraham Maslow, *Motivation and Personality* (New York: Harper and Brothers, 1954), pp. 214, 256, 296; Robert White, *Ego and Reality in Psychoanalytic Theory* (New York: International Universities Press, 1963) pp. 33–37.

44. Ibid., p. 309.

45. Ibid., p. 310.

46. Robert Lifton, *Boundaries: Psychological Man in Revolution* (New York: Random House, 1970).

47. Ibid., p. 319.
48. Ibid.
49. Ibid., pp. 319–20.
50. Ibid. My italics.
51. Ibid., p. 321.
52. Ibid., p. 323.
53. Ibid., p. 315.
54. Ibid.
55. *WB*, pp. 111–44.
56. *PP*, 2:398.
57. *PP*, 1:315.
58. Ibid.
59. Ibid., p. 316.
60. Ibid.
61. Ibid., pp. 316–17.
62. Ibid., p. 311.
63. Ibid., p. 312.
64. Ibid., p. 313.
65. Ibid.
66. *TTP*, pp. 113–29.
67. Ibid., p. 113.
68. Ibid., p. 119.
69. Victor Turner, *The Ritual Process* (Chicago: University of Chicago, 1969), pp. 95–130.
70. *TT*, p. 122.
71. Ibid., p. 339.
72. Ibid., p. 339–40.

5

Modernity and Passivity

The world for James is a pluralism of relatively independent and contending forces. It is also a world where change and novelty are pervasive characteristics of this pluralism of interacting powers. Modern life, for James, is just an extreme manifestation of the general pluralistic and changing character of all reality.

The heart of James's interpretation of modern life is a paradox. The paradox of modernity is that at the very moment when the adaptive challenges of modernity require a high degree of responsible action there are also various forces which are pushing human beings toward passivity. In the terms of more contemporary diagnoses, James was trying to create a deeper *activeness* to take the place of the superficial *activism* and overt passive fatalism which were growing in his time and which may be still with us today.

Life is pluralistic and changing and because of this it is also full of risk and insecurity—a world where there are real threats and dangers and real gains and losses. Life has always had this character, but in the context of modern life the dangers, risks, and possible gains and losses are even greater.

James had no systematic theory of modern life. Nor is it my purpose to present him as a great sociologist of the early twentieth century. But there is a sociological fringe to his thought. In addition, there are legitimate methods which lay behind his observations. For instance, there are extensions of his radical empiricism and incipient phenomenology. In addition, we see once again his diagnostic or complementary use of the sciences. Finally, there is a wide range of informal observa-

109

tions which should be given the status of loose ethological observations about the animal *Homo sapiens* in his various environments. At this level, James is the explorer and naturalist, not unlike what he was when he accompanied Louis Agassiz to the Amazon to observe tropical aquatic life.[1] But now he is studying man in his own environments.

The forces producing inaction and passivity in the modern world were, for James, largely cultural. Rigid scientific empiricism, philosophical and religious monism and absolutism, and popular Calvinism—these are three of the more prominent cultural forces which James believed were undercutting the possibility of responsible action. Dogmatic empiricism introduced the doctrine of philosophic determinism with its pessimistic belief that all so-called free (and responsible) human action is illusory. Monism and absolutism do just the reverse; they communicate the lulling idea that all change, risk, and insecurity are themselves basically illusory and that beneath the apparently transitory there is an abiding and unifying reality which assures us that indeed *all is well*. Popular Calvinism, with all of its fearful conscientiousness, was then breaking down and becoming nothing more than a superficial activism, an activism which was quickly being channeled into the frantic search for the "bitch-goddess success" and a debased quest for ease and pleasure.

Pluralism and Experience

James's earliest remarks about the pluralistic nature of reality were derived from his scientific studies in physiology and anatomy. But his mature philosophy of pluralism is based primarily on descriptions of a phenomenological kind. We will start with these descriptions and then work backward to his uses of science.

Some of his earliest descriptive analyses of pluralism came in the context of his refutations of monism or absolutism. Monism was a postition in the philosophy of religion which became widely popular in Germany, England, and the United States toward the end of the nineteenth century. It was strongly associated with the names of Spinoza and Hegel and James's contemporaries Royce, Green, Bradley, and McTaggart. Monism believed that all the individual entities and all the changes (birth, accident, evolution, decay, and destruction) which they seem to undergo are basically appearance and illusion. There is a changeless underlying totality and oneness which relates to everything and determines everything.[2] All individual and separate entities are actually manifestations of this one underlying principle or mind. Against such a view, James asserts simply that this is just not how the world appears to the mind of man, especially the mind of the common person who is unpolluted by the distorting presuppositions of idealistic philosophy. "Arbitrary, foreign, jolting, discontinuous—are the adjectives," James believes, "by which we are tempted to describe" our experience of reality.[3]

In *A Pluralistic Universe* (1909) and his unfinished *Some Problems in Philosophy* (1911) James continues to counter monism with basically phenomenological descriptions of our experience of the world. But here the argument is more precise. He does not contend that things are unrelated; he only asserts that they are not related *completely* and in *all respects*. "The same things disjoined in one respect *appear* as conjoined in another."[4] In both of these books James also consolidates a growing criticism of "conceptualism" or "intellectualism," the tendency of the mind to order experience by abstracting out certain attributes of an object and ignoring the remainder.[5] The definitions of objects which result from this process are by nature "static" and will automatically exclude the changing and discontinuous aspects of experience. Following the lead of Bergson, James asserts that conceptuality likes unity and permanence and tends to disregard both pluralism and change or novelty.[6] Concepts tend to "freeze" the living flux of experience so that neither change nor differentiation are noticed. In *Some Problems in Philosophy,* James argues that we cannot capture *conceptually* either real pluralism or real novelty and change; both of these dimensions of experience we know primarily at the level of "perception" or "knowledge by acquaintance."[7] "So the common-sense view of life is something really dramatic, with work done, and things decided here and now"—this is how the real world presents itself at this fundamental preconceptual level.

Interspersed throughout these descriptions of the pluralistic and changing character of reality, James introduces moral evaluations of monism. These evaluations are basically psychological in form and reveal a hierarchy of values which will become clearer to us as we proceed. Monism certainly gives us a vision of a secure, peaceful, and basically harmonious world. At a certain level, everyone needs this fundamental dimension of assurance. Like such religious concepts as the aseity of God or the ideas of God's love and justifying grace to be found in Lutheranism and Wesleyanism, monism conveys a sense of all-encompassing security to the people who accept it. Even today, over fifty years after the death of James, we see many phenomena which point to the recurring need for this kind of security and assurance. One could point to the return of various forms of popular mysticism with their implicit monistic assumptions; the emergence of such obviously monistically grounded groups as Hare Krishna with its "Krishna Consciousness"; the great popularity of the theology of Paul Tillich with his idea of God as aboslute, *a se,* and the "ground of being"; and monistically sounding humanistic psychologies with their ideas of a pervasive and never-failing "actualization tendency." The issue James was addressing is as relevant today as it was to his; a monistic spirituality is a major option for large numbers of people in our time.

But James did not completely reject monism and he certainly did not reject the fundamental dimension of psychological security that it conveys. He only rejected those thoroughgoing monisms which squeeze out completely any possibility of relatively independent entities and wills existing in the finite world. As he writes in the *Will to Believe,* the security which monism puts forward comes with a high price; it blinds us to the real insecurities, real decisions, "mutually exclusive alternatives" which characterize this world and require an attitude, as James says, of "Either—or!"[8] This Kierkegaardian stance of James is pervasive throughout his writings and gives his vision a remarkable similarity to much that is found in the existentialist perspective. James said more than once that pluralism is "the more moral" and monism the "more religious view."[9] James's final religious vision, as we will see later, combined the moral dimensions of pluralism and the religious security of monism by developing a concept of God as "finite" and a religious vision suggestively referred to as "pluralistic mysticism."

Monism leads to passivity and inactivity by overemphasizing the harmony and final security of the world. Scientific empiricism—another phenomenon as present today as it was in James's—has the same result but for different reasons. In this form of empiricism, things are determined completely, not so much by God or some encompassing absolute, but by the causal mechanisms of the past. The phenomenological descriptions in the *Principles* of the purposive nature of consciousness were partial refutations of the deterministic errors of this point of view. In the next chapter, I will discuss his more specifically metaphysical arguments against determinism. At the moment, it will be more profitable to make another point. Even though James both repudiated the "automaton theory" and refused to depict consciousness as a causally produced collection of atomistic impressions, James did, as we have seen, set the ground for a pluralistic understanding of consciousness. Not a pluralism of discrete ideas and causal impressions, but a pluralism of meanings and empirical selves—this was the pluralism of consciousness which James was developing in the *Principles*.

James's pluralistic understanding of the external world is supplemented by an equally pluralistic understanding of the human psyche. But here James sometimes got his logic confused. He often started with a scientific point of view and then added to it his phenomenological descriptions; the method should have been just the reverse—even on the basis of his own testimony. James frequently spoke about the relatively independent systems of our body, the variety of our instinctual impulses,[10] and the random and conflicting tendencies of our cerebral cortex[11] as though he had direct access to these mysterious unseen entities. The fact is that we know about the varied and conflicting nature of our impulses and passions by first experiencing the ambiguities, hesitations, and conflicts of consciousness. Having first experienced our pluralism of bodily impulses at the level of lived experience, we then search for more "objective" data which may explain and confirm this experience. It is then that we begin to infer the possibility of James's crucial doctrine of the pluralism of instincts or his equally important theory of the unstable, complex, and responsive cerebral cortex of humans.

As we have seen, James called mind or consciousness a "theatre of simultaneous possibility," a pluralism of contending meanings and selves. Not only does this anticipate existential-phenomenological insights into the ambiguity of consciousness and Eriksonian theories of identity confusion, it also anticipates psychosocial theories about the Protean nature of modern man. For in reality, James's phenomenology is a phenomenology of consciousness in a pluralistic and highly differentiated society. Consciousness is defined partially by its objects, and the consciousness which James describes is one related to the relatively autonomous and competing social realities of an increasingly more complex modern society.

This can be seen all the more clearly in James's remarkable chapter in volume 2 of the *Principles* entitled "The Perception of Reality." Here James lays out a highly important description of the "many worlds" in which we live. In the context of a sensitive discussion of the nature of belief, James argues that our world of experience is actually divided into several "sub-worlds" or "multiverses."[12] Some of the worlds appear as realities and some as more unsubstantial fantasies or dreams, but "the genuinely philosophic mind" must take them all as phenomena which are undeniable parts of the world and study them just in the manner in which they appear. James lists several such subuniverses, "each with its own special and separate style of existence."[13] There is the world of sense experience, the world of scientific abstractions, the world of ideal relations, of "idols of the tribe" and prejudices, of "supernatural worlds," of "individual opinion," and finally the worlds of "sheer madness and vagary."[14]

Phenomenologists such as Edie, Wild, and Gurwitsch are inclined to see James's theory of multiple worlds as an anticipation of Husserl's concept of "regional ontologies"—the idea that there are different regions of experience which have their own respective modes of appearance.[15] This may be true, but it is best not to overlook the various ways in which this is actually a phenomenology of modern experience and not something timelessly relevant to human experience in all situations and all ages. It is in the modern world that abstract scientific propositions have become differentiated and separated out of our direct lived experience of the world. It is probably only in the modern world that our tribal idols and supernatural visions have become regions of experience independent from our private opinions, our worlds of madness, and our scientific explanations. Modern man lives in a multiverse; it is not clear that all men of all ages have done so, at least not in a world so richly and discretely varied as is the modern world.

Theories of Modernity

James is weak on sociological concepts. This does not mean, however, that he is weak on social vision or sociological relevance. He had a metaphysics of pluralism and a penetrating description of the lived experience of existing in a pluralistic world, but he did not have a systematic sociological explanation of why pluralism and rapid social change were so prevalent in modern countries. He only had the direct awareness that all of reality was pluralistic and changing and that modern societies were more so.

James's pluralism, although not designed exclusively to explain our social experience, does articulate well with the dominant sociological theories of modernity developed by such sociologists as Durkheim, Weber, and Talcott Parsons. According to this tradition, a society is modernized to the extent that it has become industrialized and technologized, i.e., the extent to which it is utilizing inanimate sources of power to accomplish its work. The introduction of new, nonhuman sources of industrial and technological power, even at a very rudimentary level, tends to have two effects on a society. First, it leads to a *division of labor* in the society and a consequent *differentiation* of the institutions of the society into progressively more independent and specialized styles of existence.[16] For instance, in a primitive society the social spheres of home life, occupation, education, and religion were related intimately to one another and mutually supported each other. But in industrial societies, economic procedures have become so complex that they are pursued in factories, offices, and institutes greatly separated from both home life and religion and to some extent even from government. This increased pluralization of life frees and liberates individuals from the centers of pervasive organic control which permeate more primitive societies. Individuals are freer to act and live as independent persons. This is why a certain degree of democratization of life goes along with the increased pluralism of modern life. James himself was fully aware of this fact and realized that his metaphysical pluralism implied a method of democratically mediating between contending and competing powers. On the other hand, this same pluralism gives individuals in these societies the subjective sense of living in different spheres with vastly different goals, rules of conduct, and value assumptions. This is a source of much of the felt confusion and fragmentation which grips the life of all people in modern societies.

The second trend created by modernization is *centralization*. At the same time that the social units of a society such as education, government, economics, and religion become more specialized, the overall system becomes more centralized and bureaucratized. This is expecially true of government, but in addition centralization and bureaucratization take hold as well in the spheres of education, economics, and religion.[17] As we will see later, James's awareness of the *pluralization* of society did not blind him to simultaneous *centralizations* of power in large institutions of various kinds. In fact, this gets to the heart of his widely known antipathy to institutions. It was actually not generalized antagonism against all institutions; it was primarily a rejection of corrupting institutional "bigness" which led to irresponsible and unresponsive institutional conduct.

Modernity, Fragmentation, and Domination

James was basically an optimistic person. He had no apocalyptic vision of modern life, but he was aware of some of its dangers. In effect, he held a dialectical theory of modern life. On the one hand, modernity meant pluralism and change with their simultaneous consequences of individual freedom and personal fragmentation and confusion. On the other hand, modernity meant a growing heavy-handedness by institutions which were either becoming too large or fighting irrelevance with crude if not brutish methods.

James was much less enthusiastic than his fellow pragmatist John Dewey about the technological by-products of modern science. Even though James certainly respected science, he did not deem it a source of salvation nor did he believe its technological overflow would be our final deliverance from life's evil and hardships. Right in the middle of his lectures on *Pragmatism,* James acknowledged that science "has opened an entirely unexpected range of practical utilities to our astonished view."[18] And certainly "the practical control of nature newly put into our hand by scientific ways of thinking vastly exceeds the scope of the old control grounded on common sense."[19] But it is also true that science's "rate of increase accelerates so that no one can trace the limit" and that even in James's day there was reason to "fear that the being of man may be crushed by his own powers."[20] The practical application of science to everyday problems might be a blessing to mankind, but James was far from certain that this would actually be the case.

James was deeply disturbed throughout his mature life by the presence of a destructive dynamism in American life. Americans were far less settled than their European counterparts, seemed to be running in all directions at once, and were almost frantic after the quest of some mysterious goal. He once wrote that there is "too much fluidity" in American life. "*Tight fit* is what shapes things definitely; with a loose fit you get no results, and America is redolent of loose fits everywhere."[21] In his famous essay entitled "The Gospel of Relaxation" James protested that Americans exhibited a kind of nervous energy, anxiety, jerkiness, and lack of repose which was absent from their far calmer cousins of Western Europe. Americans seem to be "living like an army with all its reserves engaged in action."[22] They exude an atmosphere of "bottled lightning," "over-tension," and "over-contraction."[23] But this "eagerness, breathlessness and anxiety are not signs of strength"[24] but actually indicate a superficial activism which is anything but true creativity and real adaptive power. Such high tension tends to "arrest the free association of one's objective ideas and motor processes."[25] The frantic *activism* which James found in American life was an impediment to the deeper *activeness* and creativity which he felt was so important.

But James was not willing to blame this unsettled state of affairs totally on the practical innovations of modern science. There were other, *cultural* forces which aligned themselves with the practical instrumentalism of American science. James believed Americans learned their nervous activism from "imitation." James writes, "They are *bad habits* . . . bred of custom and example, born of imitation of bad models and the cultivation of false personal ideals."[26] This is James's way of saying that this style of life is a result of cultural ideals and aspirations. What cultural source does James nominate as the cause of such behavior? It is remarkable, especially when viewed from the perspective of Weber's Protestant-ethic hypothesis, to notice that James too believes that Calvinism is the final source for the activism about which he is concerned. It is the "over-active conscience" of the New England Puritan mentality.[27] This "need of feeling responsible all the live long day has been preached long enough in our New England" and a new culture proclaiming the virtues of a calmer and deeper kind of true activeness needs to emerge to take its place.[28]

In other words, the activism of a depleted Puritan heritage combined with practical science to feed the fires of runaway social change and costly personal and social fragmentation. In addition, the cultural sources for helping human beings gain more responsible control of these forces seemed lacking. Neither our Puritan heritage, scientific empiricism, nor religious and philosophical monism seemed capable of inspiring a deeper and more responsible activity of the kind needed to live in the emerging world.

But modernity brought another danger. Today we would call it "centralization" or "bureaucratization." James did not have available to him such grandiloquent terms to express his intuitions. James, as we will see more fully later, was not against institutions; he was simply skeptical of large and/or outmoded institutions. Since it is the very nature of reality and society to change, institutions which were a service in one age are bound to undergo some irrelevance in another unless they are themselves able to change and address emerging circumstances. But he was equally critical of the colossal new bureaucratic and power-hungry institutions he saw springing up in America. In a letter written in 1899, he wrote, "I am against bigness and greatness in all their forms. . . . The bigger the unit you deal with, the hollower, the more brutal, the more mendacious is the life displayed. So I am against all big organizations as such, national ones first and foremost; against all big successes and big results."[29] When institutions become anachronistic or too large and systematized, they squeeze out the vital and saving pulse of individual creativity and the adaptive alternatives which it can bring. Certainly, the individual is more fundamental than such institutions with their "herding and branding and general regulating and administering by system the lives of human beings."[30]

The charge that James is anti-institutional is not quite accurate. In his understanding of the role of habit and custom in human life and his understanding of the role of education for the activation of human potentials, we will learn how deeply James respected the place of institutions which are sensitively tuned to human needs. The more inhuman and destructive side of big governmental and business institutions James believed he saw in the American imperialistic acts of the Spanish-American War. In this kind of behavior he saw the emerging economic and technical power of modern America pressing on with almost mechanical irrationality to impose its will on other people. This kind of modernity is nothing more than "the big, hollow, resounding, corrupting, sophisticating, confusing torrent of mere brutal momentum and irrationality" which will crush all that is before it unless restrained by a deeper moral force.[31]

James and Some Cultures of Psychology

James had no definitive view of the nature of modern societies, and it is not my intention to suggest that he did. Rather,

I am arguing that psychologists—except for the very most specialized—inevitably have these larger "fringes" or "horizons" of meaning within which they place their more specifically psychological work. James's psychology is surrounded by a larger fringe of meaning about the nature of modern life, and it is impossible to capture the real thrust of his understanding of human nature without making this larger context of thought explicit.

The same is true of the cultures of psychology which will now emerge as partners in dialogue throughout the remainder of this book. The psychological cultures of detachment, control, joy, and care do not have systematic theories of modern life. But they do have implicit images about modern society which strongly color their concepts of the human.

Although psychoanalysis is a movement which has gone beyond Freud on a variety of issues, the shadow he casts is still a long one. The following remarks are restricted to Freud.

Freud's view of modern life evolved around his understanding of the superego and its role in the establishment and maintenance of civilization. The major problem of modernity would be, as Freud saw it, a problem of the control of human impulse after the traditional irrational restraining forces of the superego and religion meet their inevitable demise.

The major premise of this position is that human nature needs control. The twofold impulses of sex and aggression, which Freud described in his *Beyond the Pleasure Principle* (1920), have to be controlled if man is to live in civilized society.[32] From the standpoint of individual development, the main source of control and renunciation is the superego—a psychic structure which is developed rather early in the life of the individual child through a process of identifying with the threats and prohibitions of parents, primarily the father. At the broader civilizational level, culture and religion are the primary agencies fostering instinctual control and renunciation. Freud believed that all civilizations "must be built up on coercion and renunciation of instinct."[33] Religion is the primary institution of culture and civilization to perform this task. This is true because religion is a projection into a cosmic realm of the helplessness and guilt centered around the forbidding father and the superego which he creates. In *The Future of an Illusion,* Freud makes the surprising statement that religion "has clearly performed great services for human civilization. It has contributed much towards the taming of asocial instincts."[34] But religion, as he argues in *Civilization and Its Discontents,* has accomplished this service at great cost; it has brought about renunciations on unconscious and irrational grounds and has produced more repression, especially of the sexual instincts, than is necessary.[35]

Futhermore, science (psychoanalysis) has shown, according to Freud, that religion is an illusion. The more that the treasures of science become accessible, "the more widespread is the falling-away from religious belief."[36] But to Freud, this would only be a small problem, because the control of instincts by religious prohibition can now be replaced by control through the rational appeals of science. Freud insists that we must develop "secular motives" and "rational explanations" for the renunciations and controls which civilization requires. But even here Freud seems uncertain. He has no doubt that the educated classes can build their renunciations on rational grounds, but he is not so certain about the broad mass of human beings who have no interest in restraining their impulses and and "who have every reason for being enemies of civilization."[37] Rational education—early and plenty of it—seems to be Freud's only answer to the major problem of modern life, e.g., the revolt of the masses resulting from the demise of renunciation based on religion and the irrational superego.

It is interesting to note how different are the concerns of Freud and James on the issue of modern life. Freud is caught between the polarities of renunciation and instinctual chaos. Science will replace religion and be the source of instinctual control as it also will be the source of ethics. The weight of James's concern falls on a different note. James too is concerned with the breakdown of tradition and the demise of religion, but not for the same reasons. He has little concern for the control of instincts; he is more concerned about the adaptive challenges which rapid change and contradictory claims about truth and goodness present to human beings who are cut off from older sources of wisdom and knowledge. It is interesting

that Freud breathes not a word about these aspects of modernity. To him the modern world is the same old world it has always
been with the simple addition of scientific knowledge. But even
here, science for him was "knowledge" and there was very little
concern in his writings about science as technological power.
Freud's view of modernity will have something to do with his
final normative image of man. For clearly Freud's optimal
human being is designed to live in a considerably different
world than is the person living the strenuous life as envisioned
by James.

Along with Freud, B. F. Skinner, our foremost representa-
tive of the culture of control, is one of the most widely known
psychologists of the twentieth century. In addition, Skinner and
Freud share in the mutual concern over the control of human
behavior. Freud was interested in the control of human instincts after the collapse of religion and the cultural superego.
Skinner's interpretation of modern life is similar but not identical to Freud's. For Skinner, behavior cannot be controlled by
rational insight, as Freud hoped that it could; it can only be
controlled by schedules of environmental reinforcement which
are precise and generous. It is Skinner's belief that modern
societies do not have schedules of environmental reinforcement
which are effective enough to guide human beings amidst the
increasingly more complex and dangerous nature of modern
life.

For Skinner the problem of modern societies is their failure
to evolve a behavioral technology which is equal to the technologies derived from the physical and biological sciences. In
Beyond Freedom and Dignity, Skinner states that "a behavioral technology comparable in power and precision to
physical and biological technology is lacking," and until this is
found we are far "from preventing the catastrophe toward
which the world seems to be inexorably moving."[38] The catastrophe which Skinner has in mind is the standard range of
human problems which have become only too familiar to
sensitive human beings during the last decade—pollution, energy shortages, birth control, hunger, etc. These are problems
which neither Freud nor James considered in any depth. But
behind these problems, Skinner believes, is a more fundamental

one—how to motivate effective, long-term, and energetic human action toward the goal of solving these problems. This, as we have already seen, was a profound concern of James.

Modern societies have difficulty producing this kind of behavior because they have cultures with inconsistent and contradictory schedules of reinforcement. In *About Behaviorism* Skinner defines a culture as "a set of contingencies of reinforcement maintained by a group."[39] But cultural practices can be a "mixed bag, and some parts may be inconsistent with others or in open conflict."[40] A sick society is a "set of contingencies which generates disparate or conflicting behaviors suggesting more than one self, which does not generate the strong behavior with which a feeling of competence is associated."[41] In his own terms, Skinner is pointing to the institutional differentiation and resultant pluralism found in standard sociological literature and, in phenomenological terms, in James. Skinner wants to design a new culture and a new supporting behavioral technology to give human beings the consistent and effective patterns of reinforcement they need.

In putting the issue of the control of human behavior in the context of inconsistent, conflicting, and potentially confusing patterns of social and cultural life, Skinner is not too far from the spirit of James. Of course, for James this pluralism of conflicting and competing points of view is an *inevitable and potentially* creative aspect of life; it is out of this conflicting state of affairs that tested and enduring adaptive alternatives are born. But James would have agreed with Skinner in seeing the pluralism of competing and inconsistent experience as, beyond a certain point, fragmenting to individuals caught in such a situation. It will be one of the surprises of the coming chapters to see how close Skinner and James actually can come in appreciating the centrality of behavior and the role of habits and reinforcement in human life. There is a behaviorist *substructure* to James's image of the strenuous life built beneath a *superstructure* which celebrates the very image of man which Skinner finds so distasteful—a vision of autonomous man. The normative vision of man held by both James and Skinner can find a place for the importance of environmental reinforcements, especially in the context of the competing and conflicting forces of modern societies. The difference is that James, in a way which is logically impossible for Skinner to do, can demonstrate how individuals themselves can participate, with some freedom, in the very process of designing their own reinforcements.

A vastly different view of the environment of modern society can be found in what we called the "psychological culture of joy." In contrast to Skinner, this view sees modern society as too controlled, too oppressive, and too rigid in the expectations it places upon individuals. James had a more dialectic view of modern life: in some respects modern life is too loose and chaotic and in other respects it is too rigid and controlled. Freud was indeed interested in what Philip Rieff called "loosening the collar" of the cultural superego; but it is also clear that he didn't want to loosen it much and that his long-term view of modernity saw the control of human impulse as the major challenge of modernity.[42]

Carl Rogers is prototypical of the culture of "joy." The major cause of human self-alienation is what Rogers calls "introjected values" or "conditions of worth."[43] These terms are designed to capture how a child internalizes parental and societal values, especially those values which contradict a child's own direct bodily experience of what is valuable. This simple but tragic process, which has been pervasive throughout history but worse in modern Western societies, alienates the growing child from his own "organismic valuing process"—his own body and the values it naturally places on experiences. The child who does this is deserting "the wisdom of his organism, giving up the locus of evaluation, and is trying to behave in terms of values set by another, in order to hold love."[44] The implication throughout Rogers's writings is that, if these introjections or conditions of worth could be decreased or at least greatly reduced, the natural and automatic valuing tendencies of the organism would be sufficient to guide the individual through his growth into adulthood and, indeed, would be sufficient to guide him in the complex set of decisions necessary to live in a modern society.

The theme of modern life as overcontrolled can be seen also in Rogers's view of technology. The popularity of behaviorism in contemporary psychology is the result, Rogers believes, of the dominance of technology in our society in general. It is not surprising, he writes, "that a technologically oriented society, with its steady emphasis on greater control of human behavior, should be enamored of a behavioristic approach."[45] There is some evidence that Rogers is aware that a pluralism of competing values rather than just heteronomous control may be an immense problem for human beings in modern societies. In one place he writes that "the modern individual is assailed from every angle by divergent and contradictory value claims."[46] But it never occurs to Rogers that the problem as well as the opportunity of the modern individual might just as much be the diversity of values as it is their forceful "imposition" on the individual in the process of socialization.

This view is shared by other representatives of the culture of joy such as Abraham Maslow, Fritz Perls, and William Schutz. These three authors, along with Rogers, constitute the theoretical backbone of the so-called human-potential movement. As a movement, it is both highly important for certain types of psychotherapy and certain manifestations of the encounter-group movement. Maslow's view, although complex and difficult to classify, on the balance of things is consistent with the view found in Rogers. It is the stunting and stultifying forces of society which inhibit the deep inner growth tendencies of the individual from expressing themselves. In his *Towards a Psychology of Being,* Maslow writes that "this inner nature" is "weak and delicate and subtle and easily overcome by habit, cultural pressure, and wrong attitudes toward it."[47] Perls implies the same kind of understanding in his distinction between two kinds of morality—"introjected" morality ("somebody else's choosing that we have incorporated") and the inner morality "of the organism."[48] The implication is that society in general and modern society in particular is the source of impositions, controls, and rigidities which create a heteronomous morality. Schutz, who burst into national prominence with his widely read book entitled *Joy: Expanding Human Awareness,* suggests much the same point of view. In one place he states that producing joy and growth in the individual is primarily a matter of "undoing." "Obstacles to release must be surmounted. Destructive and blocking behavior, thoughts, and feelings must be altered."[49] Once again the larger fringe of meaning is that modern society on the whole inhibits, blocks, and restricts our freer and more spontaneous capacities for growth. In view of this analysis of modernity, it is not surprising that this culture of psychology has a normative view of man which emphasizes expressiveness, spontaneity, joy, and the liberation of the body as the general goals of life.

When we move to the last of our contemporary cultures of psychology—the culture of care—we find a different set of preoccupations than was found in either Freud, Skinner, or the contemporary culture of joy. In each of these three, antitheses of control *or* release are the fundamental rubrics for analysis, no matter how differently they are finally applied. For the culture of care, modern life is seen in terms of how it encourages activeness or passivity—categories which are also implicit in James. The major values at stake become will and freedom or their extinction rather than expressiveness and release or their control. In addition, each of these representatives of the culture of care, although loosely related to the psychoanalytic tradition, seems to have chosen slightly different ways to reconstruct it.

Extreme degrees of social differentiation and pluralism as well as breathtaking rates of social change are the major features of modern life for Erik Erikson. These forces tend to disrupt and undermine cultural traditions—the major sources of personal and group identity. What Erikson calls "identity confusion"[50] can be a pervasive consequence of these disruptions; one of the manifestations of this is an abiding passivity— an inability to "take hold" of things and to affirm a point of view. Identity confusion is a factor in the weakening of the active developmental virtues of *hope, will, purpose,* and *competence* and the final adult capacity for active *care.*[51]

Both Erikson and Fromm make a distinction between a fuller and deeper kind of *activeness* and a frantic and superficial *activism* which, in the last analysis, is really only a cover for passivity and inertia.[52] For Fromm there are two forces which push modern man toward passivity. First, there is the general "rootlessness" which comes from the more individuated and socially differentiated lives we live in advanced technological societies. And second, there is capitalism—the great force pushing toward the passiveness of consumerism and what Fromm calls the "marketing personality."[53] As Erikson wants to restore the deeper activeness of "generativity" and "care," so Fromm hopes for the emergence of a more profoundly active style of life which he calls "productiveness."[54]

But the activeness in generativity and productiveness involves a full-bodied interrelation between man's passional or instinctive tendencies and his higher capacities for volition and deliberation. It is the kind of activeness which Rollo May wants to restore with his concepts of "intentionality" and "care." This, for May, is what is needed to counteract the "schizoid" character of modern life which has developed because modern societies are in such a state of transition.[55] This is May's more dramatic way of speaking about what Erikson has called "identity confusion." But for May, as for Erikson, this diffused, confused, or schizoid mode of life leads to a deep sense of passiveness, "apathy," and "powerlessness."[56]

Regardless of the different ways they arrive at their analysis, James has in common with the culture of care a concern for a deeper kind of activeness on the part of human beings and a fear that various forces in modern life are conspiring to undermine it. Of course, James associated this incipient passiveness with forces, primarily cultural, which were especially visible in his day such as absolutistic monism, scientific empiricism, and Calvinism. These were the cultural forces which seduced the people of his day into an apathetic response to the forces of transition and fragmentation to which James was so sensitive. Of course, William James, the great celebrator of democracy, pluralism, and novelty, would not have wanted to live in a world that was otherwise. But he also knew that what injected risk and zest into life could also destroy it, as it had done to various species down through the course of evolution. His pragmatism, his radical empiricism, and his vision of the strenuous life were ways to keep this from happening to the modern person.

Furthermore, James has another thing in common with the culture of care; he settles neither on too much control nor on too much freedom or anomie as the fundamental problem of modern societies. From the standpoint of the individual, it is the sheer fact of transition itself, and the alternating pockets of arbitrary control and anomic freedom which it injects, that is the major problem. This is why both James and the culture of care avoid the extremes of the superficial analyses of the other cultures of psychology which lead them to become impaled upon the polarities of release and control. For James and the culture of care, neither more control nor more release is the answer. Rather, the answer rests in more responsibility and more ethical sensitivity, i.e., the strenuous life. Only then will modern persons be able to pick and choose between their controls and their releases in the name of a higher good relevant to the whole community of human beings.

Notes

1. Allen, *WJ*, pp. 101–16.
2. *WB*, pp. 275–85.
3. Ibid., p. 264.
4. *PU*, p. 153.
5. Ibid., p. 224.
6. See *PU*, pp. 227–52, and *SPP*, p. 151.
7. *SPP*, p. 165.
8. *WB*, p. 269.
9. *SPP*, p. 165.
10. *PP*, 2:383–441.
11. *PP*, 1:141–42.
12. *PP*,2:291.
13. Ibid.
14. Ibid., pp. 292–93.
15. Edie, "Critical Studies: William James and Phenomenology," *The Review of Metaphysics* 23 (March 1970): 506: John Wild, *The Radical Empiricism of William James* (New York: Anchor Books, 1970), p. 149; Gurwitsch, *The Field of Consciousness* (Pittsburgh, Duquesne University Press, 1964), p. 379.
16. The concept of "division of labor" was first introduced into sociology by Emil Durkheim in his *De la Division Travail Social* (Paris: Felix Alcan, 1893). For a succinct statement of how modern societies differentiate see Talcott Parsons, *Social Structure and Personality*, (New York: The Free Press, 1965), pp. 161–63.
17. James Peacock, *Consciousness and Change* (New York: John Wiley, 1975), pp. 8–9.

18. *P,* p. 123

19. Ibid.

20. Ibid.

21. Perry, *TCWJ,* 2:255.

22. *TTP,* p. 103.

23. Ibid., p. 104.

24. Ibid., p. 105.

25. Ibid., p. 108.

26. Ibid., p. 105.

27. Ibid., p. 109.

28. Ibid., p. 112

29. *LWJ,* 2:90.

30. Perry, *TCWJ,* 2:267.

31. Ibid, p. 311.

32. Sigmund Freud, *Beyond the Pleasure Principle* (New York: Bantam Books, 1963), pp. 71–78.

33. S. Freud, *The Future of an Illusion* (New York: Anchor Books, 1964), p. 5.

34. Ibid., p. 60.

35. S. Freud, *Civilization and Its Discontents* (New York: W. W. Norton, 1942), p. 51.

36. S. Freud, *The Future of an Illusion,* p. 60..

37. Ibid., p. 64.

38. B. F. Skinner, *Beyond Freedom and Dignity* (New York: Bantam Books, 1972), p. 3.

39. B. F. Skinner, *About Behaviorism* (London: Jonathan Cape, 1974), p. 203.

40. Ibid.

41. Ibid.

42. Philip Rieff, *Freud: The Mind of the Moralist* (Chicago: The University of Chicago Press, 1979), p. xxiii.

43. Carl Rogers, *Client-Centered Therapy* (Houghton Mifflin Co., 1951), p. 498, and "A Theory of Therapy, Personality, and Interpersonal Relationships as Developed in the Client-Centered Framework," in *Psychology: A Study of a Science,* ed. S. Koch (New York: McGraw-Hill, 1959), 3:226.

44. Carl Rogers and Barry Stevens, *Person to Person* (New York: Pocket Books, 1975), p. 8.

45. Carl Rogers, "In Retrospect: Forty-six Years," *American Psychologist* (February 1974), p. 119.

46. Rogers and Stevens, *Person to Person,* p. 4.

47. Abraham Maslow, *Toward a Psychology of Being* (New York: D. Van Nostrand Co., 1962), p. 4.

48. Fritz Perls, "Mortality, Ego Boundary and Aggression," *Complex* (Winter 1954), p. 46.

49. William Schutz, *Joy: Expanding Human Awareness* (New York: Grove Press, 1967), p. 20.

50. Erik Erikson, *Identity, Youth, and Crisis* (New York: W. W. Norton, 1968), p. 131.

51. Erikson, *Insight and Responsibility* (New York: W. W. Norton, 1964), pp. 111–57.

52. Erich Fromm, *The Revolution of Hope* (New York: Bantam Books, 1968), p. 12.
53. Fromm, *Man for Himself* (New York: Rinehart and Co., 1960), pp. 67–83.
54. Ibid., pp. 82–106.
55. Rollo May, *Love and Will* (London: Fontana Library, 1972), p. 17.
56. Ibid., pp. 14, 54, 61, 292.

6

Will, Freedom, and Care

Human action makes only a small difference in the course of history, but this "small difference" can make *all the difference in the world.* This is James's understanding of the role of will and freedom in human affairs. Being a scientist, James was well aware of the determinisms and regularities of human nature. But as an ethicist and metaphysician, he tried to demonstrate the reality of voluntary decisions and freedom. It is on this issue that James's almost Kantian commitment to the priority of practical moral action (practical reason) reveals itself. The logic and goals of practical reason must be dominant over the logic and purposes of theoretical reason. To live life and to survive and flourish, we must first of all seek that truth which is good before we become preoccupied with that truth which is simply factual, as important as this truth is. "Science must constantly be reminded," James writes, "that her purposes are not the only purposes, and that the order of uniform causation which she has use for . . . may be enveloped in a wider order, on which she has no claims at all."[1] The "wider order" which James has in mind is a moral order where freedom and moral consequences are characteristics of human action.

James should be regarded as first and foremost a psychologist and philosopher of the will. His massive 100-page chapter toward the end of volume 2 of the *Principles* is one of the most ambitious and successful essays on the will in modern psychology. It also may have been one of the last. Modern psychology has had very little to add—in fact, very little to say—on the subject of the will since the time of James. Caught in the

131

philosophy of determinism, modern psychology not only has neglected the study of will, it has considered the subject scientifically and philosophically unrespectable.

James's concern with the will runs throughout his writings. The strenuous life requires an active will. But James does not see the will as an autonomous inner essence which completely transcends learned responses, social conditioning, and biological impulse. The will builds on and guides the more or less involuntary dimensions of life. James's view of the will can acknowledge the reality of Skinner's conditioned responses, Marx's social determinisms, or Freud's instinctual pressures. These involuntary and conditioned aspects of life give the will its material to work on, its content, its options, and the possibilities from which it chooses. James is not a voluntarist if voluntarism means a vision of the will which sees it as completely rising above the regularities of biological and social reality. It is true that James sees only a relatively small place for the role of "free will" in the total drama of life, but the difference it makes, as I said above, makes all the difference in the world.

On the whole, James would agree with Paul Ricoeur in seeing a reciprocal relation between the voluntary and the involuntary. In *Freedom and Nature* Ricoeur writes, "Not only does the involuntary have no meaning of its own, but understanding proceeds from the top down, not from the bottom up."[2] This statement is consistent with the spirit of James's procedure. As we saw earlier, James himself believed that introspection (his word for phenomenological description) "is what we have to rely on first and foremost and always." But, as we have learned, James was not always clear about what this meant and not always consistent in its application. Yet much of his writings assumes his position on the nature of the will and his theoretical interest in the topic goes back to the beginning of his career. His article entitled "The Feeling of Effort" (1880), which was the foundation of his chapter on the will in the *Principles,* was written only two years after his early, crucial article entitled "Remarks on Spencer's Definition of Mind as Correspondence" (1878). From the beginning, James was going in two directions at once—toward a phenomenological theory of the will and a functional theory of the mind.

Therapy and Will

James's interest in the will was motivated by deep personal concerns. James was born in 1842 and died sixty-eight years later, in the summer of 1910. His life spanned the most breathtaking period of transition which history has witnessed. Nearly everyone in the Western world experienced an enormous expansion of consciousness, considerable conflict over the plethora of alternative ideologies available, and a massive assault on accustomed views of themselves and their world. James was a highly sensitive and intelligent young man who may have experienced an even more profound sense of expansion, confusion, and fragmentation than many of his contemporaries. His father was a wealthy and idealistic amateur philosopher who rebelled against his own Calvinist background and spent his life writing one book after another weaving together a philosophy composed of Swedenborgianism, Fourier socialism, and fragments from his rejected Calvinist heritage. He aspired to give his children (especially William and Henry, the two oldest) the best possible education which both Europe and the United States could offer. In an effort to accomplish this dream, Henry James, Sr., shuttled back and forth between the United States and England, France, Germany, and Switzerland looking for but never quite finding the perfect education for his two precocious sons.

Following the desires of his father, the young, charming, and somewhat immature William James broke off his late-adolescent interest in art and entered Harvard to pursue a course in science. Over the next ten years of his life, he moved from physiology, to medicine, to anatomy, to psychology and then to philosophy, never certain of what he wanted and where to take his stand. This period was marked also by disappointing trips to the Amazon in quest of zoological specimens and to Europe in quest of relief from an aching back. In his late twenties James was an unmarried, jobless, depressed, aimless, and nearly suicidal young man looking desperately for something to give his life meaning and direction. O. F. Matthiessen thinks this state of affairs was the result of his father's fanatic insistence on *being,* which made it quite impossible for his children to determine just what it was they were to *do*.[3] Erikson says James's identity confusion was the result of his father's tendency to produce a "tyranny of liberalism and a school in utopianism in which every choice was made from the freest and most universal point of view and, above all, was to be discussed with Father."[4] Cushing Strout thinks James's malaise was the result of his identification with his father, "who urged him to become a scientist, while paradoxically holding up to him the image of the metaphysician as the highest kind of mind."[5] Whatever the precise explanation, it is clear that James felt hounded by a sense of identity confusion on and off throughout his life. He once wrote, "The constitutional disease from which I suffer is what the Germans call Zerrissenheit or torn-to-pieces-hood."[6] James's sense of torn-apartness took on crisis proportions in his late twenties. He weathered the crisis, turned the corner, gained hold of his life, and developed into one of the most creative people of his time. His sense of fragmentation and diffusion was transformed into a wide and deep sympathy for the vast pluralism of lives which exists in the modern world.

But how did this change of course come about? His life was transformed by an idea—a vision. He was grasped by a conviction which gradually gave his life a deeper sense of purpose and direction. In many ways his entire philosophy is an amplification of these celebrated words which he wrote in his notebook on April 30, 1870:

> I think that yesterday was a crisis in my life. I finished the first part of Renouvier's second "Essais" and see no reason why his definition of Free Will—"the sustaining of a thought because I choose to when I might have other thoughts"—need be the definition of an illusion. At any rate, I will assume for the present—until next year—that it is no illusion. My first act of free will shall be to believe in free will.[7]

This belief in free will was what James needed to snap out of his lethargy, paralysis, and inactivity. His depression had become entangled in his mind with the ideology of determinism so fundamental to the narrow scientism of his day. This was one of the many forces of the modern world reducing human beings— and this included James—to passivity and fatalism. Holding before his *attention* the idea of free will and *acting* as though it were true constituted for James the therapy which changed the course of his life.

The Voluntary and the Involuntary

James made use of a famous example which he claimed contained an entire philosophy of the will if properly understood:

> We know what it is to get out of bed on a freezing morning in a room without a fire, and how the very vital principle within us protests against the ordeal. Probably most persons have lain on certain mornings for an hour at a time unable to brace themselves to the resolve. We suffer; we say, "I *must* get up, this is ignominious," etc.; but still the warm couch feels too delicious, the cold outside too cruel, and resolution faints away and postpones itself again and again just as it seemed on the verge of bursting the resistance and passing over into the decisive act. Now how do we *ever* get up under such circumstances? If I may generalize from my own experience, we more often than not get up without any struggle or decision at all. We suddenly find that we *have* got up. A fortunate lapse of consciousness occurs; we forget both the warmth and the cold; we fall into some revery connected with the day's life, in the course of which the idea flashes across us, "Hollo! I must lie here no longer"—an idea which at that lucky instant awakens no contradictory or paralyzing suggestions, and consequently produces immediately its appropriate motor effects. It was our acute consciousness of both the warmth and the cold during the period of struggle, which paralyzed our activity then and kept our idea of rising in the condition of *wish* and not of *will*. The moment these inhibitory ideas ceased, the original idea exerted its effects.[8]

Although James overestimated the power of his example, it does indeed suggest most, if not all, of his psychology and philosophy of the will.

First, this story reveals that James linked the will very closely to what he often called the "passional" dimension of our beings. Phenomenological description of our voluntary acts suggests that will is related closely to our subjective interests and our passions. James's concept of the will is not restricted to "deliberate volitions." In the larger sense of the word, the will is fed by our instincts, learned habits, social pressure, and emotions.[9] Making use of the so-called reflex theory of the mind then popular in physiology, James spoke in his *Will to Believe* of the mind as having three departments—perception, conception, and reaction or will. Although when James was using this model, he sometimes lapsed into quasi-mechanical terminology, the real function of the concept is metaphorical. Time and again James has demonstrated that the mind does not just *react* to *stimuli,* it *responds* to meanings. Seen from this perspective, the reflex model is a metaphor to communicate the idea that the mind responds to a perceived *world* of meanings and, furthermore, that our perceiving and conceiving natures are in the service of our responsive, passional, and willing natures. "The willing department of our nature," James writes, "dominates both the conserving and the feeling department."[10]

But all of this language is an artificial breaking up of dimensions of the mind which are really related. The main point of James's story is that we tend to respond spontaneously to perceived ideas which are not contradicted by other ideas. Our passions and desires are not just blind impulses; they are connected to objects, memories, and *ideas* of objects and memories. This is important to notice because what James says about the will at times will sound very much like behaviorism. But it is not; there is a real place for consciousness and ideas in James's theory of the will.

The deeper willing nature of the person in James's illustration is very *active* even though the person is flat on his back in a warm bed. He wants to get up; there are many interesting things to be done in the coming day. He also wants to remain in bed; the covers are so enticing and the thought of the cold room is so repelling. His subjective interests and desires abound as he lies there in all of his early-morning coziness.

That is just the trouble. The person has too many ideas. They conflict with one another and cancel each other out. If there was only one idea, he would respond spontaneously to it. James writes that "consciousness is *in its very nature impulsive.*"[11] Here James can sound almost like Freud. Freud's understanding of a "wish" *(Wunschregung)* also sees consciousness as impulsive in character and highly responsive to satisfying ideas and representations.[12]

Of course, James is not just speaking about any type of idea or representation. He is speaking about those ideas which are *memory* images of prior actions we have taken on behalf of our subjective interests. James has a *developmental* situation in mind here. The child's earliest responses to the world are direct bodily reactions to the gratifying properties of objects. But we do not characterize those acts as voluntary; in fact, phenomenological description reveals them to be involuntary. Involuntary acts are truly automatic "and (on the first occasion of their performance, at any rate) unforeseen by the agent."[13] But voluntary acts, being "intended beforehand, are of course done with full prevision of what they are to be."[14] The point is that voluntary acts which are aware of ends and consequences are built up out of involuntary acts; involuntary acts give us our fund of primary performances which are remembered and called back into action by our voluntary performances. A child sees a bright object and instinctively reaches out his hand. Almost by accident, his hand wraps around the object and the child discovers himself holding it. Possibly the next time the child sees the interesting object (or possibly after several such involuntary lucky hits) the child can begin to intend (on a very rudimentary level) to grab the object. Such examples lead James to assert that *"a supply of ideas of the various movements that are possible left in the memory by experiences of their involuntary performances is thus the first prerequisite of the voluntary life."*[15]

When one of these ideas of a formerly experienced movement is before the mind, we tend to enact directly that movement. James calls this kind of action "ideo-motor action."[16] James writes, "Wherever movement follows unhesitatingly and immediately the notion of it in the mind, we have ideo-motor action."[17] Such action is different from involuntary action; it is based on a conscious idea or thought and the consequences of the act are anticipated. Neither of these conditions obtains in involuntary action. These ideas of movement are the only precondition for voluntary action. We have no experience of commanding the act or no experience of energy going out from our brain to our limbs which calls them into action. The idea of the movement and some kinesthetic sense of its consequences is all that is necessary.[18]

But is this description adequate to James's illustration of the poor person worrying his head about whether to get up or stay in bed? James believes that we would get up as soon as the idea of doing so crossed our mind, but we *don't* because we have other ideas which contradict it. We sense the cold and this gives us the idea of another action—staying in bed. We have done both things before. We can anticipate the consequences of doing both. We are frozen in inactivity and hesitation because the two ideas inhibit one another.

How, then, does a person escape this state of affairs? The answer can be found in the following words of description. For a moment consciousness lapses and we "forget both the warmth and the day's cold; we fall into some revery connected with the day's life, in the course of which the idea flashes across us, 'Hollo! I must lie here no longer'—an idea which at that lucky instant awakens no contradictory or paralyzing suggestions, and consequently produces immediately its appropriate motor effects." And suddenly we find that we have gotten up. The "revery connected with the day's life" fills the mind. We think of all sorts of things we should do, actions we shall take and which need to be done. This intimate connection with our life-world fills our minds and we get up and start doing them. No other ideas contradict those about the activities which await us and we arise to face the day.

Will and Attention

But does this adequately describe all voluntary acts? It certainly does not and James is aware of the additional work which needs to be done. It does not account for acts of "deliberate volition"—those acts which are the province of true choice, decision, and freedom. Nor does it explain our sense of effort which introspection shows to accompany our deliberate acts.

Truly deliberate volitional acts issue out of a situation of mental conflict. The mind becomes a seat of multiple possibilities and ideas, some of which are in contradiction. This leads to an experience of unrest, hesitation, and conflict. We already have seen the many ways James's description of consciousness uncovers its potentially ambiguous, pluralistic, and conflictual nature. But consciousness can be gripped by conflict even when dominated by a single "object." In chapter 3 we learned an object is never simple. It always has a fringe, halo, or horizon. This fringe or horizon may include ideas and images in tension, if not in contradition, to the focus or topic of the object. Hence, the fringe of meaning of an idea or object may inhibit us and have sufficient strength to keep our responses in check.[19]

Regardless of the source of mental conflict, human beings, James insists, have an innate psychological need to resolve it. We cannot live with an inner sense of dividedness for long. But the resolution can come in a variety of ways. The factor of *attention* seems to be the crucial variable leading to resolution by decision. But sometimes our attention is more or less *passive*[20]; at other times it is very *active* indeed. According to the ideo-motor theory of action, whatever course of action arrests one's attention, consciousness will in fact enact it. Sometimes attention settles on a single idea for action with considerable ease. Sometimes there are so many reasons in favor of the action that attention settles easily and the deed follows smoothly. Sometimes, under the pressure of emergency or pain, attention is captured by a precipitous internal pressure or external event. Sometimes our situation throws us into a very serious, of not strenuous mood, and the gravity of the situation leads our attention to settle on a momentous, even self-sacrificial course of action.[21]

James sees our attention as somewhat passive in these types of decisions. Richard Stevens is probably correct in chiding James for failing to take full account of the ways in which we "allow our attention" to be moved in these types of decisions.[22] But James is doubtless right that attentive effort is at a minimum in these decisions. This is not the case, however, in that class of decisions which James would call fully "deliberate decisions." In these cases, our decisions are marked by a sense of "effort." But what is this sense of effort? Is it our brains sending a message to our limbs that we must act? James spends many pages demonstrating that we have no introspective or experimental evidence of this experience. Then of what does this experience of effort consist?

The experience of effort consists in *sustaining* our attention on a particular idea rather than letting it move elsewhere. In deliberate decisions, consciousness is dominated by at least two ideas, both of which are reasonable or in some way compelling. To make the decision we must "murder" the one alternative and affirm the other. We commit the deed with our attention. We affirm the one alternative by keeping our attention upon it; we vanquish the other alternative by burying it with our inattention. The excluded alternative is banished to the fringe of consciousness and there made powerless through inattention. Such an act is the highest expression of will. James writes, "The essential achievement of the will, in short, when it is most 'voluntary,' is to ATTEND to a difficult object and hold it fast before the mind."[23] This is the *fiat* of effort. Effort is continued attention to an object or idea when it might be easier to let it go. "Effort of attention," James states with solemn finality, "is thus the essential phenomenon of will."[24] And of course, according to James's theory, once the victorious alternative is definitely fixed upon, action is soon to follow.

Will and Passion

It is clear that, when James is describing the nature of deliberative decisions, he is portraying the very heart of his understanding of the strenuous life. In addition, in deliberative choices of this type we open up for ourselves alternative futures. The concept of will and the concept of time are related intimately to each other in James's thinking. A deliberative voluntary act breaks the determinisms of the past and opens a freer future. We defy the weight of instinct, habit, and social custom and fix our attention on a possibility which is not endowed with these reinforcements. There is always an element of self-sacrifice involved; it involves "deliberately driving a thorn into one's flesh."[25]

In deliberate decisions of the strenuous kind, we generally affirm some distant future good at the expense of a more present instinctual satisfaction or customary habit. James writes, "All far-off considerations, all highly abstract conceptions, unaccustomed reasons, and motives foreign to the instinctive history of the race, have little or no impulsive power. They prevail, when they ever do prevail, *with effort*."[26]

James is not saying that to choose on behalf of a distant goal, another person, or some abstract ideal of duty *always* is to choose against instinct and habit. These remarks must be placed within his larger theory of instinct, which we will consider in some detail in the following chapter. James is not taking the position of Freud that instincts are always peremptory and egoistic and always for short-term pleasure or aggression. James believes that human beings have a wide range of instincts, some of which clearly are altruistic and benevolent. Our sympathy for other people and our concern for the remote future are fed, according to James, by energy from our instincts and passions. To this extent the strenuous life is not unlike Erik Erikson's concept of generativity. Generativity—the generalized drive to care for the future of one's own children and those of others—also is in part empowered by instinctual energies.[27] James gets at this point in his chapter on the self. Here he writes,

> The sympathetic instincts and the egoistic ones are thus coordinate. They arise, so far as we can tell, on the same psychologic level. The only difference between them is, that the instincts called egoistic form much the larger mass.[28]

James seems to see the effort of attention as reinforcing—tipping the scales toward—those long-term future goals or other-regarding sympathies which are empowered by the weaker passional energies. James's entire theory of will is designed to show the possibility of free action in behalf of the abstract claims about remote and distant considerations for the future.

In effect, James is once again presenting his image of human beings as active, purposeful, and selective. We need not let the brute force of experience shape us as clay is formed in the hands of a sculptor. Our interests and attention are closely related. Out of the great mass of environmental forces which bombard us every day, our interest and attention select only a small portion to become part of our meaningful experience. James's theory of the will is designed to suggest how, out of a situation of conflicting interests, our attention can sometimes reinforce the one fed by the weaker stream of instinctual and habitual energies.

Reflections on James's Theory of the Will

In his *Love and Will,* Rollo May is basically appreciative of James's theory of the will, but he is critical of it as well. He believes that James unadvisedly makes too great a distinction between "wish" and "will"; in addition, James fails to find a place for the "imagination" in his theory of voluntary action. May is fighting the Victorian mentality which tended to see "will" as over against "wish." The Victorian believed that, in order for will to function with strength and precision, our wishes had to be repressed.[29] May believes that James's latent Victorianism shows through in his understanding of the relation of our wishing and our willing. For instance, at one point James writes, "If with the desire there goes a sense that attainment is not possible, we simply *wish;* but if we believe that the end is in our power, we *will.*"[30] But here James is not "summarily dismissing" wishes or treating them as "unreal and childlike" in the way in which May suggests. We already have seen how James believes that will in the broad sense is fed by our instinctual, passional, and wishing natures. James has a definite romantic substratum to his thought. As growing children, our bodily passions and actions give our emerging will the fund of action-ideas which makes willing possible. A wish for James is one of these action-ideas along with the impulsive power behind it. Willing is not against wishing; indeed, for James, the will builds on wishing. James's entire doctrine of subjective interests goes against May's criticism. Even in James's understanding of the more complicated processes of deliberate volition, attention never works against wishing as such, although in some instances it might reinforce a weaker wish at the expense of a stronger one.

His second criticism is related to his first. May believes that

James fails to understand the role of imagination and intentionality in our willing. May almost equates imagination and "intentionality." The following quote gives us both his definition of intentionality and his criticism of James:

> By intentionality, I mean the structure which gives meaning to experience. It is not to be identified with intentions, but is the dimension which underlies them; it is man's capacity to have intentions. It is our imaginative participation in the coming day's possibilities in James's example out of which comes the awareness of our capacity to form, to mold, to change ourselves and the day in relation to each other. James's reverie as he lay in bed is a beautiful, albeit denied, expression of it. Intentionality is at the heart of consciousness. I believe that it is also the key to the problem of wish and will.[31]

May's remarks are rather curious. There is nothing whatsoever "denied" in James's understanding of the role of "reverie" or imagination. In reality, James is quite clearly doing what May says he should but believes he fails to do. When James writes in his example that "we fall into some revery connected with the day's life," he is speaking about the very phenomenon which May says is missing. What James means by "revery connected with the day's life" is this: our *attention* begins to play over daily actions which generally occupy us. This is James's terminology for what May calls our "imaginative participation in the coming day's possibilities." From James's perspective, when our attention begins to dwell on the familiar world of everyday practical activities, all contradictory ideas are pushed into the fringe of consciousness and we spontaneously act—we get up. May's criticism flounders. James is no enemy or antagonist of May; he is in fact of the very same warp and weave.

Paul Ricoeur's criticism of James's view of the will is also curious and is, in fact, withdrawn almost as quickly as it is made. At the very beginning of his remarks, Ricoeur states with apology, "The defect of James' analysis seems to us one of language rather than of doctrine."[32] Ricoeur believes that upon occasion James lapses into the language of mental physics. It is true that upon certain occasions James refers to effort as a "force" or "quantity" added to an ideal possibility in order to strengthen it and make it prevail. But Ricoeur himself seems to realize this is just a temporary lapse and almost acknowledges that the charge that James is making an analogy between will and physical properties is unfair.[33] Ricoeur admits that James never thought of effort as a physical force. Effort has to do with attention, and attention is not a physical energy; it is a fundamental structure of consciousness.

Will and Freedom

After all that James has said about the will, he admits that on scientific grounds he has not proved, in fact cannot prove, the reality of freedom. Toward the end of both his chapter on the "Will" and his chapter on "Attention," James concedes that what appears to be effort may really be only a "resultant" of subtle associative processes which are difficult to perceive. On phenomenological grounds the experience of effort seems to be an "original force" without prior causal antecedents. Both in *Principles* and in *Essays on Radical Empiricism,* James is inclined to take the testimony of direct experience at face value. But this experience could be wrong. For instance, if alternative "Z" triumphs over alternative "A," it may be because "the associative processes which makes Z triumph are really the stronger, and in A's absence would make us give a 'passive' and unimpeded attention to Z."[34] The stronger associative correction may in fact dictate the forces of our attention.

We should not be surprised, therefore, to hear James say that "the question of free-will is insoluble on strictly psychologic grounds."[35] How could it be otherwise? Dedicated as it is to the discernment of the conditions, determinisms, and regularities of life, how can scientific psychology comprehend the dimension of freedom? By the very definition of its task, freedom is excluded from consideration. Even *phenomenological description is not enough.* Direct descriptions reveal the structure of consciousness and demonstrate the phenomenal presence of such experiences as voluntary attention and effort. But phenomenological description does not prove the reality of these experiences.

Where, then, does one turn? The answer for James is this: One turns to metaphysics, and more specifically, to ethics as a division of metaphysics. By metaphysics, James means nothing more than the rigorous task of thinking hard and straight about the fundamental presuppositions of human action seen in its broadest context. It is on the issue of free will that we see why James was not so much on the way toward a phenomenological psychology as he was toward a truly philosophical psychology of the widest scope. It combined experimental, comparative, and introspective (phenomenological) methods with a broad inquiry into the *logical* preconditions for human action.

The logical preconditions for ethical action require the belief in free will. James says that the grounds for his belief in freedom are "ethical rather than psychological" and for this reason, he "prefers to exclude them" from consideration in his *Principles,* dedicated as it ostensibly was to the idea of psychology as a scientific discipline. But, as we have seen, James never maintained this separation of psychology from philosophy—not in his *Principles* and certainly not in his writings taken as a whole. It is typical of James that as soon as he says ethical consideration should not intrude into psychological inquiry, he goes right ahead and does it. "A few words," he writes even in the *Principles,* he "may be permitted about the logic of the question."

The few comments he permits himself in the *Principles* reflect an earlier argument worked out in his "Dilemma of Determinism" (1884). The argument is basically an appeal to logic— something which is often overlooked, especially in view of James's criticism of the rigidities of theoretical reason in *A Pluralistic Universe.*[36] In criticizing theoretical reason, James is really trying to build a place for the logic of practical reason and action. His argument for freewill is basically this: (1) The more rational of two alternatives is the truer and we should therefore choose it,[37] and (2) the postulate of free will is more rational than thoroughgoing determinism because it better accounts for the brute facts of practical action.[38]

James does take a few misleading turns in his argument. His argument is easy to miss and in fact recently has been misunderstood frequently by some of his best commentators. Sometimes he seems to say that the postulate of determinism is just as much of a metaphysical assumption as the postulate of freedom and that, in the end, we must make an arbitrary choice—almost a kind of Kierkegaardian leap of faith.[39] At other times, he says that the need for rational order is a fundamental subjective interest, a structure of our very personalities. We have subjective needs for moral rationality as well as theoretical rationality; in the final analysis we must affirm those postulates which will satisfy our subjective needs for rational moral order since these needs are just as real as are our needs for theoretical order.[40] A. J. Ayer believes this is the sole grounds for James's belief in freedom and sees it as a choice on basically "emotional" grounds.[41]

The latter argument may to some extent be valid, but it falls short of a fully logical argument, which he does in fact present. The real heart of his argument is that determinism cannot explain certain obvious facts of life and for this reason it is held at the cost of self-contradiction. What are these basic aspects of experience for which it cannot account? It cannot explain that in the normal course of practical action we "approve" some things and have "regrets" about others. To regret something, for example, is to assume that something else could have been in its place.[42] Of course, the determinist cannot admit this because it would contradict the very premises of his determinism. Hence, the determinist is forced into a radically pessimistic view of the world in which there can be no regrets about anything. The logical direction of this pessimism is total inactivity or possibly even suicide. In the face of such things as violent murder or other acts of human cruelty, the determinist can only say that it could not have been otherwise. The determinist can only avoid this profound pessimism by saying that he lives, along with Voltaire's Candide, in the best of all possible worlds and that everything, although causally determined, is actually good and working for the best.

This leads the determinist to logical difficulties. If we do live in the best of all possible worlds, our regrets are mistaken. But the determinist cannot tell us to refrain from regrets without implying that we live in a world we can change—where something other is indeed possible than what does in fact exist.[43]

This, of course, the determinist cannot do and still believe that all is determined.

James's argument could be improved. But at least, in contrast to what some commentators contend, it is not just an argument based on emotional preference. In essence, he is simply saying that sooner or later, if the determinist acts at all, he will contradict himself. He will indeed make a judgment which entails regret or approval, and then he will be exposed as irrational. Hence, belief in free will is more rational than the position of the determinist. The demands of practical rationality must take precedence over the conventions of theoretical reason and science. The purposes of science are "not the only purposes."

The Heroic Life and Its Problems

James's concepts of will, attention, and effort are fundamental to his heroic view of life. But his understanding of life as strenuous and heroic is built on a general openness to experience and a basically sympathetic style of life. In addition, it is strongly contemplative. It is through attentiveness that one earns the heroic life. As attentiveness is the key to effort, it is also the key to the heroic personality. Our capacity for effort through attention keeps us from flinching and turning aside before adversity. It keeps us from fleeing the field of battle in a time of moral and spiritual struggle. When our capacity for attention, effort, and heroic action are guided by an ethic, they become the measures of the worth of a human being. James becomes positively rapturous when he writes,

> The world thus finds in the heroic man its worthy match and mate; and the effort which he is able to put forth to hold himself erect and keep his heart unshaken is the direct measure of his worth and function in the game of human life. He can *stand* this Universe. He can meet it and keep up his faith in it in presence of those same features which lay his weaker brethren low. . . . But just as our courage is so often a reflex of another's courage, so our faith is apt to be, as Max Müller somewhere says, a faith in someone else's faith. We draw new life from the heroic example. The prophet has drunk more deeply than anyone of the cup of bitterness, but his

countenance is so unshaken and he speaks such mighty words of cheer that his will becomes our will, and our life is kindled at his own.[44]

The world which the heroic individual can face is the pluralistic world of chance, conflict, and real risk about which James had so much to say. It was a world where no ultimate coherences assure life with a pregiven and effortless harmony. Even God's harmonizing activity, James tells us in his more speculative moods, does not exhaust all that needs to be done. There is room left over for man's own efforts.

James's heroism, as we have noted, has strongly ascetic overtones. This is true even though his entire theory of man gives a positive, in fact indispensable, place for human instincts, passions, and subjective interests. If James's substratum of romanticism can be kept in mind, the ascetic dimensions of the following quotation do not seem so dated. There is no more powerful passage in James's writings which reveals the full scope of his view of the heroic and strenuous life.

> Within the psychic life due to the cerebrum itself the same general distinction obtains, between considerations of the more immediate and considerations of the more remote. In all ages the man whose determinations are swayed by reference to the most distant ends has been held to possess the higher intelligence. The tramp who lives from hour to hour; the bohemian whose engagements are from day to day; the bachelor who builds but for a single life; the father who acts for another generation; the patriot who thinks of a whole community and many generations; and finally, the philosopher and saint whose cares are for humanity and for eternity,—these range themselves in an unbroken hierarchy.[45]

The heroic and strenuous life, with its orientation toward more distant ends and its care for both present and future generations, requires some capacity to inhibit that mass of impulses concerned with short-term goals. For James, however, this is never a simple matter of the spirit against the body. As we saw in the chapter on the self, the body for James is a body-self and a body-spirit. His hierarchy of heroic acts described above is brought about by one part of the body-spirit inhibiting another part. The inhibition which James has in mind is the inhibition of inattention. The positive energizing which he envisions comes from the application of our attention to these long-range goals.

Heroic images of humans have not been popular during most of the twentieth century—and for good reasons. Under the influence of Freud, we have become sensitive to the subtle ways in which appeals to self-sacrifice and ascetic denial can dominate and oppress us. We have become aware of the way unrealistic and impossible ideals can become the foundations for a morbid superego. On the other hand, the heroic life, as it was to some extent for James, can become a compensatory device to overcome one's sense of depression and passivity. James was aware that his own appeals to the strenuous life were partially efforts to fill his life with the very quality which he sometimes felt to be so lacking.[46]

But in recent decades, psychology has once again begun to exhibit models of the optimal human being which celebrate the qualities of the heroic and strenuous life. The two principal examples are Erik Erikson's concept of "generativity" and Erich Fromm's concept of the "productive" personality. Other examples could be mentioned. In addition to the work of Rollo May, which we have already cited, and the earlier work of Adler, more recently Ernest Becker and Robert Lifton also have advanced heroic images of the person. In Becker's concept of the "heroic individual" and Lifton's understanding of "symbolic immortality," we have important new versions of this *ancient* model of man.[47]

All heroic images of the human can be criticized for lifting up an impossible and highly idealistic image of man which constitutes an oppressive and guilt-producing tyranny on all those poor souls who are barely managing to keep their lives together and have no energy to move toward truly self-sacrificing and strenuous styles of life. It will be instructive to review the optimal images of the human found in the writings of Erikson and Fromm—certainly the most thoroughly worked out of contemporary heroic images of the human—to determine whether they are subject to this criticism. Then we can return to James and decide whether it applies to him.

Heroic images of the human will be oppressive unless equipped with ways of showing how average human beings can approximate certain ideals by moving forward in a gradual, step-by-step fashion. In addition, they must have ways of assigning worth and dignity to those who do not measure up to the heroic virtues of saints and reformers but who can indeed demonstrate progress in view of their beginning points, their abilities, their opportunities, and other realities of their social and ecological niche.

This is exactly the strength that Erikson's view of generativity has over Fromm's understanding of the productive personality. Fromm sees all human existence as a paradox or mélange. On the one hand, humans are a part of nature—embedded in its regularities and secure in its natural processes. On the other hand, human beings—because of their capacity for reason, imagination, and self-awareness—transcend the processes of nature.[48] However, man has a nostalgic longing for the security and union left over from his former harmony with nature. It is Fromm's conviction that union through a regressive return to nature is forever closed to man. The only way for human beings to satisfy their drive toward relatedness is through a progressive development of their capacities to contribute to the lives of others. In *Man for Himself* Fromm writes, "Productiveness is man's ability to use his powers and to realize the potentialities inherent in him."[49] In the *Art of Loving,* he writes, "Giving is the highest expression of potency. In the very act of giving, I experience my strength, my wealth, my power."[50]

Fromm and James are in agreement in seeing man as cut off from the effortless harmonies of a less differentiated existence, whether this existence be seen as an archaic union with nature (Fromm) or the security of life in a world of absolute monism (James). Both believe that humans must discover their true authenticity in a new kind of activeness—a higher manifestation of one's powers through contributions and gifts to others. But Fromm is guilty of the sin committed by most heroic views of life. His heroism becomes a tyranny of idealism. Anything short of full productiveness is "unproductiveness" and "passivity."[51] Fromm gives us no methodology for growth and no standards for measuring the relative worth and dignity of those who are less than fully productive.

Erikson is one of the few contemporary proponents of a

heroic view of man who incorporates safeguards against using it in an oppressive and heteronomous way. His protection comes from the fact that his normative view of human nature is connected with a developmental psychology. His developmental psychology gives us two things: (1) an outline of some of the developmental requirements needed to reach the ideal, and (2) a diagnostic device for measuring that we are *on the move* although we have not in fact approximated our goal.

Erikson's normative concept of man is summed up by the concept of "generativity." Erikson defines generativity as the future-oriented concern to establish and guide the coming generations of human beings.[52] In *Insight and Responsibility,* Erikson writes that "generativity, as the instinctual power behind various forms of selfless 'caring,' potentially extends to whatever a man generates and leaves behind, creates and produces (or helps to produce)."[53] This parellels closely James's view of man which we saw above when he wrote about the "father who acts for another generation," "the patriot who thinks of a whole community and many generations," and "the philosopher and saint whose cares are for humanity."

But Erikson's theory of generativity is related to his theory of human development. Generativity depends upon a fund of earlier positive resolutions to certain psychosocial crises of life. Generativity is similar to James's concept of will without the latter's more sophisticated analysis of the role that attention plays in our future-oriented acts on behalf of others. In addition, they both agree that higher levels of mature action require a prior fund of action possibilities. James speaks about this under the rubric of prior ideas of action and their consequences; Erikson does the same in the context of his theory of development. Erikson has charted a series of developmental conflicts which occur during childhood and adolescence. He points to the conflicts between trust and mistrust, autonomy and shame, initiative and guilt which occur during the first years of life. He also points to the childhood conflict between industry and inferiority, the adolescent conflict between identity and identity confusion, and the early adult conflict between intimacy and isolation.[54] For generativity to occur, the positive resolutions of trust, autonomy, initiative, industry, identity, and intimacy must predominate over their negative counterparts. Generativity as a heroic virtue does not and cannot jump out of a vacuum. There must be a prior fund of action possibilities which can be called upon to support truly mature and self-giving activity. Most heroic images of the human flounder—including Fromm's understanding of the productive personality—because of their failure to account for this need.

James's vision of the heroic and strenuous life also had the weakness of not being built upon a theory of the stages of human development. To some extent, James's view is subject to the same criticism as is Fromm's. But although James did not have a systematic theory of development, he was interested in the processes of development. In his theory of the "transiency of instincts" (which I will explain in the next chapter) we find a concept very similar to Erikson's highly important "epigenetic principle"—a concept so fundamental for Erikson's own theory of development. Furthermore, James had a profound interest in the psychology of habit. Autonomous strenuous action requires, according to James, a background of firm and stable habits. In his psychology of habits, James will have much in common with Skinner and the psychology of control. The point is that our capacity for deliberation and will, for James, is indeed small. It outstrips only slightly the fund of settled and habitual responses to the world which an individual has developed through the course of his life. James does in fact give us a vision of the possibility of heroic and even self-sacrificial action. But such action occurs only when it is preceded by a developmental history whereby our passional life has been shaped into a fund of settled and habitual potentials for action. It is out of this fund of action possibilities that our attention creates our strategies for the future.

James's image of the strenuous life can be compared profitably to the methods of a mountain climber scaling a barren and craggy cliff at an almost perpendicular angle. He starts the ascent with a great deal of equipment—ropes, pins, hammers, chains, and food, not to mention his own physical energy, his desire to succeed, and his drive to survive. His ascent is slow. At each state he secures himself with his ropes, pins, and hammer from accidental falls. His will, attention, and effort is focused on raising himself only a few inches—at best a few feet—above his present level. He regains his strength by resting on his supports. He is unable to expend these tremendous amounts of energy without interruption. Yet much of what he does seems almost automatic. Most of his voluntary activity is very much of a passive type; there are actions such as pulling his rope or grabbing his hammer which he has performed millions of times before and which come almost automatically as soon as the idea crosses his mind. His deliberate decisions are few. His decision to go on the climb to begin with may have been deliberate and marked by hesitation as he weighed the dangers against the rewards of such a venture. Midway during the climb he may have to decide to go on or return with his goals not accomplished. He may have to decide in some circumstances whether to hoist himself by eighteen inches or by only six. In short, his heroic ascent does not occur with one gigantic leap from the bottom to the top. In view of the slowness of his progress, there are times when he may look like a fool. And although the crucial variable to success is his own effort, it is also true that rest, relaxation, and his reliance on his many supports are of fundamental importance as well. Will, freedom, attention, and effort play only a small role in human life, but the role that they play makes all the difference. Such is the scope of the strenuous mood and the heroic life.

Notes

1. *PP*, 2:576.

2. Paul Ricoeur, *Freedom and Nature* (Evanston, Ill.: Northwestern University Press, 1966), p. 5.

3. O. F. Matthiessen, *The James Family* (New York: Alfred A. Knopf, 1948), p. 209.

4. Erik Erikson, *Identity, Youth, and Crisis* (New York: W. W. Norton, 1968), p. 151.

5. Cushing Strout, "The Pluralistic Identity of William James: A Psychohistorical Reading of the Varieties of Religious Experience," *American Quarterly* 23 (May 1971):143.

6. Perry, *TCWJ*, 2:679.

7. *LWJ*, p. 147.

8. *PP*, 2:524–25.

9. *WB*, p. 9.

10. Ibid. p. 114.

11. *PP*, 2:526.

12. Paul Ricoeur, *Freud and Philosophy* (New Haven: Yale University Press, 1970) pp. 134–51.

13. *PP*, 2:486.

14. Ibid., pp. 486–87.

15. Ibid., p. 488.

16. Ibid., p. 522.

17. Ibid.

18. Ibid., p. 501.

19. Ibid., pp. 528–29.

20. *PP*, 416–17.

21. Ibid., 2:531–35.

22. Stevens, *James and Husserl: The Foundations of Meaning (The Hague: Martinus Nijhoff, 1974), p. 147.

23. *PP*, 2:561.

24. Ibid., p. 562.

25. Ibid., p. 534.

26. Ibid., p. 536.

27. Erikson, *Childhood and Society* (New York: W. W. Norton, 1963), p. 267.

28. *PP*, 1:325.

29. May, *Love and Will* (London: Fontana Library, 1972), p. 205.

30. *PP*, 2:486.

31. May, *Love and Will*, pp. 223–24.

32. Ricoeur, *Freedom and Nature*, p. 176.

33. Ibid., p. 31.

34. *PP*, 1:451.

35. Ibid, 2:572.

36. *PU*, pp. 227–52.

37. *WB*, p. 146.

38. Ibid., p. 147.

39. *PP*, 2:573. Although James uses this kind of argument occasionally, it is associated most generally with his argument for religious beliefs. The idea that since religious beliefs cannot be proved on theoretical grounds, one can only be convinced of their truth by acting on them—this is an argument set forth in his essay "The Will to Believe" (1896). It is a mistake, however, to believe, as Richard Stevens does in his *James and Husserl*, that this is the essence of his argument for freedom (153–56).

40. *WB*, p. 147.

41. A. J. Ayer, *The Origins of Pragmatism* (London: Macmillan, 1968), p. 218.

42. *WB*, p. 161.

43. Ibid., p. 163.

44. *PP*, 2:579.

45. *PP*, 1:23.

46. Perry, *TCWJ*, 2:270.

47. Ernest Becker, *The Denial of Death* (New York: The Free Press, 1973), pp. 255–86; Robert Lifton, "On Death and the Continuity of Life: A 'New' Paradigm," *History of Childhood Quarterly* 1 (Spring 1974):681–96.

48. Erich Fromm, *Man for Himself* (New York: Rinehart and Co., 1960), p. 40.
49. Ibid., p. 84.
50. Fromm, *The Art of Loving* (New York: Harper and Brothers, 1956), p. 23.
51. Fromm, *Man for Himself*, pp. 62–82.
52. Erikson, *Childhood and Society*, p. 267 and *Identity, Youth, and Crisis*, p. 138.
53. Erik Erikson, *Insight and Responsibility* (New York: W. W. Norton, 1964), p. 131.
54. Erikson, *Childhood and Society*, pp. 247–69.

7

Instincts and the Culture
of Detachment

Possibly more than any other feature, psychology in the twentieth century has been marked by an awareness of the role of instincts in the mental life of man. There are exceptions to this generalization. Certainly behaviorism of the Skinnerian variety has characteristically ignored the biological and instinctual foundations of human behavior. In addition, existential and phenomenological psychologies have shown little concern with the instinctual foundations of behavior. But to the man in the street, modern psychology is very much related to the discoveries and claims of Freud. To the average man, the animal and instinctual dimensions of human motivation are the central message of contemporary psychology.

The difference between Freudian psycholanalysis and certain humanistic psychologies such as those of Rogers, Perls, and Schutz is not that the former emphasizes instinctuality and the latter, certain higher or noninstinctual dimensions of man. Rogers and others like him place as much emphasis upon the instinctual foundations of personality as did Freud. Rogers's idea of a "self-actualization tendency," taken over from the theories of Kurt Goldstein, is just as biological and instinctual as is Freud's concept of the libido, and possibly even more so. The difference between them is found in their model and theory of instinctual life—their respective understanding of the rhythms and ranges of instinctuality. Both orthodox psychoanalysis and most of the so-called humanistic psychologies function out of what John MacMurray called the "organic

156

metaphor." The difference between them is that they use different organic models as foundations for their systems. Psychoanalysis uses a tension reduction and pleasure-pain paradigm; Rogers and others use a model which emphasizes growth, unfolding, and open-ended hemostasis. Both are to some extent reductionistic in that they attempt to understand wide ranges of human behavior in analogy to the supposed functions of their preferred organic model of life.

James too had a theory about the instinctual dimensions of human existence. His specific theory of instinctuality is continuous with his functional view of mind which we reviewed in chapter 2. He developed it primarily out of a combination of his comparative and experimental approaches to psychology, but it gained its overall character from his phenomenological perspective.

It is instructive to compare Freud and James on their respective understandings of human instinctuality. The issue of the nature of human instincts offers an excellent perspective from which to view some of the major differences between James's view of the strenuous life and what I have called the culture of detachment. There are amazing similarities between Freud and James which have never been explored adequately. Of course, there are significant differences. But their differences cannot be located in the fact that Freud makes more of human instinctuality than does James. It would be a grave mistake to think that simply because James finds a place for will, attention, and freedom that he is less concerned than Freud with the biological and instinctual foundations of life. As we have seen, a coherent application of James's methodological commitments entails a thorough description of the fundamental structures of human consciousness. Of course, one discovers instinctuality in the very process of doing this; one finds it in the form of "subjective interests" and experienced appetites. But there is much one can learn about instinctuality from a comparative and experimental view as well. In sum, we will be forced to conclude that James had an amazingly powerful theory of human instinctuality—one which can now marshal support from more recent discoveries in ethology and experimental and biological psychology. It is also a theory which seriously challenges the foundations of the orthodox psychoanalytic view of human nature and much of the cultural vision which follows from it.

Freud developed his theory of instincts in the context of medical psychology. He was concerned primarily to find an explanation for such clinical symptoms as hysteria, obsessive neurosis, and the phobias. Much of his theory, however, gained the status, even in his own eyes, of a general psychology and was thought to reveal insights into man in general and not just humans in the grips of a crippling mental disease.

Freud and Instinctuality

The first major difference between Freud and James on the nature of instinctuality is this: James believed humans had a large number of instinctual tendencies whereas Freud believed human activity is motivated by no more than two types of instinctual energy, although throughout his career his mind changed about just what these two types actually were. In his *New Introductory Lectures* (1933), when he is reviewing the development of his theory of the instincts, he explicitly repudiates the kind of pluralistic thinking which one finds in James— the kind of thinking which "postulates as many different instincts as may be needed."[1] In his early theory he made a distinction between the two great classes of needs known as "hunger and love." The hunger instincts were associated with the ego and were concerned with the serious business of self-preservation.[2] The love instincts had to do with the preservation of the species and were manifested in our sexual drives and a type of energy which Freud called the "libido."[3]

This early dualism of instinctual forces began to crumble in a series of metapsychological papers written between 1910 and 1915, especially his 1914 paper entitled "On Narcissism: An Introduction."[4] Here he became convinced that the ego itself could become an object of libidinal energies. In short, the ego, he theorized, could get its energy from the id and there was no need for the additional and somewhat "uneconomical" theory that the ego had its own instincts.

But Freud enjoyed the utter simplicity of only a single type of instinct—sexuality—for only a few years. In 1920 he published his *Beyond the Pleasure Principle,* in which he proposed a new, dual-instinct theory.[5] His experiences with such phenomenon as the bewildering tendency in his patients to resist cure and to repeat compulsively their self-destructive behavior led him to hypothesize the existence of an instinct for self-destruction and death.[6] Hence, eros and thanatos—sexuality and death—became for Freud the two great classes of instincts motivating all behavior.

Most of Freud's middle career was dedicated to the study of the sexual instincts. In his "Three Contributions to the Theory of Sex" (1903) and his "Instincts and Their Vicissitudes" (1915), Freud portrayed our sexual instincts as conservative, and interested primarily in the discharge of energy and the return to a state of quiescence or equilibrium.[7] Furthermore, his observations of sexual perversions and neuroses led him to believe that the sexual instincts were highly "plastic" and fluid—easily susceptible to alteration in both "aim" and "object." In addition, the instincts were tenacious. They could be repressed but they could not be extinguished. They would always find some substitute avenue of gratification if more obvious and direct roots were inaccessible.

Freud did approach something of the spirit of James's pluralistic theory of instincts by speaking of sexual instincts *in the plural* rather than a sexual instinct *in the singular.* According to Freud, there was no one sex instinct which inevitably expressed itself through customary avenues of genital contact in heterosexual intercourse. Our sexual instincts express themselves piecemeal—bit by bit, so to speak, in the process of our development throughout infancy and childhood. Freud had a rough approximation to an "epigenetic" theory of sexual development—something that we will find also in James, although not limited to sexual development.

We also find a similar but much broader model in the writings of Erikson. By an epigenetic theory, I mean that Freud believed our sexual instincts express themselves according to a timetable which corresponds to the pace of biological growth. Sexual libido first expresses itself, according to Freud, in the "oral" regions, then the "anal" orifice, and even later it becomes centered around the sexual organs themselves—the phallus or the clitoris.[8] The development and normal integration of these component instincts is full of vicissitudes and easily arrested or derailed. Fully adult genital organization of sexuality is the result of a fortuitous set of infant and childhood experiences and by no means a simple spontaneous consequence of the aim and organization of the instincts themselves.

There is a direct relation between Freud's understanding of the instincts and his cultural vision. Freud's idea of the truly healthy individual—the person *post* psychoanalysis—sees him as transcending over and detached from both his own chaotic instincts as well as social and cultural authority. One cannot rely on one's own biological impulses for guidance because they are formless and insatiable. The instincts in relation to the ego are like the superior power of a "horse" in relation to its "rider" or like the unruly and surly masses of a steaming metropolis to the small but better organized forces of the police.[9] The instincts themselves need the guidance of either culture (in the form of the superego) or psychoanalytic insight, and preferably the latter. To depend upon external cultural and social authorities (fathers, political leaders, and kings) is to allow oneself to be robbed and deprived of the vital libidinal energies with which such external authorities are always invested.[10] Freud believed that each human being was endowed with a given quantity of libidinal energy; to invest energy in another, be it loved one, father, or civil authority, was to reduce one's pool of energy for one's own enjoyment.[11] This conflict between instinct and culture in Freud is captured well by Philip Rieff when he writes,

No small part of Freud's impact upon the contemporary moral imagination derives from his idea of the self in conflict. He conceives of the self not as an abstract entity, uniting experience and cognition, but as the subject of a struggle between two objective forces—unregenerate instincts and overbearing culture. Between these forces there may be compromise but no resolution. Since the individual can neither extirpate his instincts nor wholly reject the demands of society, his character expresses the way in which he organizes and appeases the conflict between the two.[12]

There should be little surprise that, as we saw in chapter 5, psychoanalytic "insight" and rational education were Freud's preferred methods methods to protect us from blind trust in either the temptations of instinct or the obligatory demands of culture.[13]

Rieff is correct in his judgment that Freud gave rise to an image of "psychological man" whose dominant goal in the life was to gain a little more cautious enjoyment through "husbanded energy and finessed self-consciousness."[14] Freud, according to Rieff, has taught psychological man how to defend "the private man against the demands made by both culture and instinct."[15] "Turning away from the Occidental ideal of action leading toward the salvation of others besides ourselves," Rieff believes that psychological man is now espousing the more "Oriental ideal of salvation though self-contemplative manipulation."[16] And it certainly would follow from Freud's theory of the instincts that all action in the world designed to improve or transform it would in reality be motivated by a cultural superego which was itself robbing us of our internal peace and equilibrium.

James's Instinctual Pluralism

James saw far less basic antagonism between human instincts and sociocultural reality than did Freud. Whereas the relation between the instincts and social reality in Freud is seen always under the rubrics of satisfaction or frustration, release or inhibition, for James the issues are somewhat different. For James social and cultural realities do not simply satisfy or repress instinctuality—they complete, pattern, and guide human instincts as well.

Instincts, James believed, must be defined somewhat differently for human beings than for animals. For some animals' instincts can be defined as a faculty for "acting in such a way as to produce certain ends, without foresight of the ends, and without previous education in the performance."[17] Had James stuck with this definition as applicable to humans, his view of instinctuality would have been cut off completely from consciousness, the self, and the will—all the structures of human nature which his phenomenological descriptions had revealed. But James quickly changes his tune. In man, instinct is mixed with consciousness and memory: "Every instinctive act, in an animal with memory," James tell us, "must cease to be 'blind' after being once repeated, and must be accompanied with foresight of its 'end' just so far as that end may have fallen under the animal's cognizance."[18] Hence, in humans instincts combine with experience and memory and are subject to both learning and voluntary control. In effect, James is saying that instincts in man invariably get mixed up with *meanings*. James's concept of instincts must be laid in the context of his entire theory of meanings as I outlined it in chapter three. But an example of what he has in mind is even better. The following illustration will be clearer if it is recalled that James did not believe in a death instinct in the same sense as did Freud; he did believe, however, that there were instinctive tendencies toward what he called "pugnacity" as well as toward "hunting" with all the accompanying thrills of the chase and the final kill. He writes,

> If a boy sees a fat hopping-toad, he probably has incontinently an impulse (especially if with other boys) to smash the creature with a stone, which impulse we may suppose him blindly to obey. But something in the expression of the dying toad's clasped hands suggests the meanness of the act, or reminds him of sayings he has heard about the sufferings of animals being like his own; so that, when next he is tempted by a toad, an idea arises which, far from spurring him again to the torment, prompts kindly actions, and may even make him the toad's champion against less reflecting boys.[19]

Freud's understanding of the wish *(Wunsch)* had some similarities with James's understanding of instincts. The human sexual wish (what Freud was in reality observing when he was studying instinctuality) was by definition a mental phenomenon, i.e., it was a biological impulse connected with a psychic representation.[20] But Freud never carried this insight so far as James by acknowledging that instincts in man are deeply mixed up with our general capacity to anticipate ends and consequences.

The idea that instinctuality in humans is invariably tied up with meanings is an insight which James unfortunately forgot in his theory of the emotions. Here James lapsed into one of his most thoroughgoing behavioristic moments. Rather than understanding human emotions as responses to the meaning that a situation carried for us, James saw it in reverse. In his famous chapter on the emotions James tells us we do not cry because we *perceive* ourselves to be helpless and powerless; rather, we first of all find ourselves crying and then feel helpless.[21] We do not first become afraid and then run; rather, we find ourselves running and then discover that we are afraid. James's motivation for this somewhat behavioristic theory of the emotions is simple: he is attempting to maintain his commitment to an intimate relation between mind and body. Emotions are not just mental phenomena disconnected from the body; they are part and parcel of the body and no artificial separation between mind and body can do justice to a theory of the emotions. Nonetheless, in disconnecting emotions from meanings, James here put himself in contradiction to the main thrust of his philosophical-psychological anthropology. It is now generally believed that James overstated his case. In reality, our emotions are very much bodily responses to perceived meanings. Whether we experience fear or anger when confronted by a speeding car about to run us down depends very much on our perception of the situation. If we believe that we can easily avoid the onslaught, we are likely quickly to skip to the curb and let rip a string of angry expletives at the anonymous driver. If our chances for survival seem much narrower, we may be grasped by an on rush of raw fear and leap immediately to safety with not a thought of anger in our heads. Only later, after a second look, does real anger begin to emerge. Clearly, James was on much more solid ground in the way he related his theory of instincts to the realm of meanings.

To acknowledge the role of meanings, experience, and memories in instinctuality might be construed by some people as an admission that instincts play no really vital role in human behavior. Certainly, this has been the argument of behaviorism from J. B. Watson[22] to B. F. Skinner. James anticipated this point of view and denied it flatly. There were also those who said that instincts serve no *purpose in man because* "reason" has taken their place. Against both of these positions, James asserts that human beings are in reality the richest of all creatures in their instinctual endowments. "Man has a far greater variety of *impulses* than any lower animal."[23] Man appears to hesitate, deliberate, and use his higher faculties for reason and choice not because he is devoid of instincts, but because he has so many, they come into conflict. "Nature implants contrary impulses," James writes, "to act on many classes of things."[24] An animal such as man which has all of these contradictory instincts seems to lose its "'instinctive' demeanor and appears to lead a life of hesitation and choice, an intellectual life; *not, however, because he has no instincts—rather because he has so many that they block each other's path.*"[25] Man possesses all the impulses that animals do and "a great many more."[26]

James concludes his eloquent defense of man's instinctual pluralism with a startling statement on the relation of instinct and reason which shows, more than anything I could quote, the essential difference between James and Freud on their general visions of human nature.

> In other words, there is no material antagonism between instinct and reason. Reason, *per se,* can inhibit no impulses; the only thing that can neutralize an impulse is an impulse the other way: Reason may, however, make an inference which will excite the imagination so as to set loose the impulse the other way; and thus, though the animal richest in reason might be also the animal richest in instinctive impulses too, he would never seem the fatal automaton which a *merely* instinctive animal would be.[27]

For James, man's instinctual pluralism and his capacity for reason go hand in hand. Reason is not against instinct. Reason, on the basis of its assessments, grants its reinforcing attention to some impulses rather than to others. The animal with the richest instinctuality and the greatest capacity for reason is one and the same creature—the animal called "man."

James does not pit reason against instinct. But he does pit reason on the side of some instincts against other instincts. The side that reason takes should depend upon the adaptive challenges of the situation in which an individual or group is located. Seen in this light, James agrees with Freud in seeing the need for the control of instinctuality. But Freud is finally more totalistic, in spite of his general plea for a more tolerant attitude toward sexual deviations. When Freud argues for more liberal attitudes toward sexual release and more enlightened approaches to the sexuality of infants and children, he is not arguing for the adaptive significance of instincts as such. Instincts, for Freud, seek pleasure and release; in man, the instincts have little adaptive significance in themselves. The situation is just the reverse for James. For James, our instincts are the foundations of our capacity to adapt to the challenges of our environment.

But in spite of this, not all instinctive responses are equally relevant for specific situations and some responses are, on the whole, irrelevant to almost any situation. In his early papers on evolutionary psychology, his chapter on "Instinct" in the *Principles,* and especially in his concluding chapter, entitled "Necessary Truths and the Effects of Experience," James sets forth the idea that our instincts emerge as a product of "free variation."[28] They do not come in the Lamarckian fashion as a result of repeated experiences which are passed on through the race from generation to generation. They first appear as a chance variation. A species' capacity for scent or vision is accidentally stronger, a certain fowl's sense of direction more efficient, or a dog's sensitivity to sounds more acute, by a matter of chance or accident. But if the new instinct is adaptive, natural selection preserves it, and it is then inherited by the offspring of that lucky creature.

Because ecological situations change, because the selective powers of environments alter, the instinctive responses which are triumphant in one environment may not be particularly relevant to another. And some of our physiological proclivities may be downright irrelevant or destructive. James cites our proclivity toward alcohol and certain drugs.[29] He also believed that a remnant of primitive man's highly functional instinct to hunt is still with us today. Its lurking presence casts an ambiguous shadow over our lives. It is excited easily; we can be swept up only too quickly in a pitch of warlike frenzy. But even here, because of the flexibility of our instincts and the fact that they inevitably get mixed up with meanings, these hunting proclivities can be altered to support with militant enthusiasm our highest moral ideals. This is a theme James investigates in his remarkable article entitled "The Moral Equivalent of War."

But James's measured appreciation for the adaptive functions of our instincts never led him to search for a hidden self buried somewhere in the inner biological man. To this extent, he was much closer to the moral vision of Freud than he was to Jung, Maslow, or most of the humanistic psychologists. There was no "real" or "true" self deeply embedded in our biological roots which only needs to be liberated and set free in order for man to discover his true identity. James always appreciated our instinctual and passional life. He recognized it as the mainspring of our subjective interests and our mental life. This was the romantic undertone to his vision of man. But he also realized that our instinctual inclinations are confused and complex; they need pruning and structuring. They need to become organized into more or less reliable habits.

James's romanticism is overlaid with a unique brand of asceticism which is probably neither stoic, monastic, nor Calvinistic in character. Only shortly after his search through brain physiology in the early chapters of the *Principles* in an effort to discover the sections of the brain which control our various responses to the world, he draws an interesting conclusion about the role of consciousness. A chief characteristic of the instincts and brain centers which control them is their "instability." Consciousness is needed to select and guide the random and unstable possibilities of man's rich range of reactive possibilities. James writes, "The brain is an instrument of possibilities, but of no certainties. But the consciousness, with its own ends present to it, and knowing also well which possibilities lead thereto and which away, will, if endowed with causal efficacy, reinforce the favorable possibilities and repress the unfavorable or indifferent ones."[30] In spite of the creativity which James assigns to our passional life, consciousness (and probably more specifically our attention) is needed to "load the dice" of its wide range of capacities and bring "a more or less constant pressure to bear in favor of *those* of its performances which make for the most permanent interest" of the person.[31]

Hierarchies and Schedules

James has a more positive view than does Freud of the role of the external environment in relation to the instincts. For Freud, the external world either frustrates or gratifies our instincts. James is aware of these dimensions but is concerned also with how the external environment (primarily social and cultural reality) activates, supports, and patterns human instinct. One sees this in his theory of the transitoriness of instincts. James, as did Freud and Erikson, believed that instincts emerge according to a biological timetable. He expressed the law like this: *"Many instincts ripen at a certain age and then fade away."*[32] Freud could agree with the first half of the statement, but of course would have nothing of the idea that instincts ever fade away. In addition, Freud's timetable of instinctual ripening applies only to the sexual instincts; for James, it applies to a wide range of different instinctive tendencies. But the concept is more important for what it says about the role of the environment than for what it says about instincts. James writes,

> A consequence of this law is that if, during the time of such an instinct's vivacity, objects adequate to arouse it are met with, a *habit* of acting on them is formed, which remains when the original instinct has passed away; but that if no such objects are met with, then no habit will be formed; and, later on in life, when the animal meets the objects, he will altogether fail to react, as at the earlier epoch he would instinctively have done.[33]

In stating this principle, James was anticipating a fundamental principle of modern instinct theory—a principle which, unfortunately, was lost for academic psychology for years.

In 1967 the American Psychological Association celebrated its seventy-fifth anniversary by holding a symposium on William James's psychology. In this symposium the great animal psychologist Harry Harlow contributed a highly appreciative review of James's instinct theory, especially his so-called law of the transitoriness of instincts. Harlow laments that, had he read James on instincts "earlier, he might have saved himself several years of tedious research and agonizing theorizing."[34] He further writes that "James makes a convincing case for the importance, including social importance, of the temporal sequence in which instincts develop."[35] Harlow believes that his own experiments with monkeys confirms much of James's principle. Infants raised without mothers or by cloth surrogates never developed properly and never regained the developmental losses which they had undergone. They had difficulties relating to other monkeys, never sexually adjusted satisfactorily to another monkey, and never assumed the parental role with the young. These famous experiments and others which Harlow has done exemplify very well, he feels, the wisdom of James's point of view.

Unfortunately, James never himself developed a systematic charting of which instinctive tendencies emerge first and just what the normal hierarchy of tendencies might be. This is something that Erikson did later in his epigenetic principle and his theory of the developmental stages which it accompanies. Had James accomplished this, many of the confusions in his psychology and philosophy would have been cleared up. Many of his own value assumptions entail a hierarchy of development. James is like Erikson in believing that man must achieve developmentally a foundation of basic trust before he can proceed to the higher, more heroic and ethical stages. This basic trust comes from the gratification of certain fundamental instinctive needs in a warm, secure, and stable parental matrix. James's own willingness to recognize the spiritual importance of monistic and mystical orientations to life is grounded on his awareness that the constant and secure universe which they offer meets certain fundamental human needs. But his desire to go beyond the psychology and spirituality of security reflects his awareness that humans must move toward more differentiated levels of individual responsibility. In this he is struggling to say something similar to Erikson when the latter sees the developmental stages of autonomy, initiative, and even generativity as building on late instinctual emergences but presupposing the early state of basic trust as a necessary foundation.

James lists another principle relevant to instinctuality. He calls it the principle of *"the inhibition of instincts by habits."*[36] This principle supplements but does not replace his theory of the transitoriness of instincts. The principle seems to mean at least two things: (1) that the first object which elicits a particular instinct may be the preferred object thereafter,[37] and (2) that when contradictory impulses can be awakened by the same object, the first impulse which appears actually may inhibit the emergence of the second.[38] The first principle explains such things as imprinting—for example, the tendency of newly born chicks to follow the first creature they see, be it a human, duck, goose, or its own mother. Harlow gives James high marks for recognizing the validity of D. A. Spalding's early observations on imprinting and suggests that had "Lorenz and Tinbergen ever read" James's chapter, they would have given Spalding and James the credit they deserve.[39] But the principle also resonates with the recognition within psychoanalysis of the importance in our lives of the first objects of love, our early experiences, and our initial attachments. Without positing a principle of constancy or a homeostatic conception of psychic equilibrium as did Freud, James in his own way recognized the conservative nature of instinctuality.

But the second meaning of the principle is even more important. The first impulses expressed toward an object may inhibit the expression of other possible impulses. The affection awakened in an infant toward his mother may inhibit the anger and aggressiveness which might emerge later. In the Adirondack mountains, where James spent some of his vacations, he heard stories about domestic calves becoming lost when infants. Having never developed a dependency on humans, their later fear of man is never overcome. With reference to this story and others like it, James can write, "All animals are tame (affectionate) during the earliest phase of their infancy. Habits formed then limit the effects of whatever instincts of wildness may later be evolved."[40] Harlow affirms James's position when he says, "Under normal rearing conditions fear and aggression are held in reasonable control because intraspecies affection has appeared already and established strong, positive, cohesive bonds which inhibit the expression of the later maturing antisocial instincts."[41] Our capacities for fear and aggression may indeed emerge later than our capacities for basic affection and trust. But whether fear and aggression are guided and surrounded by a context of love and affection depends as much on the environment and what it encourages as it does on the schedule of instinctive emergences themselves.

Instinctual Pluralism

But the most striking and controversial aspect of James's theory is his instinctual pluralism. James grants a relative individuality and autonomy to our instinctual tendencies. He makes no effort to reduce them all to one or two master tendencies. He is of a different mold than Freud, who subsumed all the different impulses under sex and aggression. James lists fear, locomotion, vocalization, imitation, aggression, sympathy, hunting, curiosity, constructiveness, play, and sexuality as all having instinctual roots. He discusses cleanliness and shame but sees them more as matters of social learning. But isn't such a list archaic—a relic from late-nineteenth-century psychology? Isn't Freud's sleek and efficient dual instinct theory or Goldstein and Roger's economical principle of self-actualization better?

The full range of human behavior, as well as its recognizable contradictions and ambivalences, may be served better by a theory closer to James's. Especially is this so since, in human behavior, we are not dealing directly with brute and raw instinct so much as we are with plastic tendencies which quickly get caught up into meanings and habits. James may be on solid ground with his instinctual pluralism. We now know that something like his instincts for curiosity, constructivenes, and play has received a great deal of experimental evidence. Robert White has summarized much of the evidence. Citing the observations of Lorenz, Maxwell, Butler, Berlyne, and many others on exploration and play in children and animals, White concludes that we must recognize the existence of such biologically grounded tendencies as something which cannot be reduced to the primary drives for food and sex.[42] These tendencies to explore, to build and construct things, and to play are more constant and less phasic. They do not function on a tension-reduction and consummatory pattern as do the lower instincts such as hunger and sex. In fact, they emerge and function best when our lower needs are gratified. White suggests that we posit a need for "effectance"—a need to become a cause, a center of efficacy and control.[43] When our so-called basic instincts are satisfied, these higher ones function on their own accord for the intrinsic satisfaction which their exercise affords. James's thinking is clearly in line with White's highly respected contribution to recent psychoanalytic ego psychology. In a less systematic way, this emphasis upon the reality of instinctual tendencies toward play, exploration, and manipulation can be found also in our major representatives of the culture of care, Erikson and Fromm.[44] All heroic images of man—all images of the strenuous and caring life—must find some way to state how man can move beyond the simple reduction of tension connected with our basic and most elemental instinctual needs. Freud had no way to do this short of positing complicated and highly dubious processes of sublimation and neutralization of basic libidinal energies.[45]

One might complain about other nominations for the status of instinctive behavior in James's list. On the whole, as Harlow's article testifies, something affirmative can be said for a large number of possible instincts which James believed to exist. Even something positive can be said for James's belief in instinctual tendencies toward sympathy. Although psychoanalysis has complicated ways of explaining altruistic acts which in effect deny that they have primitive instinctual bases, a broader perspective must admit that both in some animals and in humans, sympathetic and altruistic impulses exist. Certainly a mother's care for her children is an example. James also points to the way dogs and monkeys tend one another in times of sickness. Donald Campbell points out in his provocative article entitled "On the Genetics of Altruism and the Counter-Hedonic Components in Human Culture" that it is defensible on the basis of genetics to posit sympathetic and altruistic tendencies in humans at the familial level (parents for children). However, he argues that they do not extend to the wider society. People carrying genes, he continues, which predispose them to courageous, brave, and altruistic behavior do not reproduce so quickly as others because of the higher risks which beset their lives; if such individuals emerge, they are destined to die out.

General social altruism, he argues, must therefore be produced by cultural learning and experience.[46]

James would agree with Campbell. Our sympathetic impulses do not have an overwhelming genetic and instinctual foundation as far as James is concerned. The reader will remember an earlier quotation in which James asserted that both the "egoistic" and the "sympathetic" interests have an instinctual basis, but that "the instincts called egoistic form much the larger mass."[47] There are biological tendencies which orient human beings toward the strenuous life (the sympathetic and self-sacrifical life on the behalf of others), but they are not the dominant inclinations. Creation is divided and split; man's biological nature is a mélange. But this is not a latent gnostic or Manichean vision lurking in the background of James's discussion of instinctuality. Rather, it follows directly from the adaptive-evolutionary substratum of his thought. In primitive societies—simple, small and family-oriented—possibly man did not need sympathetic interests which extended beyond his family, tribe, or clan. But in modern, complex, quickly changinbg societies where family, tribe, and clan are brought face to face with the larger world, a capacity for sympathetic and strenuous activity in behalf of the whole is now needed. It is a demand which the overall situation of modernity places on man—a demand which may in fact exceed his natural inclinations.

But there is something to build on. There are sympathetic inclinations in humans, James believes, and these can be amplified and stabilized into habits and psychological structures. Whereas contemporary humanistic psychology tends toward a sweetness-and-light view of man's biological capacities for love and growth and orthodox psychoanalysis toward a biometaphysics of total depravity, James's analysis is situational and pluralistic. Both our egoistic and sympathetic inclinations have their adaptive significance, but in the context of the modern environment which man has created for himself, his egoistic tendencies overreach themselves and his sympathetic inclinations fail to have the range and depth which the situation requires. Education is needed. Culture and habit must build on the fragments of altruistic impulse which nature gives us. In seeing things this way, James is probably on better grounds than is Erikson with his concept of generativity. Generativity is given instinctual foundations in Erikson's developmental schedule; it is rooted in inclinations which may mature in adulthood and find activation in adult experiences—especially those of tending children.[48] But Erikson fails to emphasize adequately the fragility of our generative and altruistic impulses and the massiveness of other impulses which may contradict and overwhelm them.

The Moral Equivalent of War

The recent phenomenological studies of James largely have ignored what he said about instinctuality. This is a pity, for his thinking on the subject was related strongly to the functional and evolutionary dimensions of his psychology. Without emphasizing this, one misses (as most of the phenomenological studies do) the ingenious, even though unstable, synthesis of functional and phenomenological points of view. Neither Wild, Linschoten, Wilshire, Edie, nor Stevens have come to terms with the fact that James's psychophilosophical anthropology was informed significantly by his belief in man's instinctual tendency to *hunt*. After many millenia of foraging the countryside in search of both beast and fowl, certainly those primitive humans equipped with certain genes adapted to the hunt must have been selected more often by the uncompromising demands of the cruel and relentless environment. But James's belief in instinctive tendencies toward the chase and the kill should not be confused with Freud's externalized death instinct. Nor should it be equated with Konrad Lorenz's "instinct for aggression" which thirsts for expression no matter what.[49] James's instincts to fight and to hunt are far more flexible and can be inhibited, as could all his instincts, by other impulses and more pacific contexts of meaning. It is not so much that we seek the hunt; rather, once by accident or necessity the hunt begins, all the archaic reactive tendencies emerge and we are grasped by a "blind excitement . . . an excitement whose intensity is greater than that of any other human passion save one."[50] "The first blows at a prize-fight are apt to make a refined spectator sick; but his blood is soon up in favor of one party, and it will then seem as if the other fellow could not be banged and pounded and mangled enough."[51]

The older James got, the more he made out of this insight into the hunting and fighting tendencies of humans. Depressed and angered with the bellicose and near imperialistic ventures of the United States in Cuba and the Philippines and with Mexico and Spain, James became fascinated with the readiness of his countrymen to be inflamed into paroxysms of jingoistic fanaticism. In his famous essay "The Moral Equivalent of War" (1910), written near the end of his life, James looks deeply into the ambiguities of the human constitution which brings about such behavior. Modern man's readiness to respond to the prospects of war relates to the primitive's thrill over the hunt. "Our ancestors have bred pugnacity into our bone and marrow," James insists, "and thousands of years of peace won't breed it out of us. The popular imagination fairly fattens on the thought of wars."[52]

As opposed to war, however, as James was, he recognized something that the pacifist and liberal mentality completely overlooks. Man not only possesses a constitutional readiness to respond to war, it is frequently in war that he rises to his most noble moments. "War is the *strong* life; it is the life *in extremis.*"[53] It gives discipline and sense of meaning to life; it brings back a community of commitment and obligation which seems to be lacking in "pacific cosmopolitan industrialism." James anticipates Philip Rieff in his sober predictions about the collapse of communities of obligation and commitment.[54] "Where is the savage yes and no, the unconditional duty? . . . Where is there anything man feels honored by belonging to?"[55] Selected for the arduous life by centuries of struggle, man, James was afraid, would be reduced by modern urban and industrial society to either a simpering blob of meaningless passion or would be set up for jingoistic exploitation by demagogues and militarists.

The liberal and pacifistic drive to eliminate war would fail unless it created a moral equivalent to war. Such a program must bear the marks of a struggle and a fight, but a struggle and fight for moral ends. It would be a "moral equivalent to war." And then William James, the great apostle of individual freedom, democratic pluralism, and the creativity of the single person, writes a sentence which might be of interest to Chairman Mao himself: "In the more or less socialistic future towards which mankind seems drifting we must still subject ourselves collectively to those severities which answer to our real position upon this only partly hospitable globe." In effect, James is asking: Why can't those old military virtues be redirected toward new and more edifying ends? Why can't those energies which were once directed toward foreign enemies be turned now toward more subtle threats, both natural and moral, and in support of the welfare of the human community? James even goes so far as to suggest an alternative to military conscription, a conscription of youth into an army against injustice, poverty, and ignorance—the root idea of what later took the form of the Peace Corps.

Whereas Freud's understanding of the conflicts between instinct and society led him implicitly toward a culture of detachment from both, James envisioned a way to harness man's passions, even his most aggressive, into a life of strenuous commitment in behalf of the human community. What man does with his instinctuality very much depends upon the *meanings* which they come to serve. But to turn man's instinctuality to the service of a *vision* of communal commitment requires a technology for the transformation of instinct into habit. But even more than this, it requires a rational and enlightened ethic to guide them both.

Notes

1. Sigmund Freud, *New Introductory Lectures* (New York: W. W. Norton, 1960), p. 131

2. Sigmund Freud, *A General Introduction to Psychoanalysis* (New York: Washington Square Press, 1960), pp. 359–60.

3. Ibid, pp. 336–39.

4. S. Freud, "On Narcissism: An Introduction," *General Psychological Theory*, ed. Philip Rieff (New York: Collier Books, 1963), pp. 56–82.

176   PLURALISM AND PERSONALITY

5. S. Freud, *Beyond the Pleasure Principle* (New York: Bantam Books, 1963).

6. Ibid., pp. 46, 65, 67, 71.

7. S. Freud, "Three Contributions to the Theory of Sex," in *The Basic Writings of Sigmund Freud* (New York: Random House, 1938), pp. 553-619.

8. S. Freud, *A General Introduction to Psychoanalysis* (New York: Washington Square Press, 1960), pp. 312-47.

9. S. Freud, *The Ego and the Id* (London: Hogarth Press, 1957), p. 30.

10. S. Freud, *Group Psychology and the Analysis of the Ego* (New York: W. W. Norton, 1960), pp. 26-39.

11. S. Freud, *Civilization and Its Discontents* (New York: W. W. Norton), pp. 55-56.

12. Philip Rieff, *Freud: The Mind of the Moralist* (New York: Doubleday and Co., 1961), p. 29.

13. S. Freud, *The Future of an Illusion* (New York: Hogarth Press, 1957), p. 60.

14. Rieff, *Freud: The Mind of the Moralist*, p. 391.

15. *Ibid., p. 361.*

16. *Ibid., p. 392.*

17. *PP*, 2:383.

18. Ibid., p. 390

19. Ibid., p. 390.

20. Paul Ricoeur, *Freud and Philosophy* (New Haven, Conn.: Yale University Press, 1970). pp. 134-51.

21. *PP*, 1:442-85.

22. J. B. and R. R. Watson, *The Psychological Care of the Infant and Child* (New York: Norton, 1928).

23. *PP*, 2:390.

24. Ibid., p. 392.

25. Ibid., p. 393.

26. Ibid.

27. Ibid.

28. Ibid., pp. 678-88.

29. *PP*, 2:627-28.

30. *PP*, 1:141-42.

31. Ibid., p. 140.

32. Ibid., p. 398.

33. Ibid.

34. Harry Harlow, "William James and Instinct Theory," in *William James: Unfinished Business* (Washington, D.C.: American Psychological Association, 1969), p. 21.

35. Ibid., p. 23

36. Ibid., p. 394.

37. Ibid.

38. Ibid.

39. Harlow, in *William James: Unfinished Business*, p. 21.

40. *PP*, 2:397.

41. Harlow, in *William James: Unfinished Business*, p. 29.

42. Robert White, *Ego and Reality in Psychoanalytic Theory* (New York: International Universities Press, 1963), pp. 23-29.

43. Ibid., p. 33.

44. See Richard Evans, *Dialogue with Erik Erikson* (New York: Harper & Row, 1967) p. 27; Eric Fromm, *Man for Himself* (New York: Rinehart and Co., 1960), pp. 187–89.

45. See White's discussion of Freud's theory of neutralization in *Ego and Reality in Psychoanalytic Theory*, pp. 9, 168–70.

46. Don Campbell, "On the Genetics of Altruism and the Counter-Hedonic Components in Human Culture," *Journal of Social Issues* 28 (1972): pp. 21–37.

47. *PP*, 1:325.

48. Erikson, *Childhood and Society* (New York: W. W. Norton, 1963), p. 267.

49. Konrad Lorenz, *On Aggression* (New York: Bantam Books, 1969), pp. 46–53.

50. *PP* 2: 412.

51. Ibid., p. 413.

52. *MEW*, p. 5.

53. Ibid.

54. Philip Rieff, *The Triumph of the Therapeutic* (New York: Harper and Row, 1966), pp. 53, 73, 239–40.

55. *MEW*, p. 11.

8

Habit and the Culture of Control

James once wrote, "Most instincts are implanted for the sake of giving rise to habits."[1] Instincts in human beings are at best highly plastic tendencies which need to be patterned and directed by learning and reason. As important as instincts are for James's philosophical psychology, he was not an instinctual utopian in the sense that we now associate with Norman Brown and Herbert Marcuse. Nor, for that matter, would he have affinities with the biological romanticism of certain representatives of contemporary humanistic psychology. Habits and the learning of habits was a fundamental dimension of James's understanding of the strenuous life. The person living the strenuous life must be supported by a large fund of firm and reliable habits which undergird his will, but at the same time, are guided to a great extent by the will.

Habits are the result of shaping instinctual tendencies by learning. It is surprising to discover, however, that the kind of learning in which James was most engrossed was what we would call today, following B. F. Skinner, "operant conditioning." James was interested in the learning which results from the "consequences" of our actions. This is what Skinner means by operant conditioning. It is a process of producing habits by following certain types of human response with rewarding (reinforcing) consequences.[2] This heightens the likelihood of their being repeated. We first saw James's interest in the consequences of behavior in his theory of will. Voluntary action requires a fund of ideas about the consequences of prior actions. This is James's theory of ideo-motor action; once our

178

attention settles on the idea or image of the consequences of a prior act, we can intend this act again, voluntarily.

As we have noticed before, James was a romantic in his appreciation for the passional and instinctual nature of man. In the context of his writings on education, he referred to this aspect of human nature as one's "native reactions." In his warm and readable *Talks to Teachers on Psychology* (1899) James asserted that the purpose of education is to extend, complicate, and add to the native reactions with which humans are born. But like Skinner, James counsels that the first task of the teacher is to produce a response in the student. James writes that the child "must take the first step himself. He must do something before you can get your purchase on him."[3] Before a reaction or response can be complicated or added to, the teacher must first of all *get a response* of some kind. James, in contrast to certain modern distortions of the ideas of progressive education, was interested in the native response not so much for itself as he was for what could be done with it. James was no celebrant of unbridled expressiveness or uninhibited unfolding. The schedule and pattern of man's instinctual or native responses are the organic foundations upon which education and culture attach themselves. The formation of habit is crucial to the process.

This emphasis upon the importance of behavior and the consequences of action must be placed in the context of what we have already said about James. It must be set in the framework of his phenomenology of consciousness, the self, and the will. Positioned within these aspects of his philosophical psychology, James's emphasis on behavior and conduct escapes the reductionism of radical behaviorism and the contemporary culture of control. James knew the place of reward, reinforcement, and conditioning in human life without believing that they mean everything and without succumbing to the thoroughgoing determinism which frequently accompanies a behaviorist orientation. Viewed from the vantage point of contemporary options, James was a Sartre or Heidegger who also would have affirmed *most* of the Skinnerian program. He was a phenomenological and existential psychologist who also knew, as does Skinner, the role of environmental selectivity and reinforcement in the shaping of human behavior. James gives us a way of retaining the freedom, responsibility, and risk that come from European existential and phenomenological psychologies while incorporating the realism, precision, and practicality of certain contemporary behavioral technologies.

Freedom and habit were related intimately for James. The crux of this relation was stated in his famous April 30, 1870, entry in his diary. This is the same entry in which he affirmed his belief in Renouvier's definition of free will as the capacity for "the sustaining of a thought *because* I *chose* to when I might have other thoughts." Shortly after these words James wrote,

> For the present then remember: care little for speculation; much for the *form* of my action; recollect that only when habits of order are formed can we advance to really interesting fields of action— and consequently accumulate grain on grain of willful choice like a very miser; never forgetting how one link dropped undoes an indefinite number. *Principiis obsta—Today has furnished the exceptionally passionate initiative which Bain posits as needful for the acquisition of habits. I will see to the sequel. Not in maxims, not in Anschauungen,* but in accumulated acts of thought lies salvation . . . Life shall [be built in] doing and suffering and creating.[4]

The editor of this entry put the phrase "be built in" in brackets because it is difficult to read this section of James's handwritten diary. I take the sense to mean that life should "be built *up* in" doing and suffering and creating. This means that the strenuous and heroic life does not come like a thunderclap out of the heavens. It is not the product of a titanic act of will which bursts forth out of nowhere. It is a result of "accumulated acts;" we build it up slowly. It is the consequence of small decisions, modest acts of self-sacrifice, moderate asceticisms which grow, become more accustomed, and more available for fresh employment. Is this the psychology of the New Year's resolution? Is James an apostle of salvation by works? Is he a secular Pelagius opposing all our current and deeply entrenched secular Augustinianisms? Just what is James about in these arresting but strangely unfashionable remarks? We will see.

The Culture of Control

The social and psychological sciences, insofar as they have been sciences at all, have tended to regard human beings as a product of the determinisms of their past. In this sense, most of the sciences of man have contributed to the ethos of the culture of control. But behaviorism in psychology, especially the work of B. F. Skinner, has been unique in proposing a practical technology aimed at gaining control of these determinisms. Skinner believes that more control rather than less is the key to the problems of modernity. Modernity, for him, is characerrized by contradictory and confusing schedules of control. Ideologies such as democracy and Christianity which make appeals to the freedom and dignity of man contribute to this situation of conflicting and haphazard systems of environmental reinforcements. Insofar as Skinner's analysis of modern life emphasizes a dearth of adequate controls and insofar as his cure for its ills entails an increase of controls, it is justifiable to say that Skinner is a leading advocate of a culture of control. Also, in view of the fact that he is the author of a widely read utopian novel entitled *Walden Two* (1948) and two recent popular books, *Beyond Freedom and Dignity* (1971) and *About Behaviorism* (1974), all designed to propagate his vision, there can be little doubt that he is actually trying to *create* a culture of control.

Skinner's psychology builds on the work of Pavlov, Watson, and Thorndike. J. B. Watson, a professor of psychology at Johns Hopkins University during the 1910s and 1920s, may have been the most profound influence on Skinner's overall understanding of his scientific work. Watson was the first to reject systematically the idea of grounding psychology on "mentalistic" concepts and "introspective" methods. In his most important book, *Psychology from the Standpoint of a Behaviorist* (1919), he set out his program of making psychology strictly a science of the external and observable behavior of human beings, making no reference whatsoever to internal mental states.[5] Watson was the psychologist who once boasted, "Give me a dozen healthy infants, well-formed, and my own specified world to bring them up in and I'll guarantee to take any one at random and train him to become any type of specialist I might select—doctor, lawyer, merchant, and yes, even beggar-man and thief, regardless of his talents, penchants, tendencies, abilities, vocations, and race of his ancestors." It generally is agreed that his overstatement is somewhat characteristic of Watson's entire program; he had the vision, but he did not have the conceptual and practical technology to carry his behavioristic program through to a convincing conclusion.

Pavlov, the great Russian scientist who discovered the phenomenon of the conditioned reflex, was probably a more profound influence on Skinner. But even here, Skinner developed a theory of learning considerably at variance with Pavlov. Pavlov worked with the so-called stimulus-response (S-R) paradigm. Pavlov studied how learning occurred when secondary (conditioned) stimuli were paired with the main (unconditioned) stimuli which produced a certain response. Even though Skinner as a student was vitally interested in Pavlov (he claims that Pavlov's signature was the only one he ever collected), Skinner gave up studying the so-called stimuli which produce behavior.[6] He began, instead, to study the consequences of behavior, regardless of how it was produced. He soon concluded, along the lines of the Columbia University professor E. L. Thorndike, that it was the "effects" of an action which led it to become a repeatable and hence learned behavior. But even Thorndike had certain mentalistic concepts associated with his Law of Effect or "trial-and-error learning." From a strictly behavioristic position, it makes no sense to speak of an emitted response as a "trial" or even of an unrewarding consequence as an "error."[7] Even these words imply an internal, mentalistic perspective which is ruled out by strict behaviorism.

In the psychology of B. F. Skinner, *methodological* behaviorism has turned into *radical* behaviorism. Skinner is not just saying that internal mental states such as thoughts, motives, emotions, and intentions, are to be disregarded for the purposes of scientific work; he is saying that such phenomena do not exist. Whatever behaviors we construe to be thoughts, emotions, feelings, intentions, etc., can really be explained as contingencies of environmental reinforcement or selection.[8]

Skinner is thoroughgoing and uncompromising in pushing the radical behaviorist point of view.

In emphasizing the reinforcing and selective power of the environment, Skinner believes he is faithful to the essential thrust of Darwinistic thinking. Skinner's contingencies of reinforcement are analogous to Darwin's natural selection. Both concepts, taken by themselves, imply a thoroughgoing environmental determinism. In *About Behaviorism* Skinner writes, "There are remarkable similarities in natural selection, operant conditioning, and the evolution of social environments."[9] In his fascinating essay "A Lecture on 'Having' a Poem," he writes, "The Law of Effect, formulated nearly three quarters of a century ago by Edward L. Thorndike, owed a great deal to Darwinian theory, and it raised very similar issues."[10] But in reality, Skinner is closer to the relentless environmental determinism of Herbert Spencer than he is to Charles Darwin. As we saw in chapter 2, James demonstrated how Spencer's environmental determinism took into account only half of the Darwinistic paradigm. It emphasized natural selection, but at the complete exclusion of spontaneous variation. The same is true of Skinner. The mysterious inner processes which lead us to vary our responses to the environment in the first place are ignored completely by Skinner. In many ways, as we will see, James's answer to Spencer may provide at least the outlines of an answer to Skinner.

Operant conditioning—the reinforcement of a response by the environment—works in different ways, according to Skinner. In fact, charting the variety of operant reinforcements goes to the heart of Skinner's contribution. And his discoveries should in no way be discounted or minimized. The importance of an action's consequences for learning is an idea that others had before Skinner. Thorndike had it and, as we will see, James had it, too. But to say this should not detract from the brilliance and uniqueness of Skinner's work, for it was Skinner, and no one else, who developed this idea into a fundamental technology for the control of human behavior. It is certainly not my intention to say that James anticipated Skinner. But it is my intention to say that James could have appreciated Skinner's position. Furthermore, James could have taken Skinner's contributions and put them in a broader philosophical and psychological context. In this way, he could have made them usable without becoming entangled in a web of self-contradictions and without obscuring certain wider dimensions of human freedom and responsibility.

Skinner distinguishes between positive reinforcement (a reinforcement which is added to a response) and negative reinforcements (a reinforcement which involves the removal of a painful or aversive stimulus). Giving a child a piece of candy would be a positive reinforcement; removing a loud noise, a threat, or a headache would be a negative reinforcement.[11] In addition, Skinner differentiates between continuous and intermittent reinforcements. Of the latter, there are reinforcements which follow an "interval" schedule and those which follow a "ratio" schedule.[12] Skinner has discovered which schedules produce the most energetic, sustained, and efficient responses. It is just this level of practicality which makes his research so usable to a wide variety of enterprises such as psychotherapy, governmental programming, and industrial management.

Surprisingly, Skinner has his own vision of the strenuous life. He uses the words of Darwin to convey his desire for a culture which will produce the largest possible number of "highly intellectual, energetic, brave, patriotic, and benevolent men."[13] Skinner wants to produce a nation of individuals with "strong behavior," a nation of persons who are more concerned about the "future of the culture" than they are about "their own actualization and fulfillment."[14] Of course, it is absurd for Skinner to use such a word as "concern" because this implies all the qualities of attention and freely chosen sympathy which Skinner's entire system makes impossible to conceive. This would not be the case, however, for an approach such as James's.

James and the Importance of Behavior

James has many affinities with the culture of control. In fact, he often has been accused of being a behaviorist and of having inspired behavioristic tendencies in contemporary psychology.

We saw in chapter 2 and the chapter on the will how James emphasized, although never exclusively as do the radical behaviorists, the importance of an action's consequences and the significance of the selective power of the environment. In our earlier discussion of the self, we saw how James *appeared* at times to reduce it to the physical movement of the head and throat when speaking or breathing. Here, it should be recalled, I suggested that James is really only arguing that consciousness should never be conceived as separate from the body—and the *lived* body, not the mechanical physical body—at that.

Even in his essay entitled "Does 'Consciousness' Exist?," James appears to take the classic behavioral position that there is no such thing as consciousness at all. But of course, he is really taking a position which we recognize today as essentially phenomenological. He is saying that consciousness does not exist as a separate or "aboriginal stuff" completely independent of the objects in the world which it perceives.[15] Here he is trying to build up his celebrated concept of "pure experience"—the idea that at our most primitive level of perception we make no distinction between our thoughts of an object and the object itself.[16] In this essay, and in other parts of his *Essays in Radical Empiricism,* he is not really taking the classic behaviorist position. Although consciousness as an empty, separate, and diaphanous substance was denied in James's later philosophical psychology, consciousness as a "function" was not. A bit of pure experience which is not in itself separated into consciousness and content can, at subsequent levels of reflection, serve two functions. From one perspective, it can function as consciousness, thought, or a state of mind; from another perspective, it can function or be counted as the object itself.[17] James is here trying to overcome Cartesian dualism and the dichotomy between subject and object which it entails. Behaviorism attempts to avoid Cartesian dualism by reducing mind to the physical components of behavior—object, environment, and the movements of the objective body. Mentalism tries to escape Cartesianism by reducing the mind to "ideas" and states of consciousness. James's doctrine of pure experience agrees with the thrust of current phenomenology and British philosophical psychology in arguing that both radical behaviorism and mentalism are false to the true facts of experience.

But the main point where James would have become truly friendly with the Skinnerian culture of control is on the importance of the consequences of behavior. The consequences of our actions rebound upon us and form and shape us. New "sets" in the brain are produced by the "motor effects" of our actions.[18] The organism grows in the direction of its functions. James quotes with approval the French saying *La fonction fait l'organe* ("Function makes the organ").[19] Or again, he writes "that *our nervous system grows to the modes in which it has been exercised* expresses the philosophy of habit in a nutshell."[20] In speaking about how to form new habits or break old ones, James advised the reader to accumulate "all the possible circumstances which shall reinforce the right motives; put yourself assiduously in conditions that encourage the new way."[21] All of this is James's far less precise and systematic way of talking about such Skinnerian business as arranging the contingencies of the environment to guarantee that desirable behaviors get reinforced and undesirable ones do not.

James develops a powerful and basically moral argument on behalf of the role of habits in human life. Habits add to both the firmness and flexibility of our efforts to adapt creatively to our worlds. Habits economize the energies expended in our efforts to handle life. If we had no habits, no more or less fixed and automatic routines, we would have to focus attention on our every movement and make conscious decisions about even our most insignificant acts. Life would be a mass of studied efforts and anguished decisions about directing our rich and complex impulses and needs. On the basis of James's theory of the plasticity and instability of instincts and cerebral sensitivity, we should not be surprised to see him write, "Man is born with a tendency to do more things than he has ready-made arrangement for in his nerve-centres."[22] "If practice did not make perfect, nor habit economize the expense of nervous and muscular energy," James tells us that human beings "would therefore be in a sorry plight."[23]

Habits free our attention for more important things. In this way they add to the flexibility and adaptability of life. Far from binding us into rigid and neurotic patterns of dumb automatism, habits make it possible for us to do some things without attending to them, thereby enabling us to apply our attention over a wider field. If we had to think about every act of dressing ourselves, deliberately directing our attention to our shoes and then the laces, making separate decisions about each pull of the string and each knot we tied, this simple morning activity would be burdened with the pain and insecurity experienced by a beginning pianist forced to play a concerto by Liszt each morning before breakfast. The poor creature would be exhausted before getting to his first cup of coffee. Habits literally free us from stupifying preoccupations with each and every literal detail. To this extent, an animal which cannot develop habits cannot truly be free. James's understanding of the relation of habits to freedom and the creative life is vastly different from the near equation of habits to neurosis which one finds both in orthodox psychoanalysis and much that passes under the banner of humanistic psychology.

James saw our habits as punctuated and encompassed by orienting moments of free attention and decision. Generally, it is a voluntary act or decision which sets a chain of habitual responses in process. A voluntary act of attention does not doggedly follow and initiate every step of the chain of habitual reactions, but it starts the process moving. "In habitual action," James writes, "the only impulse which the centres of idea or perception need send down is the initial impulse, the command to *start*."[24] But no sooner has the "conscious thought or volition instigated the "habitual movement, than the process takes over and functions on its own. It happens, according to James, because each movement in the chain engenders a bodily sensation or feeling which becomes the signal or starter for the subsequent movement.[25]

The pianist voluntarily sits down at the piano and then wills to play a piece. This sets in motion a long string of tested and habitual movements. The sensation of the preceding movement is the cue for the following one. So goes the process until the piece is finished. Conscious attention does not instigate every movement. But in spite of this, it does get the entire process in motion in the beginning, and it may interrupt and set things in order when the more mechanical processes break down. So it is with the golfer and his swing, the carpenter and his hammering, the knitter and her needles. It must be readily admitted that each of the detailed movements in these complex actions are not directed by "distinct volitions." "The will, if any will be present, limits itself to a *permission* that" the distinct movements "exert their motor effects."[26]

James's concept of learning and habit does not exclude the functioning of the will. In fact, it presuppose the will as determining its direction and the purposes to which it is put. In addition, habit and reinforced learning need not reduce the range of freedom. In James's view of things, they actually increase it by liberating consciousness from mechanical detail and by backing up decision with the force of firm and tested sequences of action. In James's theory, the power of habit and the culture of control are put into the service of the will and the kingdom of conscious ends. "The more of the details of our daily life we can hand over to the effortless custody of automatism," James exhorts, "the more our higher powers of mind will be set free for their own proper work."[27]

Creativity and Control

Habits are a method for saving up the wisdom of experience. In our fund of habits we have a bank of more or less successful responses to the environment which we can draw on as conditions warrant. Of course, there can be habits which are not so much successful possibilities of action as they are aimless rituals designed to ward off anxiety and threat. Unfortunately, James did not have much to say about this kind of habit. It was to be the destiny of medical psychology primarily under the leadership of Freud to illumine the dynamics of habits of this kind, habits which we now are prone to call obsessive or compulsive neuroses. But we have, in recent decades, been so conscious of these more debilitating habits that we have almost lost sight of habit in the sense that James conceived it.

Habits make it possible for us to confront a wide range of novel situations with a storehouse of action possibilities which are more precise and more tested than brute instinct alone. The recognition of this fact has been long in coming, but we will see the return of the day when to speak of creating good habits in ourselves or our children will not be construed as Victorian repressiveness. Habits tested in one situation are usable in another. The running we learned in the backyard playing "kick-the-can" can be later used on the football field or in times of war to escape the enemy. Habits have an intimate relation to the phenomenon of culture even though they are not quite identical to it. Culture stores up for a society the values and patterns of behavior which experience has selected as serviceable. A society attempts to instill its culture into the thought, feeling, and conduct of its members, especially its children. Habit is the behavioral counterpart of culture. In defending the role of habit in the life of the individual, James is in fact also defending the role of culture in the life of society. In one place he writes, "Habit is thus the enormous fly-wheel of society, its most precious conservative agent. It alone is what keeps us all within the bounds of ordinance."[28] Nor is habit contrary to the exigencies of a pluralistic and quickly changing society. Habit stabilizes us and makes us resistant to needless, haphazard, or unwise change. On the other hand, it protects us from facing novelty *de novo*. It gives us a fund of responses, some of which may be relevant to the fresh challenges we face.

But the contemporary culture of control, especially as represented by Skinner, only sees half of the story. It has helped us once again to see the importance of learning, habits, environmental selection, and reinforcement—aspects of life which latent romantic and individualistic tendencies in American culture can easily overlook. But there is at least half of mental reality which Skinner leaves out and which James, in spite of his deficiences, can help to restore. Skinner, for all practical purposes, gives us an empty organism and disregards the active, purposeful, and striving character of the human being. It is just this side of human nature which James invested so much time in elucidating and which served to balance his own behavioral orientation. James, in contrast to both Spencer and Skinner, developed a model of behavior built around analogies to both poles of evolutionary theory—spontaneous variation and natural selection. At the level of his phenomenological descriptions, he depicted consciousness as active, moving, directional, interested, and selective. Consciousness is primarily characterized by subjective interests related to objects (meanings) in the world. Both spontaneous variation and natural selection have endowed man with a great variety of native instincts and interests. James even saw our instincts as naturally organizing themselves into schedules of developmental tendencies. All of this suggests that we bring a great deal to the reinforcements of the environment and that, in fact, what we find to be reinforcing greatly depends on what we wish for, want, and strive for to begin with. Or as James would say, what we find reinforcing depends very much on the nature of our "practical interests."

Furthermore, as we have seen, James places his theory of habit in the context of an understanding of the will and a metaphysical defense of freedom. But in spite of all this, the question of creative thinking is still an issue. How does one go beyond the customary and habitual to think of something new—a novel solution to a difficult problem? James's discussion of the will and freedom do not in themselves answer this question.

To find a solution to a problem is very similar, James tells us, to recalling a forgotten name. In both instances, we are "straining" and "pressing" toward something that is "absent," we are trying to fill a "gap" in consciousness.[29] Voluntary attention functions in both types of mental operation but does not explain the total process. In the case of recall, attention searches over a great number of things, places, or people "associated" with the absent name. Finally, when enough associations are gathered, James assumes that the proper neural pathway is energized and the forgotten name suddenly "appears" in consciousness. James's major point here is this: "All these added associations *arise independently of the will,* by the spontaneous process we know so well."[30] All that the will or attention does is *"to emphasize and linger over those which seem pertinent, and ignore the rest."*[31] Will has a place, but it is not everything.

Finding the unknown solution to a problem is similar to recalling a forgotten name except for one crucial difference. In memory the answer is in fact there but temporarily absent; in creative thinking the solution is not *there at all.* To solve a problem, we fix our attention on the goal we want to achieve and on the relations and conditions which we know the solution must fulfil. We know that the solution must fulfil such and such a known condition, it must be related to so and so, it must do this or that, but just what the answer is we do not know. But by fixing our attention on *what we do know,* by concentrating on the associations of the unknown answer, we gradually find ourselves spontaneously coming up with hypotheses. For James, there is an analogy between the blind hypotheses of creative thinking and the spontaneous variations of evolution. After years of concentration and turning over various alternatives in his mind, the creative thinker comes up with one which seems to *fit* the known conditions of the solution.[32] Once again, much of the creative process seems to be random, blind, and unconscious. Attention and purpose come at the point of concentrating on the end and the known conditions, relations, and associations of the unknown solution. Some of these associations may have the status of habits or conditioned learnings. But a habit or a conditioned learning does not explain our capacity to will a solution and to attend over long periods of time to the conditions which the solution must fulfil.

James is obviously trying to synthesize a theory of purposeful reasoning and problem solving with an evolutionary model of thinking. Today, this model of thinking has been greatly refined by cyberneticists. The respected psychologist Donald Campbell refers to it as the "blind variation and selective retention" theory of creative thought.[33] It has much to do with "trial and error" theories of thinking. Campbell points out that Charles Darwin and Alexander Bain made early contributions to this theory of creative thinking, both of whom James read and quoted extensively. Other early forerunners of the theory were Paul Souriau, H. Poincaré, and Ernst Mach. More contemporary contributions have come from E. L. Thorndike, E.C. Tolman, Campbell himself, and many others. Although the model is far more accurate today than it was when James worked with it, his phenomenology of will and attention and his understanding of their role in purposeful, creative thinking are still not taken with sufficient seriousness in the more mechanistic versions of the theory.

James could have agreed with the culture of control that habit and environmental reinforcements are crucial for the strenuous life. Habit and reinforcement have an indispensable role to play in the development of firm, consistent, long-term behavior aimed toward distant future goals on behalf of the wider human community. Both James and Skinner were interested, in their respective settings, in producing people with the capacity for this kind of behavior. James understood the necessity of organizing one's environment, epecially in a chaotically changing and pluralistic society, to reinforce the psychological structures and habits which one considers important for modern living. But James had a way of getting out of the self-contradition which besets the advocates of radical behaviorism. Because of his phenomenology and philosophy of freedom, James can demonstrate that humans have sufficient autonomy to enter into the deliberative exchange required to design consciously the supportive and reinforcing environment which they believe essential for their life together in a modern world. James could have joined with Skinner in the call for a more rationally planned environment. But he had ways of demonstrating how humans have enough freedom, transcendence, and rationality actually to accomplish such a feat. Skinner and the culture of radical behaviorism challenge us to design an environment with appropriate reinforcements, but fail to demonstrate how we can liberate ourselves sufficiently from past conditioning to do anything new or different. A culture of control is impossible without being placed first of all within a culture of freedom. The presupposition behind Skinner's appeal for more satisfying and consistent reinforcements is the belief that humans have enough freedom not only to respond to the challenge but to plan cooperatively and democratically what kind of supports they want for their life together.

In the end, however, James would have believed that a *thoroughgoing* culture of control was impossible. The processive, changing, and pluralistic nature of all existence make a thoroughly rationalized life completely impossible. Routine, pattern, rationalization, and predictable patterns of reinforcement have their place, but they can never be the entire story. The colliding and contending individuals of a pluralistic universe must undergo a never-ending process of readjustment, reorientation, and restructuring. To adapt creatively to such a world, we must have resources for changing our habitual responses, acquiring fresh ones, and consolidating the new ones into firm and effective approaches to the world. It is precisely the nature of man to go beyond simple reactions to the brute contingencies of the physical environment; man can also create a culture with artificial reinforcements which can be established or reorganized on the basis of hypotheses about the present and future which his own purposeful creativity develops. It is the failure of the culture of control to understand this truth which makes its image of man and modern society finally so very mistaken.

Notes

1. *PP*, 2:402.
2. B. F. Skinner, *Science and Human Behavior* (New York: The Free Press, 1953), p. 65.
3. *TTP*, p. 20.
4. *LWJ*, p. 148
5. J. B. Watson, *Psychology from the Standpoint of a Behaviorist* (Philadelphia: Lippincott, 1917).
6. Skinner, *Science and Human Behavior*, p. 65.
7. Ibid., p. 64
8. Ibid., p. 257–82.
9. B. F. Skinner, *About Behaviorism* (London: Jonathan Cape, 1974), p. 205.
10. B. F. Skinner, *Cumulative Record* (New York: Appleton Century Crofts, 1972), p. 353.
11. Skinner, *Science and Human Behavior*, p. 73.
12. Ibid., pp. 99–106.
13. Skinner, *About Behaviorism*, p. 205.
14. Ibid., p. 206.
15. *ERE*, p. 4.
16. Ibid., p. 5.
17. Ibid., pp. 9–10.
18. *PPI*, p. 124.
19. Ibid., p. 109.
20. Ibid., p. 112.

21. *TTP*, pp. 34–35.
22. Ibid., p. 113.
23. Ibid.
24. Ibid., p. 116.
25. Ibid.
26. Ibid., p. 118.
27. *TTP*, p. 34.
28. *PP*, 1:121.
29. Ibid., p. 584.
30. Ibid., p. 586.
31. Ibid.
32. Ibid., p. 589.
33. Donald Campbell, "Blind Variation and Selective Retention in Creative Thought as in Other Knowledge Processes," *Psychological Review* 67 (1960):380–400.

9

Body, Reason,
and the Culture of Joy

At first glance it would be easy to think that James might have the most in common with the psychological culture of joy. By the culture of joy, I have meant a loosely associated group of influential psychologists who share two common attitudes. First, they share a view of a man that sees his inner biological makeup as full of rich and creative potentials which are straining to express themselves. The release of these potentials brings enormous quantities of spontaneous joy and a deep sense of personal fulfilment. Second, they believe that these basic potentials will indeed express themselves if a warm environment is provided and the oppressive hand of tradition and cultural expectations is stayed. Psychologists such as Carl Rogers, Fritz Perls, William Schutz, and, to a lesser extent, Abraham Maslow, can be associated with this view.

All of these psychologists belong to a wider movement generally called humanistic psychology. James is cited often as a precursor of humanistic psychology, and on the whole, this judgment is correct. Humanistic psychology is defined frequently by first distinguishing it from psychoanalysis and behaviorism. It is alleged that psychoanalysis and behaviorism reduce man to either biological drives or environmental reinforcements; the human being as a center of freedom, creativity, and initiative is either ignored or altogether denied to exist. Humanistic psychology is supposed to study man's higher capacities for freedom, agency, love, joy, and wonder. It entertains a more encompassing image of man than either psychoanalysis or behaviorism. In this broad sense, humanistic psychology includes most of existential and phenomenological psychology (May, Binswanger, Boss, Sartre),[1] research in altered states of consciousness (Ornstein, Tart),[2] certain aspects of psychoanalytic ego psychology (Erikson, White),[3] so-called neo-Freudian psychology (Horney, Sullivan, Fromm),[4] as well as the figures I will talk about in this chapter—Rogers, Perls, Schutz, and Maslow. When humanistic psychology is seen from this encompassing perspective. It safely can be said that James himself was a broadly humanistic psychologist.

There are certain ways, however, in which these four figures, although clearly a subculture within the broader movement of humanistic psychology, exemplify a type of thinking considered prototypical of humanistic psychology. It is the purpose of this chapter to suggest that a genuine humanistic psychology would shun some of the biases of the "culture of joy." The psychology of James, in spite of his many points of agreement, reveals ways in which the culture of joy is not so humanistic as some might think. There is among these psychologists a curious romanticization of human biological potentials; James could sympathize with this tendency up to a point, but finally would repudiate it. In the last analysis, the culture of joy posits an internal biological valuing mechanism which, with a minimum of conscious deliberation, guides humans into making choices and decisions which are simultaneously personally satisfying and socially responsible. This is not just a strategic hypothesis limited to the context of psychotherapy with individuals and groups. It is for them a fundamental assumption about human nature.

There is an additional hypothesis connected with the culture of joy which is more implicit than explicit. It is the assumption that, if everyone relies on this biological valuing process, there will flow from it an almost utopian harmony of interests, wants, and desires. In this literature there is the remarkable implication that, when all people are fully aware of their own organismic needs and completely attuned to their own valuing processes, an almost preestablished harmony of wants and desires will reign over society and conflict will be at a minimum if it does not altogether disappear. James could affirm this last assumption even less than he could the first.

There are important differences in the image of man, society, and modernity between James and the culture of joy. As I have pointed out before, there is a romantic foundation to James's concept of the human. But above this, there is an ascetic superstructure which celebrates the virtues of nonrepressive inhibition, deliberation, directed will, and rational reflection. For James, neither internal balance nor external harmony with the world and society can be achieved by the effortless unfolding of biological potentials in the simple way envisioned by the culture of joy. Although James makes no artificial and primordial distinction between the body and the mind, there are, he believes, functional distinctions which can be made between our reflective processes and direct organismic experience. James would agree with the culture of joy that our reflective processes are both motivated by and must take account of our organismic needs. James is forever saying this when he speaks about the motivated nature of consciousness and the importance of subjective interests for thinking and choosing. But he is also aware that organismic needs can conflict both with one another and with those of our fellow human beings. Hence, our valuing processes must be *reasoned* as well as *felt;* they must lead to conclusions about the *morally good* as well as about the *organismically satisfying.* The valuing processes of the person living the strenuous life entail delicate and complex acts of balancing subjective interests with rational assessments about the long-term consequences of one's acts and wishes for one's self and the wider community. Arriving at our judgments about the good is always a process of compromise where some desires are expressed, others restrained, and still others carefully patterned to complement the health and happiness of the larger community.

James would agree with the statement of Brewster Smith when he doubts that "the 'wisdom of the body' (and the untutored mind) is sufficient for the valid guidance of significant human choice."[5] He would also sympathize with Smith when he suggests that humans may not have the evolutionary-biological equipment to handle the recent drugs or the new complex human "relations of an interdependent urban society."[6] Smith writes, "In evolutionary terms, these human relations are almost as new as saccharine."[7] James even might go so far as to affirm Smith's harsh characterization of this type of psychology as "pseudobiologistic."

The difficulty with the brand of humanistic psychology in the culture of joy is its failure to affiliate with a broader philosophical psychology. James Dagenais in his *Models of Man* has made this point; he believes that there must be "a return to, or a rediscovery of, the foundations of third force psychology."[8] Dagenais believes that the roots of this culture of psychology go back to the phenomenological studies of Brentano, Stumpf, and the gestalt psychologies of Wertheimer, Koffka, and Kohler. This is true to a considerable extent. It also may be that James and his brand of philosophical psychology can contribute to a better foundation for the more lasting values of the culture of joy.

Similarities and Differences

The psychology of Carl Rogers vividly and succinctly exemplifies most of the features common to the culture of joy. One of the most prominent aspects of Rogers's psychology is a phenomenological orientation similar to the incipient phenomenology of James. James, of course, was not the inspiration for Rogers's phenomenology, although Rogers's phenomenological descriptions of the self, as was pointed out in chapter 4, must have been influenced by James—but only indirectly through the work of George Herbert Mead. Rogers's phenomenological orientation came most immediately through a book entitled *Individual Behavior: A New Frame of Reference for Psychology*[9] (1949) by Donald Snygg and Arthur Combs, the latter of whom had once been a student of Rogers. These thinkers were in turn influenced in their phenomenological thinking by the so-called field or gestalt psychologies of Lewin and Kohler and, to some extent, Wertheimer and Kohler. It seldom is realized that Lewin, Kohler, Wertheimer, and Koffka had all, at one time or another, been students of the great German advocate of empirical phenomenology, Carl Stumpf. In addition to being one of William James's closest European friends and admirers, Stumpf had been a student of Brentano at the same time as Edmund Husserl. But on the whole, Rogers (as was the case with Perls, Schutz, and Maslow, who were also influenced by the gestalt psychology stemming from these figures) was not deeply familiar with the European backgrounds of his phenomenology.

Rogers believed that psychology as a science should use both phenomenological and objective methods of investigation.[10] But by phenomenological, Rogers had nothing very rigorous or specific in mind. Sometimes phenomenology was for him a method of grasping a person's "subjective experience."[11] This, of course, should be distinguished from James's level of "pure experience," which was for him the most primordial level requiring description. Subjective experience, as he explained in his *Essays in Radical Empiricism*, was already a result of a secondary process of reflection which breaks up the more primitive level of pure experience where subjective and objective have not yet been differentiated.[12] Sometimes Rogers uses phenomenology to refer to a method for grasping the structure of a person's "internal frame of reference." By this, Rogers means a person's "perceptual field"—the peculiar way in which an individual *perceives* his or her experience.[13] Rogers believed that behavior was a response to one's field of experience "as perceived."[14] This is Rogers's way of speaking about what James held in his theory that humans live in and respond to a world of meanings. James and Rogers also share the belief that descriptive methods in psychology are not incompatible with the use of objective methods as well.

In addition, both James and Rogers could agree that psychology, in spite of its provisional use of the hypothesis of scientific determinism, must presuppose the more fundamental reality of human freedom. Most of the time Rogers builds his argument for freedom on loosely phenomenological grounds. James, it will be recalled, did the same; the difference is, however, that this was only half of James's case for freedom. Rogers argues for the reality of freedom in the context of comments about deterministic assumptions within the modern behavioral sciences and about the growing control over human life which these sciences are exerting. Rogers sees modern societies as becoming at all levels increasingly more controlled. He places the blame largely on the shoulders of fellow behavioral scientists—such as Skinner—with their uncritical deterministic assumptions and their penchant for inventing technologies for control.[15] Against such assumptions, Rogers, like James, accepts at face value those "compelling subjective experiences" in which a person feels "within himself the power of naked choice."[16] In one of his many essays dedicated to this theme in *On Becoming a Person,* Rogers writes, "To believe, as Skinner holds, that all this is an illusion, and that spontaneity, freedom, responsibility, and choice have no real existence, would be impossible for me."[17] Rogers argues explicitly—or what James asserted in his essay "Sentiment of Rationality"— that scientific enterprises always are motivated by prescientific value judgments and perferences. Even the aim of "theoretical rationality," James points out, is a prescientific "interest."[18] Rogers echoes the same idea when he writes, "In any scientific endeavor—whether 'pure' or applied science—there is a prior personal subjective choice of the purpose or value which that scientific work is perceived as serving."[19] The major difference, however, between James and Rogers on the issue of freedom is this: James, as we saw above,[20] goes beyond phenomenological description of the lived reality of freedom and argues on metaphysical grounds that determinism is logically incompatible with the possibility of practical moral rationality and action.

Both Rogers and James believe that humans are capable of far greater levels of functioning than is generally the case for the majority of people. Humans are capable of much more than low-level preoccupation with sustenance, protection, and security. This conviction is shared also by Maslow, Perls, and Schutz. But there are significant differences between James and the culture of joy on how these more expansive horizons of human potential are envisioned.

For instance, Rogers's concept of the "fully functioning" person suggests that this optimal state occurs when the individual is freed from anything which obstructs his complete "openness to experience."[21] This means getting as close as possible to what James talks about as "knowledge by acquaintance" and "pure experience." But James was far more aware than Rogers that these levels of perception are only relative and that in reality there is no possibility of confronting experience without some degree of selectivity. Complete openness to experience, for James (as for Freud), would overwhelm the organism with a barrage of unassimilable stimulation.[22] Although Rogers talks about this level of experiencing in absolute terms, in ways James did not, both would agree that *some degree* of openness to experience is fundamental to creative living.

But Rogers takes the idea much further and makes it the systematic touchstone for the release of human potentiality. When one is completely open to experience, all the necessary data and information for a decision are available to the organism.[23] Under optimal condition, it is for Rogers the "organism" or body which makes the decision. When this is the case, creativity will emerge and the person will move toward the *process* of functioning fully.

James's approach to these higher "reaches" of human functioning is vastly different. In 1906, only four years before he died, James delivered a speech entitled "The Energies of Men." The speech expressed a concern which was implicit in many of his writings: Why is it possible for humans sometimes to summon enormous amounts of energy, far exceeding their normal levels? It was the phenomenon of the "second wind" which fascinated him most; he argued that humans living in a modern world need to apply its mysterious secrets to the realm of moral living.[24] James was interested in the "quality," not the "quantity," of energy expended and believed that each person had great reserves which could be called forth under certain conditions.[25] The conditions for the release of this energy were notably different for James than the safe, warm, and permissive environment which Rogers believes necessary for the fully functioning person to emerge, although as a preliminary factor this is important for James as well. But assuming a person has enjoyed a reasonable level of warmth and safety in early life, it is demanding circumstances and commanding ideas which are the chief factors calling out these deeper forces of energy and creativity. These circumstances and ideas evoke emotions and excitement which carry us far beyond our customary levels of activity. As James writes, "Excitements, ideas, and efforts, in a word, are what carry us over the dam."[26] Rogers romanticizes the creativity of the body devoid of commanding symbols and provocative circumstances; James celebrates the role of gripping ideals and the unusual trials of life as factors calling forth our deeper energies.

The Wisdom of the Body

There is a pervasive body romanticism which runs throughout the culture of joy. There is the belief that hidden deep down in the genes, chromosomes, and instincts of every human being is a "true self," an inner core of personality which, under certain conditions, can come to the surface. This conviction is summed up in the phrase "the wisdom of the body." There is also a widespread, although expanded, use of Kurt Goldstein's concept that human behavior is motivated by one all-encompassing tendency toward "self-actualization."

Humanistic psychology need not entail a body romanticism and body mysticism in the sense found in the culture of joy. In its more existential and phenomenological forms, such as the psychologies of Sartre, Boss, and Binswanger, it does not. It does in the culture of joy because of its fondness for a certain type of organic metaphor built around the idea of an "actualization tendency," or tendency toward "self-actualization." A great deal of modern thought about the human "self," according to John MacMurry, has centered around some form of organic model borrowed primarily from biology, anatomy and physiology.[27] Concieving of the self in analogy to a biological form can take different directions because of the variety of organic models which contemporary science offers. The culture of joy does not use the homeostatic and tension-reduction model employed by Freud and much of scientific psychology. Nor does it use the model of free variation and natural selection bequeathed by Darwin and employed in reversed form by James himself. Rather, psychologists such as Rogers, Perls, Schutz, and Maslow use the model of the actualization tendency—the idea that the human organism is oriented toward growth, expansion, and sociality and that it contains within it an internal valuing process which can constitute a safe and productive guide to all of life's decisions.

There is, of course, nothing wrong with supplementing one's psychology of human nature with organic analogies in order to clarify the functioning of the human self. James does this, and it has been my argument that James's tendency to supplement his phenomenological descriptions of consciousness, will, attention, and the self with an organic metaphor borrowed from Darwin gets to the very heart of his strength, especially in comparison with most purely phenomenological and existential psychologies. In addition, the concept of an actualization tendency has some advantages and for some purposes is a very enlightening metaphor indeed. But in the culture of joy, the metaphor of the actualization tendency has become overextended and romanticized. In addition, the emphasis upon the harmonizing, balancing, and value processing capacities of the body obscures the real and necessary role which reason and reflection must play in the drama of human decisions.

In his widely read book entitled *Client-Centered Therapy* (1951), Rogers lays down a basic principle about motivation: *"The Organism has one basic tendency and striving—to actualize, maintain, and enhance the experiencing organism."*[28] Rogers originally employed this concept of motivation because it explained, and I think correctly, certain observations he found in therapy, i.e., that people generally want to get better and the therapist usually can depend on a "forward-moving tendency" within the client pushing him or her toward health. In the context of psychotherapy, Rogers observed a general tendency toward "growth," "maturity," greater "differentiation," greater "independence" and "self-regulation," and higher degrees of "socialization, broadly defined."[29]

Rogers's belief in an actualization tendency was supported, he was convinced, by several significant authorities. Hobart Mowrer, Clyde Kluckhohn, Harry Stack Sullivan, Karen Horney, and Andras Angyal are thought by Rogers to hold something like it. But Kurt Goldstein, in his remarkable book entitled *The Organism* (1939), is the preeminent source of the asserted that the goal of the "normal life is toward activity and idea for Rogers as he is for all the members of the culture of joy. In the context of working with severely brain-damaged soldiers after World War I, Goldstein became convinced that much of the motivation theory of his day applied more to the severely ill, sick, and traumatically injured than it did to individuals in a reasonably healthy condition. For instance, tension-reduction models of motivation applied very well to those who, because of sickness and injury, could not handle tensions and who struggled for survival by maintaining things in an unchanged state.[30] In addition, it is precisely the sick and injured who seem pulled by a variety of separate impulses which they seem unable to control.[31] In contrast to this, normal and healthy activity seemed to Goldstein far more coordinated and holistic. To explain this, Goldstein posited an "actualization tendency" and asserted that the goal of the "normal life is toward activity and progress."[32] Furthermore, the tendency of healthy activity is not the reduction of tension; rather, the normal organism attempts to maintain tension and to "actualize itself in further activities, according to its nature."[33] In reality, however, Goldstein does not deny that there can be different instinctive tendencies which can be stimulated by diverse environmental situations; he simply is maintaining that in healthy organisms there must be some higher "agency which makes the decision in the struggle between the single drives."[34]

Stated at this level, the idea of an actualization tendency means little more than that all living organisms have a general tendency to maintain an integrated and relatively open relation with their environment. But Rogers and the culture of joy make much more than this out of the principle. Rogers believes that this actualization tendency provides all humans with an "organismic valuing process" which makes it possible for them to sift through their experiences to determine which truly will be enhancing for the organism as a whole. One of the main outcomes of psychotherapy is a heightened capacity to trust this organismic valuing process rather than the "introjected" values which a person may have incorporated from parents and culture. The client on the way to health becomes once again like the infant in his value judgments about experience. Rogers wants to convince us that "just as the infant places an assured value upon an experience, relying on the evidence of his own senses, . . . so too the client finds that it is his own organism which supplies the evidence upon which value judgments may be made."[35] In his essay "The Therapist's View of the Good Life," Rogers says that the good life for the fully functioning person is "that which is selected by the total organism."[36] Fully functioning persons are able increasingly to "trust their total organismic reaction to a new situation" because they have learned that "doing what 'feels right' proves to be a competent and trustworthy guide to behavior which is truly satisfying."[37] Frequently Rogers suggests that the wisdom of the body is greater than the mind. In his essay "Toward a Modern Approach to Values" (1964), he assures us that, if the fully functioning person "can trust all of himself, his feelings and his intuitions may be wiser than his mind, that as a total person he can be more sensitive and accurate than his thoughts alone."[38] In his psychology, the actualization tendency is submitted as the grounds for a total ethic in a modern and quickly changing society. There is little doubt, we are safe in assuming, that this goes far beyond any ambitions for the concept which Goldstein ever hoped for or, for that matter, wanted.

A similar tendency to extend some simple ideas derived from gestalt psychology to a much wider field can be found in the writings of the popular guru of the encounter culture, Fritz Perls. Using the thinking of Goldstein and the theories of gestalt psychologists such as Wertheimer, Köhler, and Lewin, Perls applied the principles of their work to the general field of psychotherapy. Once again, the organism appears as a remarkably accurate balancing and harmonizing instrument. Perls uses the word "self-regulation" rather than Goldstein's concept of "self-actualization." The idea of self-regulation is given a distinctively gestalt definition in *Gestalt Therapy* when he writes, "In the struggle for survival the most relevant need becomes figure and organizes the behavior of an individual until this need is satisfied, whereupon it recedes into the background (temporary balance) and makes room for the next *now* most important need."[39] Perls is like Rogers in that he audaciously extends his theory of organismic self-regulation into the higher realms of ethics. In fact, it is his position that cultural tradition and the realm of "ethics" are a positive hindrance to the real foundations of morality found in the self-regulating capacities of the body.[40] In his essay 'Morality, Ego Boundary and Aggression," he identifies morality with "external" and heteronomous control of behavior and sees it as the enemy of the true and authentic regulation of behavior by the gestalt-forming and self-regulating needs of the organism as a whole.[41]

In the writings of William Schutz and Abraham Maslow the situation is more complex but still adds up to a body romanti-cism and an overgeneralization into areas of morality and ethics of the truth about the self-regulatory capacities of the body. Faith in the mystical "wisdom of the body" can be found in almost every page of Schutz's highly popular *Joy* and *Here Comes Everybody,* even though little explicit use is made of Goldstein's principle of self-actualization. Maslow, on the other hand, makes considerable use of Goldstein and follows Rogers and Perls in extending the idea into arenas of ethics and moral values.

In a 1958 article entitled "Psychological Data and Human Values," Maslow speaks of the universal goal toward "self-actualization" and becoming "everything that a person can become."[42] He compares it to how "an acorn may be said to be 'pressing toward' being an oak tree, or that a tiger can be observed to 'push toward' being tigerish."[43] Maslow, however, is far more sophisticated than Rogers and Perls in specifying a developmental sequence and a hierarchy of needs which must be met before the higher levels of self-actualization can be attained. Furthermore, Maslow is more elitist than the other members of the culture of joy. He is clearly of the opinion that not everyone can actualize himself with equal power and preci-sion. Some people, Maslows believes, are "better choosers" than others. This conviction led Maslow to his famous studies of so-called self-actualizing people.[44] "It is the free choices of such self-actualizing people," Maslow proclaims "that can be descriptively studied as a naturalistic value system."[45]

Yet Maslow's more sophisticated body romanticism is ac-companied by the culture of joy's characteristic understanding of the passive role of the environment in supporting the pro-cesses of self-actualization. "Man is ultimately not molded or shaped into humanness, or taught to be human. The role of the environment is ultimately to permit him or help him to actualize his own potentialities, not its potentialities."[46] Whereas James could follow Darwin in emphasizing both the inner proclivities of the organism as well as the selective and reinforcing power of the environment in the formation of our humanness, Maslow is paradigmatic of the culture of joy in celebrating the classic paradigm of the acorn and the tree. Little wonder, then, that the culture of joy sees oppression and overcontrol as the fundamental problem of modernity and wider ranges of unfettered actualization of the body as the most powerful cure for its many ills.

The Triumph of the Ascetic

A brief summary of several points already made in our earlier discussions of James will suffice to crystallize his differences from the culture of joy. His major difference, however, will be developed in the following chapter on ethics. James makes a basic distinction between *good* as felt organismic satisfaction and *good* as moral or ethical action. The culture of joy in general fails to make this distinction. James would agree with the culture of joy that good at the level of organismic satisfaction is relevant to the determination of the morally good, but the two are not identical. The morally good has to do with the determination of rules and principles which reconcile conflicting felt goods in the context of specific environmental challenges and possiblities. The good man for James is not only the person who knows what he feels and is aware of his organismic satisfactions, he is aware also of the larger reality of conflicting goods and can envision acceptable common principles which will enhance the amount of good experienced by all. To do this, some felt goods must be held in check or denied altogether. Others must be patterned and channeled with regard to time, place, amount, and frequency. All this requires processes of moral reasoning which go beyond the simple awareness of "organismic experiencing." The person living the strenuous life is aware of his felt satisfactions, but he is also able to order and restrain them through a more inclusive process of moral reasoning. In the strenuous life, the romantic idea of the wisdom of the body suffers a limited defeat before the forces of a modest but persistent asceticism of reason, attention, and will.

Even though felt satisfactions find a place in James's normative view of the person, James never overestimates the raw biological potentials of man. In reality, the culture of joy, in spite of its aspirations to recover a humanistic psychology, tears the human body out of its world of meanings where James in fact locates it so firmly. James's most basic discussion of the body is in the context of his description of the "material self." The material self is the living body related to all the other material objects—clothes, home, children, spouse, mother, father—with which the body feels identified. Since this is really the way we experience our bodies, it is not clear that we ever can "feel" our "organismic experiencing" completely devoid of these basic relations and identifications.

Furthermore, although James always emphasized, both in his early dualistic period as well as his gradually emerging phenomenological orientation, the functional unity of body and mind, he continued to envision consciousness as a special instrument of the body performing tasks somewhat distinguishable from other bodily functions. James, in a manner quite similar to Goldstein's tendency toward self-actualization, posited a thrust within the living body toward self-integration and wholeness. But in spite of this drive toward integrity, James believed there existed a variety of ways this could be easily and even naturally disrupted. We have seen how he believed it the task of consciousness to order man's highly sensitive and unstable cerebral hemispheres through exercising powers of selectivity over the plethora of environmental stimuli.[47] We have reviewed also James's theory of the plasticity, pluralism, and transitoriness of instincts and their susceptibility to confusion and conflict. In contrast to the apostles of joy, for James culture and learning, when flexible and amenable to alteration in changing circumstances, do more to order conflicting bodily tendencies than they do to disturb the deeper regulatory capacities of the organism.[48]

Although James believed in the existence of impulses towards play, curiosity, and constructiveness—tendencies similar to the ones which some theorists, especially Maslow, associate with the higher reaches of self-actualization—he also believed in other massive tendencies toward egoism and the excitement and exhilaration of war, combat, and the hunt.[49] Sympathetic tendencies exist in the bodily orientations of humans, but self-regarding and self-protective impulses are greater still. Learning, culture, inspiring circumstances, commanding ideas, enlivening meanings, and processes of reason and decision are finally for James the realities which structure and pattern the body toward significant action. In the end, James is so very close and yet so very far from the central images of the culture of joy.

Notes

1. Rollo May, *Existence* (New York: Basic Books, 1958); Ludwig Binswager, *Being-in-the-World,* ed. Jacob Needleman (New York: Basic Books, 1963); Medard Boss, *Daseinsanalyse and Psychoanalysis* (New York: Basic Books, 1963); Jean-Paul Sartre, *Being and Nothingness* (New York: Citadel Press, 1966).

2. Robert Ornstein, *The Psychology of Consciousness* (San Francisco: W.H. Freeman and Co., 1972); C.T. Tart, *Altered States of Consciousness* (New York: John Wiley, 1969).

3. Erikson, *Identity, Youth, and Crisis* (New York: W. W. Norton, 1968); Robert White, *Ego and Reality in Psychoanalytic Theory* (New York: International Universities Press, 1963).

4. Karen Horney, *New Ways in Psychoanalysis* (New York: W. W. Norton, 1939); H. S. Sullivan, *The Interpersonal Theory of Psychiatry* (New York: W. W. Norton, 1953); Erich Fromm, *Man for Himself* (New York: Rinehart and Co., 1960).

5. Brewster Smith, Humanizing Social Psychology (San Francisco: Josey-Bass, 1974), p. 176.

6. Ibid., p. 177

7. Ibid.

8. James Dagenais, *Models of Man* (The Hague: Martinus Nijhoff, 1972), p. 33.

9. Donald Snygg and Arthur Combs, *Individual Behavior: A New Frame of Reference for Psychology* (New York: Harper and Bros., 1949).

10. Carl Rogers, "Two Divergent Trends," *Existential Psychology,* ed. Rollo May (New York: Random House, 1961), pp. 86–87.

11. Carl Rogers, "Toward a Science of the Person," *Behaviorism and Phenomenology,* ed. T. W. Wann (Chicago: University of Chicago Press, 1964), pp. 101–11.

12. *ERE,* pp. 32–33.

13. Carl Rogers, *Client-Centered Theory* (Boston: Houghton Mifflin Co., 1957), p. 491.

14. Ibid., p. 492.

15. Carl Rogers and Barry Stevens, *Person to Person* (New York: Pocket Books, 1971), p. 43.

16. Carl Rogers, *On Becoming a Person* (Boston: Houghton Mifflin Co., 1961), p. 192.

17. Ibid., p. 391.

18. *WB*, p. 70.

19. Rogers, *On Becoming a Person*, p. 391.

20. See above, pp. 161-64.

21. Rogers, *On Becoming a Person*, p. 187.

22. *PP*, 1:402.

23. Rogers, *On Becoming a Person*, p. 189.

24. *MEW*, p. 36.

25. Ibid.

26. Ibid., p. 38.

27. John MacMurry, *The Self as Agent* (London: Faber and Faber, 1957), p. 33.

28. Rogers, *Client-Centered Therapy*, p. 487.

29. Ibid., p. 488.

30. Kurt Goldstein, *The Organism* (Boston: Beacon Press, 1963), p. 197.

31. Ibid., p. 203.

32. Ibid., p. 197.

33. Ibid.

34. Ibid., p. 203.

35. Rogers, Client-Centered Therapy, p. 523.

36. Rogers, *On Becoming a Person*, p. 187.

37. Ibid., p. 189.

38. Carl Rogers, *Person to Person* (New York: Pocket Books, 1971), p. 15.

39. Frederick Perls, Ralph Hefferline, Paul Goodman, *Gestalt Therapy* (New York: Dell Publishing Co., 1951), p. 11.

40. Ibid., pp. 9 and 247.

42. Frederick Perls, "Morality, Ego Boundary, and Aggression," *Complex* (Winter 1954), p. 51.

42. Abraham Maslow, "Psychological Data and Human Values," *Toward a Psychology of Being* (New York: D. Van Nostrand Co., 1962), p. 145.

43. Ibid., p. 151.

44. Abraham Maslow, *Motivation and Personality* (New York: Harper and Brothers, 1954), pp. 199-234.

45. Maslow, *Toward a Psychology of Being.*, p. 149.

46. Ibid., pp. 151-52.

47. *PI*, 1:139.

48. Ibid., p. 121.

49. *P*, 2:411-13.

10

Ethics and the Strenuous Life

James does not derive all of his normative image of the human from his psychology. The total picture requires his *philosophical psychology* and his *ethics*. James's image of the strenuous life is especially influenced by his ethics. The contemporary sciences of man proceed by a method considerably different from James's. They try to drive images of the healthy, normal, or average human being from their explanatory theories. The purely psychological aspects of James's thought—his functionalism, his experimentalism, and his incipient phenomenology—all point toward the normative vision of the strenuous life. But this vision is not completed until we gain an understanding of James's ethics. Ethics or moral philosophy goes beyond both empirical explanation and phenomenological description. Ethics was, according to James, an effort to think metaphysically about the nature of free and responsible human action. Metaphysics, as we saw earlier, is an "unusually obstinate attempt to think clearly and consistently" about some of the basic assumptions behind various aspects of experience. Ethics is the attempt to think "clearly and consistently" about the conditions of moral action and, as such, is something which transcends both scientific explanation and phenomenological description.

It is James's ethics which gives the final justification for the strenuous life. Man's nature as revealed by James's psychology seems to require an ethical life, but only ethics itself portrays the positive content of this life. James's psychology revealed the selective character of the human mind, its tendency toward the future, and toward decision and choice. It revealed man's pluralism of interests, his variety of empirical selves, the reality of the will and attention, and the purposeful and meaning-saturated nature of consciousness. All of this suggests that humans are capable of the strenuous life and require it in order to live coherent and meaningful lives. But the real necessity of the strenuous life comes from the nature of communal exis-tence—the fact that humans with their conflicting range of wills and desires must find ways to mediate and harmonize their differences.

James, then, was a precursor of what Brewster Smith was calling for in our opening chapter. Smith suggested that our normative images of human nature should be derived from our ethics and political philosophy. He could have named other normative disciplines such as theology or philosophy of re-ligion. His point still stands: psychology can tell us if humans are capable of this normative vision and what conditions are necessary to bring it about. The normative disciplines, however, should have the central role in specifying the final content of this normative life. If the modern social sciences—especially the psychologies and psychotherapies—took this seriously, they would be far more tentative about their concepts of human nature and would turn far more frequently to the normative disciplines for consultation about their guiding images.

Ethics and Metaphysics

The central task of ethics is metaphysical and has to do with the definition of such words as "obligation," "good," and "ill." James's ethics are continuous with that broad philosophical school called "utilitarianism." To underestimate the impor-tance of the generally utilitarian character of James's ethics, as John Wild does, is to do violence to the foundation of James's moral philosophy.[1] On the other hand, Wild is certainly correct in showing that James's emphasis on the self-sacrificing nature of the strenuous life goes beyond the simple principle of utility. James's utilitarianism is crowned with an existential ethic of decision, risk, and sacrifice.

In his major statement on ethics, "The Moral Philosopher and the Moral Life" (1891), James rejects the idea that ethical obligation impinges upon our finite lives from some supersensible realm of eternal ideas.[2] Morality springs from the specific situation of conflicting desires and claims between concrete human beings. James writes, "Without a claim actually made by some concrete person there can be no obligation, but . . . there is some obligation wherever there is a claim."[3] Claim and obligation are "coextensive terms" and the idea that our sense of obligation stems from some "overarching system of moral relations, true 'in themselves'" is a fiction.[4] Morality results from finite humans' adjusting their respective senses of good with one another. And then James adds a startling footnote. "Whether a God exist, or whether no God exist, in yon blue heaven above us bent, we form at any rate an ethical republic here below."[5] The ethical life does not depend upon the idea of God, but James did believe that the concept of God adds energy and perseverance to the moral life.

But if ethics involves the adjustment of conflicting goods, how does James characterize the nature of good? Here James's democratic and pluralistic instincts become so blatantly visible that they almost lose their credibility. He finds difficulty with a large number of standard attempts to define the good—such as the self's happiness for the moment, happiness in the long run for self and others, adding to one's perfection and dignity, harming no one, being in accordance with universal law or the will of God, or promoting the survival of the human species. The definition he offers in their place is this: *"The essence of good is simply to satisfy demand."*[6] The moral philosopher should begin with the assumption that all demands are *"prima facie* respectable."

James's motives for saying this are easy to discern and of a piece with the rest of his philosophy. James takes all experience seriously even though he recognizes that only some experiences can stand the test of time. His radical empiricism, as he neatly summarized it in *The Meaning of Truth,* entails the idea "that the only things that shall be debatable among philosophers shall be things definable in terms drawn from experience."[7] The positive side of this principle is that philosophy should base itself on the broadest possible range of experience; no experience should in principle be excluded from consideration. In claiming that no demand should be prima facie excluded from consideration as good, James is bringing the spirit of his radical empiricism into his ethics. Furthermore, such an openness is consistent with James's ubiquitous pluralism. James resists the idea of an a priori scale of values derived from either God or man which would exclude automatically the claims of particular persons or segments of society. And most importantly, James is exercising that sympathy with the experience of others which he described so beautifully in "On a Certain Blindness in Human Beings." Our own practicality, our own selective attention and subjective interests, as necessary as they are, lead us to go through life "blind to the feelings of creatures and people different from ourselves."[8] James here is trying to devise a democratic and pluralistic ethic. The first step of such an ethic is to take seriously and empathically the elemental experiences about the good which all people, no matter how diverse, seem to have.

But the first step is by no means the last step. There is much more to discerning the *morally good*. James is making a distinction between the *good* and the *morally good*, a distinction worked out in detail by James's eminent student and biographer, R. W. Perry.[9] In some ideal world such as Freud's realm of hallucinated wish fulfilment, one could imagine that all goods demanded might be fulfilled. "But this world of ours is made on an entirely different pattern,"[10] James tells us. "The actually possible in this world is vastly narrower than all that is demanded."[11] Tragic choices must be made. Shall we choose this person or that person for our lifetime mates? We can't have both. Shall we be a lawyer or a doctor, follow this career or that, cherish this value or that value? Shall we eat gluttonously or remain slim, smoke to our hearts content or retain clear and vital lungs? We must choose, and in the process of choosing, something is always lost, always sacrificed. "Some part of the ideal must be butchered. . . . It is a tragic situation."[12]

It is precisely this recognition that the moral way is a tragic way which separates James so decisively from the culture of joy. The culture of joy is right in believing that our own intuited organismic experiencing is the source for our primitive apprehensions of the good. But they are wrong to believe that these primitive apprehensions are the same as the *morally* good.

How then do we proceed? How do we arrive at the morally good? James answers this question by asking another, "Since everything which is demanded is by the fact a good, must not the guiding principle for ethical philosophy . . . be simply to satisfy at all times as many demands as we can?"[13] "That act must be the best act," James insists, "which makes for the best whole," awakens the "least sum of dissatisfactions," prevails *"at the least cost,"* and "by whose realization the least possible number of other ideals are destroyed."[14] The morally good, then, has to do with those acts and rules which are the most inclusive of the non-morally good.

This definition of the morally good gives James an affinity with that tradition of utilitarian ethics associated with Jeremy Bentham and John Stuart Mill. In spite of this, James had reasons for keeping his distance from these eminent British philosophers. Utilitarianism relied too heavily upon associationism for its psychology and the naïve principle that pain and pleasure were the sole motivating forces for humans. We have seen James's antipathy to associationism, but he was equally critical of the pleasure-pain theory of human motivation. In addition to basic physiological pleasures and pains, James argued that humans have a whole range of subjective interests which include such things as the desire to play, aesthetic interests, and the desire to know. One might call these pleasures but in a vastly different sense than the simple physiological drives such as food, thirst, and sexuality. Our experienced goods and ideals have many sources, only a few of which result from the rhythms of our basic physiological pains and pleasures.

Regardless of these differences, James's definition has obvious affinities with utilitarianism. Frankena reminds us that utilitarianism associates the moral end with "the greatest possible balance of good over evil in the world as a whole."[15] Of course, there are many kinds of utilitarians and it is difficult to know in just which direction James was going. John Roth believes that he was close to situation ethics—a kind of "act utilitarianism," which focuses upon specific acts in specific situations and sees moral rules and principles only as suggestive rules of thumb.[16] But I see James as closer to "rule utilitarianism"—an approach which asks not which *act* but which *rule* will bring the greatest good.[17] The rule utilitarian devises and follows the best rules to cover a range or class of situations; he does this even though he realizes that situations change and that eventually amended sets of rules must be created. In the meantime he follows the most workable rules—the rules which bring about the best and most consistent set of consequences.

There is far more emphasis upon the importance of shared rules in James than most commentators have recognized. We already have seen the great emphasis he places upon habits. Habits, of course, are not the same as rules, but they are the characterological counterpart to rules. Handling situations according to established habits and rules greatly minimizes the energy we might otherwise waste making new decisions and developing fresh strategies of action. Just as James once said that habits are society's "enormous fly-wheel, its most precious conservative agent,"[18] he could have said the same about rules.

The difference between the act utilitarian (the situation ethicist) and the rule utilitarian is a respect for tradition and culture. James had a respect for tradition and culture in a way quite analogous to his respect for habit. Within both we find concealed an appreciation for the place of rules in the ethical life. In this sense, James was a conservative and held a conservative view of the role of culture in the human pilgrimage. Certainly James was a pragmatist and in this sense an experimentalist, but it is surprising to see how conservatively he interpreted his pragmatic approach to ethics. Like certain contemporary theorists such as Clifford Gertz[19] and Karl Popper,[20] James believed that a society's culture was a storehouse for the generally successful rules and traditions which had established a workable equilibrium of inclusiveness. Culture is the fund of rules and customs which have been selected by the feedback of time and experience. Although the moral philosopher should realize that cultural rules are in principle revisable, he should begin by assuming the general validity of the inherited tradition. James writes these words on behalf of tradition:

So far then, and up to date, the casuistic scale [of tradition] is made for the philosopher already far better than he can ever make it for himself. . . . The presumption in cases of conflict must always be in favor of the conventional recognized good. The philosopher must be a conservative, and in the construction of his casuistic scale must put the things most in accordance with the customs of the community on top.[21]

Changes will inevitably occur, but the change which James envisions is an orderly shift from one set of cultural rules to another. Just "as our present laws and customs have fought and conquered other past ones, so they will in their turn be overthrown by any newly discovered order which will hush up the complaints that they still give rise to, without producing others louder still. 'Rules are made for man, not man for rules.'"[22] As the old rules inevitably "weight upon" and even "repress" certain goods, the new rules will do the same. Every set of rules and its institutional embodiments—be it private property, marriage, taxation, socialism or whatever—sacrifices some goods in the hope of a more inclusive order. The innovator and experimentalist must not be against rules. "We may," as James argues, "replace old 'laws of nature' by better ones."[23] He does this not to get rid of rules or to handle things in an arbitrary, subjective, and personally idiosyncratic way; he does it to find more workable shared rules for a more inclusive order.

The Ethics of Reform

James's words about the role of the innovator and reformer remind us of his essays written several years earlier, "Great Men and their Environments" and "The Importance of Individuals." In chapter 2 we saw how they signal James's great concern with the role of the creative individual in social and cultural change. But he had a basically conservative view of the entire process. Much that occurs today in the name of social change and experimentation would have struck James as bizarre if not downright dangerous. The truly creative individual is rare. He must approach his task with humility and an appropriate sense of finitude. Note the cautious tone when James writes, "Every now and then, however, some one is born with the right to be original, and his revolutionary thought or action may bear prosperous fruit."[24] But such a person "risks much when he breaks away from established rules and strives to realize a larger ideal whole than they permit."[25] James concedes, however, that "the *highest* ethical life—however few may be called to bear its burden—consists at all times in the breaking of rules which have grown too narrow for the actual case."[26] But the person who aspires to be a real innovator, a true breaker of rules and finder of new ones, must follow "one unconditional commandment, which is that we should seek incessantly, with fear and trembling, so to vote and to act as to bring about the very largest total universe of good which we can see."[27] One does not break rules in the name of self-realization or self-actualization. One does not break rules in the name of short-term gains for oneself and one's close associates. One does this only when it benefits the whole community in the long run.

Still James can be criticized for not stating so clearly as is needed the role of substitute thinking and action in the process of experimentation. James writes in one place that social experiments "are to be judged, not *a priori*, but by actually finding, after the fact of their making, "how much satisfaction and how much pain they create.[28] James overstates the case when he says that "no closet-solutions can possibly anticipate the results of trials made on such a scale."[29] James is fully aware in his other writings that part of intelligent thinking, even in the area of morality, involves a substitute process of trial and error whereby the consequences of certain actions are imagined and calculated symbolically prior to the action itself. Although James should have stated this truth more emphatically, in the context of his discussion of morality his basic point is correct: the feedback of experience is of fundamental importance in establishing the truth of any moral claim. We will discuss this point further when we review James's pragmatic theory of moral truth.

James also failed to emphasize the importance of environmental *context* in his formal ethical discussions. Yet in reality this theme runs throughout his writings and gets to the heart of his emphasis on the *consequences* of a moral act. In fact, a better statement of his true understanding of moral behavior might go something like this: *There is a dialectical relation between nonmoral and moral good. Moral good refers to those principled acts which implement for a community the highest and widest organization of nonmoral good possible in a given environment with its particular resources and limitations.* Although there are certain abstract principles which may apply to any enviroment, James's implicit ecological persepective makes allowances for particular sets of rules for specific environmental niches. But everywhere, to implement a high level of general good, some claims must be sacrificed. For James, the concept of moral action and the idea of sacrifice are intimately related.

Identity and the Strenuous Mood

Ethics, for James, is the key to personal identity in a pluralistic and changing world. But for ethics to reconcile the value conflicts within our empirical selves, it must be undergirded by the supports and demands of a personal God.

The question of personal identity was of uppermost concern in the closing paragraphs of "The Moral Philosopher and the Moral Life." These pages are the vital center of James's thought and the key to his message to modern man. He describes the perennial experience of man—man the creature with multiple selves attached to conflicting values and interests. This is the situation already described with meticulous detail in his groundbreaking chapter on the self in the *Principles.* His material self may conflict with his social and spiritual selves or one of his many social selves may be in tension with the others. James is depicting a persistent characteristic of human existence, but one exacerbated by the pluralism of modern communities and values.

James is more explicit than thinkers such as Erikson and Lifton in defining modern identity confusion as basically an ethical problem. Even the solitary individual is in a moral situation if his or her various selves with their differing values are in conflict with one another. This is a "real" ethical situation because the community of conflicting values has not been internalized within the mental life of the single person. James writes about such a person as follows: "His self of one day would make demands on his self of another; and some of the demands might be urgent and tyrannical, while others were gentle and easily put aside."[30] Since man is a creature with multiple selves which reflect the social demands of the world around him, "Obligation can thus exist inside a single thinker's consciousness."[31]

If a multiple sense of obligation can exist within a single person, how does one find peace and identity? James's answer is this: "Peace can abide with him only so far as he lives according to some sort of a casuistic scale which keeps his more imperative goods on top."[32] In other words, the individual finds harmony and identity only insofar as that person has an ethic, a casuistry and method for making decisions and ordering his life into a hierarchy of goods with the more inclusive ones at the highest point on the scale. The more pluralistic our experience of the world, the more is it the case that the royal road to wholeness is through the ethical life.

There will be, of course, an element of "cruelty" in the ethical life. Some values will suffer and be sacrificed. Certain values and interests which we cherish will be "wounded" and eliminated upon the altar of decision. "It is the nature of these goods," James writes, "to be cruel to their rivals."[33] Our higher ideals call out all the "mercilessness in our disposition, and do not easily forgive us if we are so soft-hearted as to shrink from sacrifice in their behalf."[34] Is this the Freudian exclusivistic and punitive superego? Not quite, for it is a decisiveness already built on the way of democratic openness and sympathy. It has more to do with what John Wild has pointed out so correctly. James's utilitarianism ultimately leads to an existential ethic of self-sacrifice and commitment. Sacrifice is the presupposition of raising the general good of the whole. Sacrifice of some of the goods to which we are attached is the presupposition of personal identity as well. The wholeness of the community and the wholeness of the self must come, for James, through the narrow passage of ethical decision.

In these concluding paragraphs of this seminal essay, James frequently speaks of the ethical life as the "strenuous mood."

"The deepest difference," James tells us, "in the moral life of man is the difference between the easy-going and the strenuous mood."[35] The easygoing mood is essentially a mood of "I don't care." It is a genial but uninvolved mood which glides along the surface of life but never becomes committed to its deeper trials and sufferings. John Wild is accurate in saying that James's understanding of the easygoing mood corresponds to Kierkegaard's theory of the aesthetic life;[36] both the easygoing and the aesthetic life try to minimize the necessity of decision and commitment.[37] Even though James believed that man's nature and the conditions of his world call for the strenuous life, it is by no means inevitable; the easygoing mood can be chosen as well. Its manifestations take a great variety of forms. James finds it in the complacency and superficial optimism of monistic rationalism. He detects it in the fatalism and the lack of interest in the future implicit in scientific determinism. He found it in the dripping aestheticism of the art buff; he even distrusted his own experience of the aesthetic mode of life which his stays in Florence and Rome led him to live.[38] He found it in the romanticism of a Wordsworth and a Whitman. And finally, as we will see in some detail in our final chapter, he found it in the religion of the "healthy-minded" and the "once-born" (in contrast to the religion of the "sick soul" and the "twice-born") which he describes in his *Varieties of Religious Experience.*[39]

The strenuous life is the opposite of the easygoing mood. It is an attitude of care and involvement in both the present and the near and distant future. It entails living by a hierarchy of values which will permit the maximum enjoyment of good both in the present community and in the communities of the future. The person living the strenuous life is willing to undergo sacrifice and hardship for this end. "The strenuous life," James contends, "makes us quite indifferent to present ill, if only the greater ideal be attained."[40] In his essay "The Sentiment of Rationality" (1879), James anticipated his idea of the strenuous mood. He discusses a "mood" of moral "seriousness,—which means the willingness to live with energy, though energy bring pain."[41] "Anaesthesia," James believes, is the "watchword" of the easygoing mood, whereas "energy" is the key word "for the moralist" living the strenuous life.[42] Energy as the mark of the strenuous life is a theme which James later pursued at length in his "The Energies of Men" (1906). But the energy and activeness of the strenuous mood is not a frantic activism of the "American way"; it is a calm and settled activeness which uses the deepest energies of a person and is guided by an ethical casuistry designed to maximize the good enjoyed by all.

James often conceived of the strenuous life in analogy to a battle. It has a martial quality to it. In spite of James's openness to a variety of claims about the good, in spite of his extensive sympathy for variety, in spite of the ways in which his doctrines of pure experience and knowledge by acquaintance led him to an appreciative consciousness as the first step in moral awareness, in the end the fully ethical mentality drives toward a fairly explicit sense for the difference between "good" and "evil." We have seen in his "The Moral Equivalent to War" how James believes that humans have a fundamental hunger for conflict and strife. James wanted to turn this tendency toward pacific and moral ends. The person living the strenuous mood responds to the moral life like a soldier to the call of battle. The strenuous mood, James writes,

> awakens at the sound of trumpets, ha, ha! it smelleth the battle afar off, the thunder of the captains and the shouting. Its blood is up; and cruelty to the lesser claims, so far from being a deterrent element, does but add to the stern joy with which it leaps to answer to the greater.[43] . . . For this reason, the strenuous type of character will on the battle-field of human history always outwear the easy-going type . . . and prove victorious in the end.[44]

Identity and the Function of Religion

Ethics and the moral life may be the key to identity for James, but religion plays an important supporting role. James is interested in determining the conditions of the strenuous life. Religion, especially the kind of personal theism associated with popular Christianity and Judaism, was to James indispensable for inspiring and maintaining the strenuous life. But his position is subtle; in many ways ethics is autonomous from religion. The formula goes something like this: *The content of the moral*

*life comes from man's autonomous practical reflection about
the reconciliation of disparate human goods, whereas its major
inspiration comes from our experience of a supportive but
morally demanding personal God.*

"The capacity for the strenuous mood," James believes,
"probably lies slumbering in every man."[45] But it must be
awakened. We already have seen how James believes that there
are instinctual foundations behind the human capacity for
sympathy and the parental response to the needs of infants and
children. The moral life has something to build on in man's
biological constitution. In addition, in the final chapter of the
Principles and the opening paragraphs of "The Moral Philosopher and the Moral Life," James advances a theory about
how man's capacity for abstract comparative judgments in the
realms of both science and morality arise through the "back
door" of the brain by the mysterious processes of free variation.[46] But in spite of these constitutional givens which man
brings to the strenuous life, more is needed to inspire it and
bring it to its highest pitch. It needs our "wilder passions" and
"higher fidelities" for "justice, truth, or freedom" to awaken it.
A dramatic view of life is needed to bring it forth. Where all is
flatness and uneventful serenity, the strenuous mood will lie
slumbering. James's revulsion to the beatific ambiance of the
Chautauqua setting spelled out in his "What Makes a Life
Significant" and his thirst for an existence of real challenges and
risks, of real goods and evils, testifies to his belief that a life of
vivid contrasts is necessary if the strenuous mood is to flourish.[47]

But most important for the activation of the strenuous life is
the idea of God. Here his argument becomes almost Kantian.
The idea of a morally sensitive God who both supports and
demands an ethical life from all humans instills within us a
seriousness which exceeds that produced by any other source.
In a purely finite world, it is easy for man to play fast and loose
with his ideals; there is no greater power to survey his deeds and
make him accountable for his acts.

This too is why, in a merely human world without a God, the
appeal to our moral energy falls short of its maximal stimulating

power. Life, to be sure, is even in such a world a genuinely ethical
symphony; but it is played in the compass of a couple of poor
octaves, and the infinite scale of values fails to open up.[48]

The idea of God is not necessary to make our world ethical; our
human claims on one another do this. The idea of God is
necessary to elicit our deepest ethical commitments.

But wouldn't the claims of a remote posterity do as well?
Wouldn't the idea that the children of the next generation or of
a hundred years from now inject an element of transcendence
over our present needs? Wouldn't this inspire us to care for the
future as well as the present? This is certainly an idea growing in
power amidst the present ecological crisis with all of its sad
prophecies about the catastrophes to befall future generations.
It is certainly the major grounds for the ethical appeal in
Erikson's idea of generativity.[49] James obviously is attracted by
this "humanistic" ground for our care and responsibility for the
future; it is implicit in much of his writings. The test of moral
truth, he tells us, is the experience of the race as a whole over
time; it entails the collaboration of generations of parents and
children.[50] But finally the "claims of a remote posterity" (the
"last appeal of the religion of humanity") is not sufficient to
arouse our deepest moral commitments.[51] We do not "love
these men of the future keenly enough." They are abstract and
distant, and whatever their claims on our present behavior, it is
all too easy to avoid them and to occupy ourselves with the
present. We may love and sacrifice for our own children, but it
is difficult for the great mass of people to go beyond this to
sacrifice for our children's children, and their children, and very
few of us can demonstrate much care and concern for the
remote posterity of others.

James believes that a personal God is necessary to bring forth
our higher ethical deeds. He works especially hard in his
Pluralistic Universe to describe the kind of God which corre-
lates with the strenuous life. This is a God who contrasts
remarkably with the totally infinite and omnipotent God of
classical theism and rational monism. It is a god who is infinite
in some respects and finite in other respects. It is a God who is
growing and changing and open to the contributions of human

beings. But even more specifically, it is a God who enters into human experience as a claimant, as a personal being who makes demands on human beings in a manner quite analogous to the way fellow humans lay their claims on each other. When we believe this about God, all of life takes on a deeper seriousness. James insists that "when . . . we believe that a God is there, and that he is one of the claimants, the infinite perspective opens opens out."[52] Our ethical ideals take on a new "objectivity and significance" and begin to utter a "tragically challenging note of appeal."[53]

Clearly, James's vision of God has important similarities with the active and personal God of ancient Judaism and early Christianity. It was an image of God which James derived from his own cultural tradition and his phenomenology of the religious experience of prominent individuals nurtured by this tradition. James did not give us in his *Varieties of Religious Experience* or other religious writings a description of the full range of religious phenomenon. It was actually a selective picture which primarily concentrated on relgious experience in the context of Judaism and Christianity. Although limited as a truly adequate psychology of religion, it had the merit of focusing the most available alternative religious visions within the Occidental tradition. Even though his psychological and phenomenological work is biased, it must be distinguished from his philosophy of religion. His own constructive concept of God clearly belongs to the latter enterprise. Yet some people might ask, Is James's image of a finite, personal, and morally serious God nothing more than the superego God so exhaustively depicted in the writings of Freud? Is James's language about God simply a different way of speaking about the internalization of the forbidding and demanding figure of the father?

There is some truth in such a charge. Both James and Freud held an ethical interpretation of God, although Freud tended to read it in a negative and James in a positive light. Freud saw the ethical God as associated with the superego and its unconscious prohibitions against the chaos of human desires. James saw the ethical image of God not so much as implanting prohibitions as presenting a general positive challenge to humans to live the morally serious life. In the end, James was somewhat blind to the numberless ways in which the Judeo-Christian image of an ethical God has been associated with the maintenance of archaic taboos and systems of irrational prohibitions. On the other hand, Freud was not so open as he might have been to a philosophical cleansing of this concept of God—one which would wash away its more repressive features.

Certainly this is the path chosen by James. The ethical life requires the seriousness of a personal and morally sensitive God. But for James, God does not actually tell us what to do. Our actual moral judgments are autonomous from the specifics of divine command. Religious people cannot invoke the mind of God or a special revelation from Him in an effort to authenticate their moral judgements. "Meanwhile," James writes, "exactly what the thought of the infinite thinker may be is hidden from us even were we sure of his existence; so that our postulation of him after all serves only to let loose in us the strenuous mood."[54] The religious ethicist, "whenever he ventures to say which course of action is the best, is on no essentially different level" from the secular thinker.[55] His appeal must be what will yield the widest good for the most humans here on earth. He must make his judgments in the context of actual claims between different human beings. His judgments must attempt to reconcile goods and interests in this world. God sets before each human being the choice "between life and good, and death and evil" and challenges this person to "choose life that thou and they seed may live." But the content of the specific moral decisions which we must make are very much a matter of man's finite moral inquiry into the good. Man needs God to help him take seriously and live faithfully by the principles which his own practical reason tells him is the highest and best. Or to say it somewhat differently, *God reinforces our free decision to transcend ourselves and focus our attention upon the needs of others, both in the present and in the distant future.*

Truth and the Strenuous Life

James's theory of truth is the most difficult and controversial aspect of his thought. In addition, it is often seen as a legitimation of the most materialistic and crassly instrumental aspects of American culture. In his rambunctious style as a popular lecturer, James referred to the truth as the "cash value" of a concept.[56] At other times, the truth was that which was "expedient"[57] or what gave "satisfaction" to a person using a particular idea.[58] Taken in the proper context, all of these characterizations of truth can be defended, although they are not without difficulty. Taken out of context, they are open to serious criticisms, if not downright ridicule.

Seen in its broadest context, James was developing a theory of truth to correspond with his evolutionary and adaptive theory of mind. But as we have seen, his functional view of mind was related intimately to an incipient phenomenology. The same can be said for his pragmatic theory of truth. In spite of his claims that his pragmatism and radical empiricism could stand independently of each other, his pragmatic theory of truth was closely associated with his doctrines of pure experience and knowledge by acquaintance.

James's main problem was that he failed sufficiently to distinguish the different types of truth which he had in mind. James's theory applies to three kinds of truth; these in turn correspond very neatly to his three departments of the mind. There is scientific truth, which corresponds to the perceptual and sense-receiving department. There is logical truth, which corresponds to the cognitive or organizing department of the mind. And there is moral truth, which corresponds to the active and volitional functions of our mental life. In all three instances James associates the truth with what is "workable." But he frequently failed to point out that "workability" has a different meaning for each of the three types of truth.

As early as his crucial essay "Spencer's Definition of Mind" (1878), James defined the truth as that which "in the long run . . . works best."[59] In this context, and throughout his writings, James's emphasis on workability and consequences is an effort to incorporate the idea of natural selection into his theory of truth. The "True" refers to those beliefs and actions which get us into a life-promoting relation with the environment. James was developing a basically ecological and adaptive theory of truth. The true is what makes possible the satisfaction of the maximum amount of human interests consonant with survival within a particular environment. The true is not just what helps us to survive; it is what gives us the fullest and most just expression of human interests while permitting us to survive in specific environments. This is what James means in his lectures on *Pragmatism* (1907) when he says that pragmatism is primarily a "method"[60] and that it focuses on the "practical" differences which a theory makes.[61] As a method, it moves away from "first principles, 'categories,' supposed necessities," and concentrates on "last things, fruits, consequences, facts."[62] This is also what he is saying when he insists the true is that which "helps us to get into satisfactory relations with . . . our experience,"[63] and when he recklessly states that the true "is only the expedient in the way of our thinking, just as 'the right' is only the expedient in the way of our behaving."[64] Of course, with regard to this last definition, he adds an often forgotten qualifier—"expedient in the long run and on the whole course."[65]

But without some further distinctions which James did not always provide, his theory of truth is open to serious misunderstanding. For instance, scientific propositions can be true without being particularly relevant, adaptive, or fruitful for the enrichment of human life. A certain formula in physics when tested may create an enormous atomic explosion which will destroy the population of an entire city and maybe an entire nation. Several such explosions could wipe the human race off the face of the earth. Such a formula would be true in the sense that it adequately accounts for certain processes in nature, but it can hardly be said to have beneficent consequences or fruits. Workability in the area of scientific truth means that the proposition brings us into contact with the reality to which the proposition refers. It makes it possible for us to *do* something with that reality. Our proposition leads to a discernible difference in our experience. In an early essay entitled "The Function of Cognition" (1885), James says that a proposition is true if it leads us to "knowledge by acquaintance" with the object of reality to which it refers. The proposition must "resemble" the object, but it must also "operate" on the object. It must make a detectable difference in our experience of the object or our experience of some reality which is continuous with it.[66] In other words, as A. J. Ayer has pointed out so appropriately, scientific truth refers to propositions which can be "corroborated by our sense-experience,"[67] although "sense experience" has a broader meaning in the context of James's radical empiricism than it does for Ayer's logical positivism.

The difference between James and a philosopher such as Ayer is that the former sees scientific truth as only a small part of a larger framework of truth. Yet both Ayer and James would agree that there are additional truths which are primarily of a logical kind. James believed the mind was endowed with innate capacities to make comparative judgments.[68] This capacity to compare and contrast, to discern differences and similarities, is "brain born" and does not derive from experience as such; it is an accidental product of the evolutionary processes of spontaneous variation. These capacities of the mind for abstract comparison and classification are the foundations of the pure sciences of logic and mathematics. In this realm something is true not because it agrees with the facts of experience, but because it is internally consistent and follows the law of logic and generalization.

But there is a third arena of truth. This is the area of moral truth, the kind of truth which James was most concerned about and which he believed to be the most important. Here our capacity, once again, for abstract comparison plays an important role, although it does not tell the entire story of how moral judgments are made. Experience is important for the testing of moral ideas, but experience itself does not give us our capacity to make abstract comparisons about justice. James points out that sometimes humans find themselves making judgments about justice which exceed the moral level of their previous experience. He writes, "Little by little there dawns in one the judgment 'nothing can be right for me which would not be right for another similarly placed" or "the fulfilment of my desires is intrinsically no more imperative than that of anyone else's."[69]

When this happens, the entire mass of habitual experience gets overturned. In holding such a position, James is going beyond the associationists of his time and behaviorists such as Skinner in our own day who would explain the origin of moral judgments as totally a consequence of the coupling and conditioning of experience. In addition, James is anticipating the view of such structuralists as Piaget and Kohlberg, who believe that our capacity for moral judgments comes from the maturing of cognitive capacities which are fundamental structures of the human mind.[70]

But although these capacities for comparative judgments are important to explain the origin of moral judgements, they do not constitute a theory of moral truth. Moral truth has to do with moral principles which are "workable." But workable now means something different. *A moral idea is workable if it leads to a higher level of enduring "satisfaction" of a wide range of human interests for the total community in the context of a given environment.* James nowhere quite gives this definition of moral truth, but it is a faithful summary of his various remarks taken as a whole. There is something correct but also short-sighted in Ayer's belief that for James "it is an essential characteristic of religious and moral theories . . . to satisfy our emotional and practical demands."[71] The implication is that, if a moral truth satisfies an emotional demand, then moral truths are primarily a matter of personal taste, have little public significance, and are primarily matters of private concern. This is really not what James had in mind. Moral truths have to do with the satisfaction of basic human interests and needs. Emotions are a part of this, but James also is speaking of such things as our basic physiological needs, our aesthetic and cognitive needs and interests, and our needs for moral coherence. These are not just arbitrary personal tastes. Their satisfaction has to do with the very survival of man as a human being. Moral truths have to do with our strategies of adaptation to our environments, our calculated risks to enjoy the greatest amount of good that is possible in the context of certain environments and conflicting claims and demands.

Moral truth deals with our rules for anticipating the future consequences of our actions. Here James is correct. We can never really know the consequences of our moral judgments until we act on them.[72] To this extent, in the moral sphere we always have to act with an element of faith; we necessarily must make decisions and take action before all the evidence is in. As James points out in his famous essay "The Will to Believe," in the moral sphere we are makers of truth, not just its recorders.[73] At best, our moral principles are strong probabilities. Because we have acted on these principles in the past and certain beneficent consequences have followed, we can expect the same in the future. If conditions change and we must develop new moral propositions, only the test of time[74] and the repeated living out of the principle by generations of human beings actually can confirm it as useful for the increase of good among man.[75] Moral questions are forced upon us and are momentous in their importance for our lives. They have to do with not only our happiness, but with our very survival. This is why they are the central questions of human life, more important, in the final analysis, than questions which deal solely with scientific fact. For James, scientific rationality was subordinate to moral rationality. He felt this so strongly that he sometimes made the mistake of reducing the true in every sense of the word to the good.[76] Although James clearly was wrong in stating the case so strongly, he was right in holding that the endless and aimless stockpiling of knowledge will not in itself promote the human good.

Pragmatism and Care

Far from being a method to promote materialistic, short-termed goals of power, convenience, and thoughtless expediency, James's pragmatism was a method for handling life's inevitable vicissitudes in a responsible manner with an eye to the long-range effects of our acts. James's radical empiricism led him to believe that there were certain continuities and basic orders to experience to which humans must attend in directing their action. But experience cannot be received simply and passively as if the basic harmonies which life requires have only to be discovered and not achieved. *There are continuities and orders to be discovered, but there are others which must be achieved.* Pragmatism was a method for achieving these super-added harmonies which are necessary for a truly human life.

In making moral judgments, James's pragmatism keeps its eye on consequences for both the "immediate practical foreground" and the "remote" perspective of the future.[77] The sense for the future as a permanent feature of the human mind is something James investigated in considerable detail in the *Will to Believe* and his "The Perception of Time" in *Principles*.[78] In one place he writes, "The permanent presence of the sense of futurity in the mind has been strangely ignored by most writers, but the fact is that our consciousness at a given moment is never free from the ingredient of expectancy."[79] James's pragmatism is tied inextricably to his philosophy of free will and indeterminism, however small these elements of life may be. It also is tied to a belief in the possibility of a better world tomorrow, no matter how realistic it is about the impossibility of banishing suffering and evil from the face of the world forever. "This regulative notion of a potential better truth to be established later" turns pragmatism toward "concreteness of fact, and toward the future."[80] Not that pragmatism turns away from the past. We already have seen the many ways in which James placed a conservative interpretation on his theory of cultural change. The past is respected as a storehouse of truth. "I have already insisted on the fact that truth is made largely out of previous truths."[81] Moral truth, in spite of the importance of the past, is ever in the "process of mutation" no matter how slow and imperceptible it may be. For the same reason, the self and the identity of the self also are always in a process of mutation. This is why ethics and a God who demands the ethical way become the key to the maintenance and reconstruction of identity for human beings in the modern world.

The Heroism of the Common Person

All of this, as we have seen before, amounts to a heroic view of life. But James's view does more than celebrate the role in adaptation and social change of the "great men" of history or the creative individuals of special talent who so obviously affect our lives. It also places great importance on the undramatic, minute, but indispensable daily acts which imperceptibly change some situations for the better or help other situations of good to endure against formidable odds. These are the people who contribute to that great mass of care which gives any viable society the firmness and flexibility to continue its pilgrimage from generation to generation. In his popular lecture "What Makes a Life Significant" (1899), James brings up once again a theme which is pervasive throughout his writings. There is a heroism of the common person as well as a heroism of the great leaders of history. Our general blindness to the experience of others causes us to frequently overlook this truth. There is risk, drama, care, concern, and a prudent eye to the future in the life of the commonest laborer. Riding on a train one day after a bland experience at a beatific but stultifying Chautauqua, James was ruing the loss of the heroisim he imagined to exist in an earlier and more unruly day. In a flash, he realized he had been blind to the "great fields of heroism lying round" about him.[82] And then James writes,

> And yet there it was before me in the daily lives of the laboring classes. Not in clanging fights and desperate marches only is heroism to be looked for, but on every railway bridge and fire-proof building that is going up to-day. On freight-trains, on the decks of vessels, in cattleyards and mines, on lumber-rafts, among the firemen and the policemen, the demand for courage is incessant: and the supply never fails. There, every day of the year somewhere, is human nature *in extremis* for you. And wherever a scythe, an axe, a pick, or a shovel is wielded, you have it sweating and aching and with its powers of patient endurance racked to the utmost under the length of hours of strain.[83]

But James is not just romanticizing in a Tolstoyian fashion the virtures of the life of labor. Nor is he presenting here a subtle defense of the exploitations of industrial capitalism. In fact, in this very article he acknowledges that some form of socialism is the necessary wave of the future. "Society has . . . undoubtedly got to pass toward some newer and better equilibrium, and the distributions of wealth has doubtless slowly got to change."[84] But this, James insists, as good and important as it will be, will not in itself give meaning to the life of the great mass of people performing the menial tasks of this world. Their lives will take on true significance when they are grasped by an "ideal." It must be an ideal flexible enough to allow novelty and change, and it must be an ideal which is capable of some degree of implementation in reality. To hold ideals is not itself equivalent to living the strenuous or heroic life. In order for life to take on true meaning and significance, there must be some "marriage" between our ideals and our active capacity to make some progress toward their realization. In contrast to the contemporary cultures of detachment, control, and joy, James's holds out for a positive place in life for the role of ideals. And of course, the ones most central to him where the ideals associated with the ethical and strenuous life.

Notes

1. John Wild, *The Radical Empiricism of William James* (New York: Anchor Books, 1970), p. 276.
2. *WB*, p. 194.
3. Ibid.
4. Ibid.
5. Ibid., p. 198.
6. Ibid., p. 201.
7. *MT*, p. 36.
8. *TT*, p. 113.
9. Roger Hancock, *Twentieth Century Ethics* (New York: Columbia University Press, 1974), pp. 68-74, Perry reference on "Intention between moral and nonmoral good."
10. *WB*, p. 202.
11. Ibid.
12. Ibid., p. 203.
13. Ibid., p. 205.
14. Ibid.
15. William K. Frankena, *Ethics* (Englewood Cliffs, N.J.: Prentice-Hall, 1973), p. 34.
16. John Roth, *Freedom and the Moral Life: The Ethics of William James* (Philadelphia: Westminster Press, 1969, pp. 18-20.
17. Frankena, *Ethics,* p. 39.
18. *P*, 1:121.
19. Clifford Geertz, *The Interpretation of Culture* (New York: Basic Books, 1973), p. 33-86.
20. Karl Popper, *Objective Knowledge* (Oxford: Clarendon Press, 1972), pp. 106-52.
21. *WB*, p. 206.
22. Ibid., p. 206.
23. Ibid., p. 208.
24. Ibid.
25. Ibid., p. 206.

26. Ibid., p. 209.
27. Ibid.
28. Ibid., p. 207.
29. Ibid.
30. Ibid., p. 211.
31. Ibid.
32. Ibid.
33. Ibid.
34. Ibid.
35. Ibid.
36. Wild, *The Radical Empiricism of William James*, p. 276.
37. Ibid.
38. Perry, *TCWJ*, 2:252.
39. *VRE*, pp. 76–139.
40. *WB*, p. 211.
41. Ibid., p. 86.
42. Ibid., p. 107.
43. Ibid., p. 213.
44. Ibid.
45. Ibid., p. 221.
46. Ibid., pp. 185–89; *PP*, 2:672–75.
47. *TT*, p. 135.
48. *WB*, p. 212.
49. Don Browning, *Generative Man* (New York: Delta, 1975), pp. 162–66 and 179–217.
50. *WB*, p. 108.
51. Ibid., p. 212.
52. Ibid.
53. Ibid.
54. Ibid., p. 214.
55. Ibid.
56. *P*, p. 46.
57. Ibid., p. 145.
58. *WB*, p. 76–80.
59. *CER*, p. 66.
60. *P*, p. 42.
61. Ibid., p. 47.
62. Ibid., p. 47.
63. Ibid., p. 49.
64. Ibid., p. 145.
65. Ibid.
66. *MT*, p. 28; also in *P*, pp. 41–64.
67. A. J. Ayer, *The Origins of Pragmatism* (London: Macmillan, 1968), p. 202.
68. *PP*, 2:643.
69. Ibid., p. 673.
70. Jean Piaget, *The Moral Judgement of the Child* (New York: The Free Press, 1965); Lawrence Kohlberg, "From Is to Ought," *Cognitive Development and Epistemology*, ed. Theodore Mischel (New York: Academic Press, 1971).

71. Ayer, *The Origins of Pragmatism*, p. 196.
72. *WB*, p. 11.
73. Ibid., p. 20.
74. *WB*, p. 207.
75. Ibid., p. 205.
76. *P*, p. 59.
77. *P*, p. 86.
78. *WB*, pp. 76–79; *PP*, 1:605–42.
79. *WB*, p. 77.
80. *P*, p. 146.
81. Ibid.
82. *TT*, p. 134.
83. Ibid., p. 134.
84. Ibid., p. 145.

11

Mysticism, Saintliness, and the Strenuous Life

The full title of James's Gifford Lectures (1901–1902) was *The Varieties of Religious Experience: A Study in Human Nature.* It often is suggested that the word "varieties" signals his pluralistic emphasis carried over to the study of religion. Yet the subtitle of the book is even more revealing. It suggests that the volume is as much about "human nature" as it is about religion. Certainly, *Varieties* is a book on the psychology of religion; but more than that it deals with what man's religious behavior teaches us about his nature. *Varieties* takes the data of religion and puts them to the service of James's philosophical-psychological anthropology. James's turn from the philosophical psychology of *Principles* to *Varieties* is not unlike Paul Ricoeur's shift from the philosophical study of the will to the study of religious symbols in *Symbolism of Evil.*[1] The early and the later writings in both cases are really different approaches to the study of human nature.

Some commentators believe James's study of religion was motivated by the unconscious hold his warm, erratic, and spiritually preoccupied father[2] had upon him. Certainly his father's religiosity had much to do with motivating James's interest in religion. James took special recognition of his father's largely unsuccessful writings by editing and introducing them in a volume entitled *The Literary Remains of the Late Henry James* (1885).[3] It is also true that from the beginning of his career James was seeking an epistemology and world view large enough to grant an honorable role to religion in human affairs. But to admit this does not mean that James simply was playing out his father's religious vision. Henry, Sr., was a rebellious Calvinist who was attracted by Swendenborgian spirtualism and Fourier socialism. His religious vision emphasized the grandeur of God, the impotence of the human will, man's determinism by both his racial inheritance and the rule of God, and the inevitability of God's victorious redemption of man and the world. William, on the other hand, believed in the efficacy of individual action, the reality of freedom, the cooperative relation between God and man, and the possibility—but by no means the inevitability—of man's final salvation. William James was indeed his father's son, but he was certainly not his father's duplicate.

In *Varieties* and his other religious writings, James achieved a synthesis between a mystical and an ethical view of life. His vision of the strenuous life was located firmly within a broader mystical vision of life. His emphasis on responsible individual action on behalf of the wider community was undergirded by an equally strong accent upon the mystical presence of God, the twofold sense of God's gracious support and ethical demands, and a wider sense of belongingness which the mystical experience inspires. His form of mysticism is a "pluralistic mysticism" in contrast to a "monistic mysticism"; it is a mysticism which envisions God as one, albeit the greatest, individual amongst a community of individual centers of power. In the pluralistic view, God enters into human experience as an individual; man and God influence each other much as humans relate to and influence one another. In the monistic view, God becomes equal to the whole of things; finite human consciousness is a mere moment, thought, or dimension in the life of God. Pluralistic mysticism portrays a dramatic and interactive view of the relation of God and man. Monistic mysticism depicts a static and deterministic relation between the divine and the human whereby self-discovery of one's essential identity with God is the key to the spiritual life.

On the whole, James brings mysticism into the service of the strenuous and ethical life. The mystical experience—that boundary-breaking experience of sensing a deeper unity of relatedness with God and the world—makes a definite contribution to the strenuous life. It gives us a broader sense of relatedness to the whole of life. That person whom we help in not just a separate and foreign object we feel obligated toward; rather, he or she is someone to whom we feel related and attached. Our involvement with another person flows from our participation in the other's life and not simply from some arid sense of duty. For this reason, the mystical experience can charge the ethical act with a heightened sense of spontaneity and joy. It can enrich the strenuous life by bestowing a sense of security and a feeling of relaxation. The mystical experience can mitigate the strain stemming from the challenge and effort of the ethical mode of existence. It can give us an intrinsic experience to stand on and, if need be, even rest on. It can bestow a present affirmation and security, a refuge and haven, which the ethical life requires if it is to survive its ordeals and trials.

This, of course, is James's normative view of the possibilities of mysticism. All mystical experience does not accomplish such wonders. James's pragmatic evaluation of religious ideas and experience leads him to a high appreciation of the mysticism associated with the popular theism of Judaism and Christianity. It is a mysticism flowing from the Jahwistic concept of God found in ancient Judaism and carried through into early Christianity. This is a unique form of mysticism largely confined to the popular religious experience of the West. It is different from the monistic mysticism of philosophical idealism and certain forms of Hinduism.

Pluralistic mysticism was the type James believed most relevant for life in the modern world. If pluralism and change become all the more aggravated in modern societies, ethical human action becomes even more important if we are to achieve the partial harmonies which life requires. But it is precisely in the environment of modernity that we profoundly need the present security, affirmation, and support which the mystical experience conveys. It is only pluralistic mysticism—the mysticism of the Jahwistic tradition whose personal God is both gracious and demanding—which dialectically conveys this twofold experience of mystical support and ethical demand.

James's philosophy of mysticism is relevant to the contemporary hunger for transcendental experience. The emerging interest in the Eastern meditational psychologies (the Yogas, Zen, Kundalini, Satipatthana, and others); the rediscovery of Western mystics such as Saint John of the Cross, Teresa of Avila, Meister Eckhart, and Johannes Tauler; the popular interest in altered states of consciousness produced by drugs and the growing scientific study of these states,[4] all signal a vast new cultural reorientation away from exclusive preoccupation with technical rationality and a fascination with nonrational or transrational mystical phenomena. It is difficult to see just where these new probings are taking us. There is the distinct possibility that the mystical state can be raised up as an end in itself. There is the possibility that this preoccupation can create a new quietism and a mystical detachment from the evils and challenges of mundane existence at a time when they require a steady hand of active ethical endeavor. Mysticism does not always accompany and inspire service to one's fellow human beings. If we are to believe Arthur C. Danto in his *Mysticism and Morality,* Eastern mysticism is very seldom associated with a truly ethical and transformative vision of life. Danto believes that most Eastern mystical philosophies lack both a belief in the reality of the will and the possibility of free action which can reduce specific evils in this world. Without these "over beliefs," mystical orientations have no truly moral view of life. As Danto writes, "I believe that generally the mechanism of the will is considered the enemy of ultimate happiness throughout the East."[5] But then he adds, "it is extremely difficult to derive a moral philosophy on the basis of this if the very possibility of morality presupposes the mechanism of the will."[6] It is precisely because monistic philosophies, whether mystical or rationalistic, are unable to certify a place for the will that James believed they were so inimical to the truly ethical and strenuous life.

James and the Phenomenology of Religion

I agree with James Edie's belief that James was an early practitioner of the phenomenology of religion.[7] Just as phenomenological description was James's first step in his psychology, so it was in his study of religion. But James took a different approach than did the phenomenolgists of religion such as G. Van Der Leeuw, Joachim Wach, Mircea Eliade, and Rudolph Otto. These great scholars were closer to the phenomenology implicit in Dilthey's *Verstehendepsychologie* and primarily spent their time discerning the morphologies to be found in religious symbols, texts, and institutions. Although James can be criticized for not taking seriously religious symbols and sacred texts, his own method can yield important fruits. James took his radically empirical or phenomenological attitude directly to religious experience itself. In this, as Edie suggests, he was closer to the phenomenology of Husserl had the latter applied it to the study of religion. In the early pages of *Varieties,* James announces he will study the meanings and forms of "religious feelings and religious impulses" experienced by "articulate" individuals.[8] He will not study origins and he will not concentrate on explanations. He will attempt to make empathic "existential judgments" about the nature of religious phenomena before embarking on the more evaluative task of making "spiritual judgments" about its worth and usefulness.[9] He will first examine the "immediate content of the religious consciousness,"[10] take the "experiential point of view,"[11] and aim simply at "the description of the phenomenon."[12] One can even find in James's methodology the supreme principle of phenomenology which was so visible in his chapter on the stream of consciousness—the importance of *intentional objects* for forming the structures of consciousness. James believes there are no religious emotions as such. Religious emotions are simply our natural emotions such as love, fear, or awe "directed to a religious object."[13] "All our attitudes, moral, practical, or emotional, as well as religious, he tells us, "are due to the 'objects' of our consciousness, the things which we believe to exist, whether really or ideally, along with ourselves."[14] This is why James, in keeping with his radical empiricism, takes quite seriously the reality of the divine in the experience of human beings. James writes, "It is as if there were in human consciousness *a sense of reality, a feeling of objective presence, a perception* of what we may call *'something there,'* more deep and more general than any of the special and particular 'senses' by which the current psychology supposes existent realities to be originally revealed."[15]

But James's phenomenology of religious experience is highly selective. On the whole, it is limited to a description of religious expressions found in the Western tradition. More than that, it is limited to options confronting James and his contemporaries at the end of the nineteenth century. The *Varieties* is not a systematic analysis of the elementary forms of religious consciousness along the lines given by scholars such as Durkheim, Weber, Van Der Leeuw, or Eliade. James's selection of religious expressions was based on personal and historical reasons; they were options confronting him and the contemporaries of his day—Lutheranism, Wesleyanism, Christian Science, the romantic religiosity of Wordsworth and Whitman, revivalism, Calvinism, and certain forms of Catholic and Oriental mysticism. Regardless of this biased choice, the analyses were empathic and largely phenomenological. *Varieties* undoubtedly helped James and some of his contemporaries understand the religious options which were available. It is a book for modern man and still relevant to some of the choices facing our present age.

James can be criticized for having an overly individualistic definition of religion even though it follows logically from his decision to study religious experience. His definition of religion as dealing with the experience of "individuals in their solitude" in relation to whatever "they may consider divine" unfairly disregards corporate, social, and institutional forms of religion. But this criticism is mitigated when we learn that the majority of the experiences James studies belong to religious leaders or founders—individuals whose religious experience and personal gifts enabled them to acquire followers, start trends, or establish movements. To this extent, *Varieties* should be read in the context of James's early articles on "Great Men and Their Environment" (1880) and "The Importance of Individuals" (1890). As we have seen, in these essays James was pursuing the question of the role of individuals in social change. This is the proper framework in which to read *Varieties*. James is studying from the inside the experience of creative religious people. He was analyzing from the inner perspective individuals not unlike the charismatic and prophetic personages who affect social changes and whom Weber studied sociologically in his monumental monographs on religion.

The Nature of Spiritual Judgments

James not only described religious experiences, he attempted to find a philosophical ground for selecting those with the more valid claims. He is interested not only in the morphologies of religious experience; he is concerned with how environments should test, evaluate, and select those expressions most efficacious for the human pilgrimage. The environment he has in mind is both the external world and the surrounding followers which the articulate religious individual may attract. How do they make their evaluations and choices? How do they discern the constructive from the destructive? James believed religion could be both. Along with Freud, Jung, and most modern scholars dealing with religion, James fully realized the potentially destructive consequences of certain religious forms. So religions must be evaluated. In fact, James proposed an academic discipline which would be called the "Critical Science of Religion."[16] Such a discipline would make some of the "spiritual judgments" which religious claims need to confront.

To make critical judgments about religion, one must go beyond description.[17] This is an insight which contemporary academic studies of religion frequently fail to recognize. With the demise of theology and the rise of the scientific study of religion, the critical evaluation of the *worth* and *value* of religion languishes. James's proposal for a critical science of religion held these two dimensions together. Within this new discipline, the philosophy of religion would be in intimate contact with the actual study of the facts and forms of religion. The philosophy of religion primarily would be concerned with the *value* of religious beliefs and practices, although the question of truth would not be neglected. In this, James's vision of the philosophy of religion differs considerably from recent fashionable trends in Anglo-American philosophies of religion, where the question of the cognitive validity of religious beliefs is the dominant preoccupation. James can be faulted for not raising the question of the factual truth of religious beliefs as directly as is necessary. Just as he did in the area of morality, he tended to confuse the question of truth with the question of value and workability. Nonetheless, he did raise an important philosophical question about the human worth of religious ideas and practices which philosophy, because of its unimaginative preoccupation with cognitive truth, has failed to advance. The logical positivism of A. J. Ayer would say that morality and religion have in common the fact that both deal only with emotional interests.[18] James would rephrase this by asserting that both have to do primarily with *human values*. But whereas this is the end of the conversation for logical positivism, James would see this as the beginning of the real task of philosophical reflection.

James's pragmatic evaluation of religion follows rather neatly the three departments of the mind implicit in *Principles* and explicit in *Will to Believe*. "Immediate luminousness, . . . philosophical reasonableness, and moral helpfulness" are the three criteria for judging the validity of religious ideas and practices.[19] Clearly, these three criteria correspond to the perceptual, cognitive, and active (volitional) departments of the mind. The individual's intrinsic experience of insight and truth (luminosity) has a claim in the area of religion, just as it does in other spheres. But it cannot stand alone. The origin of a religious claim in mystical intuition, pontifical authority, or supernatural revelation does not in itself authenticate it just as its origin in a neurotic, sick, depressed, or otherwise pathology-ridden mind does not in itself invalidate it. In addition, to be considered valid, a religious idea must *make sense* in the light of other known truth. In this criterion, we see that James is indeed interested in the possible factuality of religious ideas. Of course, the direct phenomenological experience of the "presence" of the divine is a kind of factuality, but James seems aware that this could prove illusory. He wants more. The structures and consequences of religious ideas must correspond to other known facts. In *Pluralistic Universe*, he even speculates with ideas of God which might "explain" the cosmology of the universe, although even here his primary concern is to find an image of

God to correspond with man's moral experience.[20] But the major criterion by which religious experiences are judged is "moral helpfulness." This is the principle of workability once again, applied in a broad, almost ecological sense. The value of a religious experience is found in *"the way in which it works on the whole."* In his "Pragmatism and Religion" (1907), he says a religious claim is valid if "consequences useful to life flow from it."[21] In the end, all religious claims, be they mystical, supernatural, Christian, or Buddhist, must be judged with this principle most in mind. "By their fruits ye shall know them, not by their roots."[22] All the way from the Bible to Jonathan Edwards's *Treatise on Religious Affections,* this is the principle which James believes men resort to in the final analysis. Just what this means and how it works will be the task to demonstrate in the remainder of this chapter.

The Twice-Born and the Strenuous Life

In preparing for his Gifford Lectures on religion, James rummaged through a wide range of religious literature, personal testimonies, devotional tracts, and scriptures from various faiths. Two broad forms of spirituality began to emerge. One was "healthy-minded" or "once-born" religion and the other was the spirituality of the "sick soul" or "twice-born." James does a convincing job of demonstrating that these two broad orientations can be found in the religious history of mankind. They also correspond to two life orientations which James elaborated in his psychological and ethical writings. The religion of the sick soul or twice-born is clearly a religious manifestation of the strenuous life and the attitude of "I care." Healthy-mindedness, on the other hand, has close analogies with the less involved and less morally concerned attitude of "I don't care." But in saying this, I must add that James did indeed respect healthy-mindedness, although in the end he believed twice-born religion was the more profound. The values of healthy-mindedness have their place within the religion of the sick soul, just as the attitude of "I don't care" should be a moment within the more encompassing orientation of "I care."

In the same fashion and for some of the same reasons, James preserves the values of monism by organizing them as elements or aspects of his pluralistic theism.

The religion of the healthy-minded is that vigorous, full-bodied, fresh-air, and optimistic type of religious sensibility which sees life as good, nature as beneficent, and God as intimately, affirmatively, and even mystically related to all his creatures.[23] This uncomplicated sense for the goodness of creation is bought at the cost of a certain amount of blindness and disregard to the reality of evil in this life. Liberal Christianity of his day; the nature romanticism of Emerson, Whitman, and Wordsworth; the mind-cure movement, Christian Science, and Divine Healing; Bishop Berkeley's transcendental idealism and Vedantism are all examples which produce the once-born type of spirituality. In our own day one could add the optimism and romanticism of such diverse phenomena as the counterculture, the human-potential movement, certain strands of humanistic psychology, various forms of progressive education, and the new and popular meditational psychologies.

It is not that evil is denied completely by healthy-minded religion; rather, one does not concentrate and dwell upon it.[24] On the whole, most once-born individuals are pluralistic enough to believe centers of evil independent of God do indeed exist in this world.[25] But healthy-minded religion was a form of positive thinking. It involved a banishment of evil from one's mind and a settling of one's thoughts on the good and the spiritual. Healthy-mindedness was a kind of symbolic behaviorism built around the power and efficacy of the "idea" and the "ideal" over our conduct.[26] We become what we think. We become what we set our minds upon. The popular "mind cure" movement of his day was the best example of this doctrine. One becomes *reinforced* by the ideas that one *chooses* to hold one's mind upon and one gradually becomes shaped into their image.

It is obvious why James was attracted by healthy-minded religion, especially the mind-cure movement of his time. It brought into focus many of the things James stood for. It held a place for the will and the will's capacity to center attention on one thing. It exemplified James's theory of how our beliefs both shape ourselves and form the world around us—an idea which ran through his essays in *Will to Believe*.[27] It found a place for James's implicit behaviorism; we are free to choose the ideas by which we live, but once that happens, habits and an artificial environment of supports may form around us which sustain us in our path.

On the whole, healthy-minded religion is not associated with a thoroughgoing monistic view of God and the world. Monism believes that God is the immutable, unchangeable, totally perfect, and completely self-sufficient All-in-All. There is nothing really outside the life of God, and humans at the deepest levels of their personalities are so completely one with the Divine Life that they are in reality mere aspects of the very body of God itself. Obviously, a religion with a monistic superstructure has difficulty locating evil outside of God; God ends up, in some manner, as himself the author of life's moral infirmity and natural suffering. Healthy-minded religion does not, on the whole, go that far. But it does have certain affinities with monism. There is a strong, although largely naturalistic, mystical strain in once-bornness which puts it near the inevitable mystical overtones of monism. In addition, some of James's criticisms of monistic mysticism apply equally well to the natural mysticism of healthy-minded religion.

In the reports and descriptions which James quotes we find loads of monistically oriented statements. Some are clearly "mystically" monistic as well. "God then fills the universe alone, so that all is from Him and in Him, and there is nothing that is outside."[28] One of James's personal friends writes that the only "foundation for wholeness" lay in this fact "of impregnable divine union."[29] The mind-cure movement is clearly a religious movement, James tells us, and holds the "Doctrine of the oneness of our life with God's life."[30] In *Varieties, Pragmatism*, and his essay "The Absolute and the Strenuous Life" (1906), James's pragmatic critique of monism argues that such luxurious basking in the security and immutability of an all-encompassing oneness lulls our spirits into quietism, indifference, and blindness to the reality of danger and evil in the world.[31]

Monism, however, does serve an important function. The security and support that it conveys gives us a "moral holiday" from the risks and moral demands of the pluralistic and strenuous path.[32] But it can serve this purpose only if it is subsumed theism, pluralistic mysticism, and the ethical mode of life. Or to say it differently, as he does in "The Gospel of Relaxation," the feelings of security, indifference, and "not caring" which can accompany mystical monism are worthy if they are moments within the larger context of "caring."[33] If our energies are already at a high pitch of tension, if we are already in a conscientious and disciplined attitude of care and concern, then the moment of security, relaxation, and trust which monism (or healthy-mindedness) affords can indeed give a boost to a life of responsibility and engagement.

James points out time and again that when the will is at a high pitch of disciplined concern, then the mystical moment of relaxation and indifference frequently can serve to *release* those accumulated energies which our earlier periods of strain and effort have built up.[34] This is especially important for his entire discussion of conversion.[35] But without this context of willed care and concern, the security which monism grants can indeed lead to an enduring attitude of quietism and indifference to the real suffering in this world. James subsumes both the values of healthy-mindedness and mystical monism to the wider religio-cultural context of a modified inner-worldly activism and asceticism. Just as in his psychology, romanticism was taken into yet subsumed beneath the strenuous life, in the setting of his religious discussions healthy-mindedness and mystical monism are included in, yet subordinate to, his vision of twice-born religion and the popular theism and mystical pluralism with which it is associated.

It is instructive to illustrate these points more concretely. James appreciates the Augustinian-Lutheran strand of theology with its monistically oriented emphasis on the supportive grace and justification of God. But in the end, James is as dialectical as Luther. On strictly pragmatic grounds, James wanted the emphasis upon God's loving acceptance held in perfect tension with an emphasis upon his transcendent demand for the ethical and strenuous life.[36]

But what is James's understanding of twice-born religion— the religion of the sick soul? His description runs like this. In the religion of the sick soul one finds individuals haunted by a deep sense of the risk, danger, and pervasive moral evil which runs through the world.[37] These are people possessed by a divided self. They are the examples par excellence of man as *homo duplex*.[38] They seem to have no natural sense of unity and coherence to their lives. They are ridden by an inner instability, tension, and conflict between the various elements of their lives.[39] Just as Kierkegaard and the existential theologians such as Marcel, Bultmann, and Tillich were aware of the ubiquitous role of existential anxiety (James called it anhedonia) in the authentic religious life, James assigned it an essential role in the experience of the twice-born.

James found a wide range of examples of the sick soul. Tolstoy, Bunyan, St. Paul, Henry Alline, St. Augustine—the experiences of these and others are described in some detail. An anxiety attack which James himself had as a young man is disguised in the form of some mysterious "sufferer" who recorded the experience in French.[40] Along with this, James must have been aware of a similar experience of terror and existential *angst* which his father had described so vividly years before.[41]

James's personal struggles and the anxiety, indecision, and dividedness which marred his early manhood, doubtless elicited his sympathy for the sick-soul mode of life. But his reasons for seeing it as the profounder style go beyond his personal predilections. They stemmed from his pragmatic test of religious truth. But they also related to his general philosophical psychology and what it taught him about the human animal in a world of evolutionary change. Man is a *homo duplex*. James could affirm this just as easily as could St. Paul, St. Augustine, Luther, or Kierkegaard. Under the influence of Kierkegaard, most post-liberal twentieth-century theology has retrieved the Pauline-Augustinian vision of the ambiguity and dynamic duality of the human will. But the Niebuhrs, Tillichs, and Bultmanns of the neo-orthodox period could have turned to James as easily as to Kierkegaard or Heidegger. And had they done so, they would not have separated themselves from a modern world view so profoundly as they did.

The dramatic and articulate examples of human dividedness found in certain religious expressions James believed were vivid

manifestations of a *general human condition*. Healthy-mindedness has the capacity to blind itself to this condition, but it is
nonetheless present in us all. "Now is all of us, however,
constituted, but to a degree the greater in proportion as we are
intense and sensitive . . . does the normal evolution of character
chiefly consist in the straightening out and unifying of the inner
self."[42]

But the dramatic examples teach us the most profound
lessons. James quotes St. Paul, "What I would, that do I not;
but what I hate, that do I." James refers to St. Augustine's
description of himself as having "two wills, one old, one new,
one carnal, the other spiritual," and adds the further remarkable comment that it "was myself indeed in both the wills."[43] In
less theological language, James describes the sick soul as
"simply a man of sensibility in many directions" whose "feelings
and impulses are too keen and too discrepant mutually."[44] He
may be a person with at least two "hostile selves, one actual, the
other ideal."[45]

The more extreme forms of the sick soul express in vivid relief
a universal truth about the self—it is an unstable, heterogeneous, and conflictual phenomenon. This is the self which
James discovered and wrote about in his psychological studies.
It is also the self which he finds in a wide range of religious
expressions. This is the self we saw in James's earlier descriptions of the material, social, and spiritual selves, all of which
could be organized around different centers of value. This is the
self which James described on phenomenological grounds as "a
theatre of simultaneous possibilities"[46] stretched out on a world
of myriad and conflicting meanings.[47] This is also the self whose
physiological foundations are heterogeneous and pluralistic. It
is a self built on a highly sensitive cerebral cortex ready to be
pulled in different directions by a plethora of environmental
stimuli.[48] And this is the self with pluralistic instinctual foundations, a self which has instinctual foundations behind both its
egoistic *and* its altruistic tendencies, even though the former are
so very much in greater supply.[49] In other words, for James, his
phenomenological description of the level of human meanings,
his physiological and comparative explanations of man's psy-
chobiological makeup, and his analysis of man's religious

experience are all "diagnostic" or "complementary" to one another.[50] No wonder that James believed *homo duplex* was closer to the true character of human nature!

The highest levels of spirituality emerge from an honest confrontation with the evil in oneself and the world. The highest levels are attained through a process of becoming. They do not come naturally. We acquire these levels through decision, effort, and struggle. Even for James it is a process much like Kierkegaard's description of the move from the aesthetic to the ethical and then to the higher levels of religions A and B; it is a process brought about by ever-deepening levels of inwardness, effort, and choice.[51] James discusses this process under the rubric of conversion, but he already has said much about the process in more secular terms in his psychological and ethical writings.[52] He uses his field theory of consciousness first presented in *Principles*.[53] Conversion comes about when some idea or value which has been peripheral to consciousness (or maybe has even been subconscious or subliminal), makes a shift toward the very center of consciousness.[54] The conversion process may be slow and gradual *or* sudden and dramatic. It almost always is preceded by a period of intense struggle when a person is either trying to *escape* a feeling of guilt and incompleteness or *attain* through an act of will some positive goal. The moment of conversion (and in some instances it may be only a faint and final "jerk") frequently comes at the point of exhaustion, the very moment when we give up our willed efforts and permit ourselves to relax, sometimes into the loving and accepting arms of a Supreme Being. At that moment our early *strenuous efforts* seem to continue their work subconsciously. We may experience these unconscious forces as *grace* and *providence*. And of course, James never denies—in fact, he positively suggests—that this subconscious process may indeed be assisted by a wider and deeper divine being with which our subliminal lives are continuous.[55]

The Saint and the Strenuous Life

James dedicates two chapters to a description and evaluation of saintliness. In many ways, they are the center of *Varieties*. At first glance, his descriptions of saintliness sound quaint and dated, something which might flow naturally from the pious atmosphere of the nineteenth century. Our contemporary sensibility influenced as it is by psychoanalytic modes of thought, calls out for dynamic explanations, causes, and accounts of hidden impulses and unconscious forces. James's emphasis is just the opposite. He concentrates on descriptions of the essence of saintliness and evaluates consequences and results. Before launching into his descriptions, he quickly hints at his evaluative conclusions: "The best fruits of religious experience are the best things that history has to show. . . . Here if anywhere is the genuinely strenuous life."[56]

"Saintliness" is a word for the highest fruits of religion. It occurs when "spiritual emotions are the habitual centre of the personal energy."[57] By "spiritual emotions" James means a sense of being grasped by an ideal power which leads one to self-transcendence in acts of sacrificial love. His descriptions sound abstract when stated by themselves; only the concrete material itself makes them truly convincing. Then, even the most reductionistic and skeptical among us may become persuaded that a truly higher life can be found amongst the saintly. A feeling of being part of a "wider life," a sense of continuity with an "ideal power," new heights of "elation and freedom," a new sense of "yes" toward the world and a new shift toward "loving and harmonious affections"—these are some of the marks of the true saint.[58] Such qualities frequently are accompanied by an ascetic capacity for self-sacrifice, endurance, and fortitude; a reduced sense of dividedness; and a newfound "charity" and "tenderness" for one's fellow creatures.[59]

Most interesting for our purposes is the "organic" relation he discovers between the saint's mystical experience and his positive feelings of love for mankind. This mystical experience need not always be acutely religious. But in these spiritual experiences, whatever their character, the knotty boundaries of the self dissolve and one senses a melting into a large unity with the world. James writes,

> Religious rapture, moral enthusiasm, ontological wonder, cosmic emotion, are all unifying states of mind, in which the sand and

grit of the selfhood incline to disappear, and tenderness to rule. . . .
The faith-state is a natural psychic complex, and carries charity
with it by organic consequence. Jubilation is an expansive affection, and all expansive affections are self-forgetful and kindly so
long as they endure.[60]

But James stops short of saying that the mystical state inevitably produces the thoroughly ethical attitude. There are differences between monistic and pluralistic mysticism in their
respective capacities to give rise to the truly ethical and strenuous life. Mystical tenderness and the melting of the self's
boundaries are *not equivalent* to the properly ethical stance. As
we have seen, ethics involves specific judgments of value which,
in themselves, no religious experience can produce. But the
mystical experience can *incline* us toward the sense of sympathy
which ethics requires; and even then, some mystical experiences
are more potent in this respect than others. There is little doubt
that James makes ethics the measure of religion. At the same
time, he does not reduce religion to ethics. Religion gives our
ethics a sense of spontaneity, joy, and durability which ethics
and the strenuous life by themselves will surely lack. [61]

The chapter on "The Value of Saintliness" is the most
exciting in the book. Here James turns to the serious business of
making "spiritual judgments" about the human worth of the
best manifestations of religion. In these pages, the full force of
his concern with the social consequences of religion emerges.
James's full-bodied and multivalued pragmatism becomes the
measure. Religion, like ethics, is measured by the range of
human values it promotes which are consistent with each other
and with the demands of survival in various contexts and
environments.

In evaluating the social usefulness of the saint, James makes a
startling statement: "There is, in short, no absoluteness in the
excellence of sainthood."[62] In fact, the belief that there is any
one ideal type of human being is wrong. "According to empirical philosophy . . . all ideals are matters of relation."[63] He
agrees, for once, with Herbert Spencer, who held that "ideality
in conduct is altogether a matter of adaptation."[64] Statements
such as this demonstrate how James anticipated what we called

in chapter 1 the "transactional systems" approach to normative thinking about human nature.

So the question is *not* "Should everyone become a saint?" The answer, from James perspective, is "obviously not." Every society needs a multiplicity of types of personality and in our present moment of history, a society with a majority would probably collapse. But this does not mean that the saint has no role to play in the contemporary world. In addition, it does not mean that a little more saintliness in us all would be a bad thing. In fact, it would be a good thing. The saint serves an important function in social evolution. Seen from a narrow perspective, and from the standpoint of the individual saint, saintliness is not very adaptive. The St. Pauls, St. Francises, and St. Bernards of this world are in many ways the most vulnerable of people. But from a larger perspective they contribute greatly to the creative adaptiveness and social evolution of the wider community. In contrast to Nietzsche, who downgrades the saint and extolls the virtues of the "strong men" of history, James believes that the saint is adapted to a "millennial society." The following words state with exceptional power James's pragmatic and ecological view of the value of the saint for social evolution.

> It is meanwhile quite possible to conceive an imaginary society in which there should be no aggressiveness, but only sympathy and fairness,—any small community of true friends now realizes such a society. Abstractly considered, such a society on a large scale would be the millennium, for every good thing might be realized there with no expense of friction. To such a millennial society the saint would be entirely adapted. His peaceful modes of appeal would be efficacious over his companions, and there would be no one extant to take advantage of his non-resistance. The saint is, therefore, abstractly a higher type of man than the "strong man," because he is adapted to the highest society conceivable, whether that society ever be concretely possible or not.[65]

Sainthood as a general idea does much to upgrade the level of society. Particular individuals as saints may be "large enough" actually to inspire the rest of us poor mortals. But in certain circumstances, and in the context of particular needs, some aspiring saints "may appear more insignificant and contemptible . . . than if he had remained a worldling."[66]

The relationship of saintly characteristics to other values is the key to the saint's true worth. If certain qualities of the saint such as charity, purity, devoutness, and asceticism are rigid ends in themselves and largely isolated from other human values, then the saint may actually be destructive to the human community. The qualities and actions of the saint must undergo intellectual criticism just as must all other aspects of life. If the saint's intellectual outlook, is "too narrow," devoutness can become fanaticism, purity can become the blind repudiation of the external and discordant, and charity a subtle way to undermine the potential autonomy of the weak. The saint's actions must be judged from a variety of perspectives, just like the actions of any other person. In one place James writes that conduct, including that of the saint, must be measured from three perspectives: "the actor, the objects for which he acts, and the recipients of the action."[67] In order for an act to be truly good, "intention, execution, and reception, should be suited to one another."[68] Saintly virtues and good intentions are not enough. Actions must fit an environment and a context. Attention must be paid to consequences. Once again, James is concerned with the feedback of experience, the selective power of the environment, and the results over time of our actions. All of these elements—so consistent with his broad evolutionary world view—are brought to bear in determining the value of the saint.

James gave considerable care to his evaluation of the asceticism of the saint. Asceticism is at the heart of the capacity for self-sacrifice. Without a capacity to sacrifice some goods in the name of other, more inclusive ones, no redemptive action in history is possible. We have seen throughout James's psychological and philosophical works a concern to rehabilitate modern man's respect and capacity for the ascetic impulse. This plea reaches its highest pitch in these pages. James makes no defense of the wilder excesses of the ascetic life; asceticism, just like all the other saintly virtues, is no end in itself. But in its more reasonable forms, the ascetic orientation meets a great need in man. Within reason, human beings court the "arduous." In addition, the reality of evil tends to pull from us the heroic and self-saccrificial response. Asceticism is one of the essences of "twice-born" religion and the "strenuous life."[69] As against this, the lack of capacity for sacrifice and inner rigor of the easygoing and healthy-minded attitude seems pale indeed. In contrast to the asceticism of the strenuous life, the easy optimism of the healthy-minded "is mere syllabub and flattery and sponge-cake in comparison."[70] The world "is essentially a theatre for heroism. In heroism, we feel life's supreme mystery is hidden."[71] The individual who is willing to "risk death, and still more if he suffer it heroically, in the service he has chosen" is consecrated forever.[72]

In a manner reminiscent of Kierkegaard's "knight of faith,"[73] James makes a remarkable synthesis between religious and military images of the good person. As we have seen, the strenuous life, especially when lived in the religious context, is the true "moral equivalent of war."[74] This is the first time the phrase appears in James's writings; it later became the title of an essay published after his death in 1910. The possibility of synthesizing the disciplined heroism of the soldier with the tenderness and ethical sensibility of the saint was evidently an idea which lingered in the back of his mind during the last decade of his life. We have already seen how James believed that man is basically a hunter and aggressor and that, although these drives may not rage to express themselves at all times, they are there slumbering and ready to be exploited. War and the military are schools for the training of this "aboriginal instinct."[75] But now we need a new asceticism of the strenuous life which will put the discipline and sacrifice of military heroism into the service of the ethical mode. This is James's solution to overcome the passivity and frantic quest for ease, wealth, and pleasure which James saw developing in modern societies. This is James's new cultural vision created out of the intellectual sources available to him—his descriptions of human consciousness, his evolutionary models, and his phenomenology of saintliness.

Mysticism and Modernity

But the ascetic, heroic, and even martial character of the strenuous life should be, in James's vision of things, undergirded by a sense of mystical participation in the whole of life. One sees this everywhere in the writings of James, in spite of his differential evaluation of mysticism and his reluctance to discuss his own mystical experiences.[76] One can see it in the importance he assigns to knowledge by acquaintance, in the respect for the givenness of experience implicit in his radical empiricism, and in his explicit statements about the role of mysticism in human life. Without the security, sensitivity, and breadth of sympathy which the mystical orientation can give, the strenuous life can degenerate into a tension-ridden activism which is the last thing that the modern world needs. The present preoccupation with the hypertensive features of modern life suggests there is enough frantic, guilt-produced, and misdirected activism as it stands without adding more. The problem of modern life is how to restore a deep sense of peace and a high level of ethical awareness to the demands for action which modern societies necessarily place upon us. A new respect for the mystical orientation may help bring the balance to our lives which modernity requires.

James's phenomenology of the mystical experience is still widely quoted. His descriptions have all the more bite because he compared the mystical experience to other altered states of consciousness such as sudden insight, the *déjà vue* experience, alcoholic intoxication, the experience of ether, and his own experience with nitric oxide. The mystical experience is marked by a high degree of *ineffability*; it is difficult to convey with words and must be experienced directly before its quality truly can be known. Even though largely ineffable, mystical states have a *noetic* quality and allegedly convey a sense of knowledge and insight into the true nature of the world. Mystical states are *transient* and occupy consciousness for relatively brief periods of time. Furthermore, although mystical states are frequently (although not always) preceded by intentional preparations which entail discipline, active concentration, and focused attention, the final mystical state itself is distinctively *passive*. The mystic "feels as if his own will were in abeyance, and indeed sometimes as if he were grasped and held by a superior power."[77]

James adds to these main descriptive features of the mystical experience several additional comments. The ineffability of the mystical state is related to the collapse of the subject-object structure of reality in the mystical state. In mystical experience, the "opposites of the world" which characterize ordinary perception are melted into a unity.[78] As James says, based upon his own experience with nitrous oxide, the "keynote to the experience is invariably a reconciliation."[79] Some reports of mystical states contain within them the seeds of a monistic view of the world. This was the case with the earlier reports of Benjamin Paul Blood, whose writing influenced James so profoundly. In his own anesthetic experience under the influence of ether, Blood experienced the loss of his own sense of selfhood and a merger of his self with the larger universe and with God.[80] In fact, in some mystic states, the person loses his experience with the smaller God of theism and finds this God "swallowed" up by a larger God equal to the whole of the universe.[81] Even though there is what James called a "theoretic drift" in mysticism toward monism,[82] he believed that on the whole the experience itself testifies only to a unifying relation with a larger power. Whether or not the larger power was interpreted monistically depended on additional "over beliefs" which are added to the mystical experience itself.[83]

A major characteristic of certain mystic states is also one which makes them relevant to the strains of modernity. Mystical experiences can convey a marvelous sense of security to the person undergoing them. This is the way Benjamin Blood described it. "The lesson is one of central safety: the Kingdom is within."[84] Another person described his experience as a "state of peace and joy and assurance indescribably intense."[85] In the mystic experience one can feel that contact has been made with the very ground of existence—the very foundation of reality. This relation with what Tillich would later call "the Ground of Being" conveys a sense of existing beyond the risks and dangers of finite life.

In explaining the mystical state, James resisted the temptation to write it off as a regressive or otherwise pathological condition. The classical Freudian explanation, which sees mystical experiences as recapitulations of the oceanic states of infancy where no clear boundaries are experienced between the child and his loving mother, were never entertained seriously by James. Rather, the reality of mystical experiences forced James to theorize that humans have several different levels or states of consciousness in addition to the ordinary waking consciousness of everyday life.[86] The stream of consciousness which he described in *Principles* is but one of several possible modes of consciousness. Yet, even though James admitted that mystic states relativized the exclusive claims of ordinary consciousness, he gave the latter priority in the final courts of philosophic judgment. This should not be forgotten. It gets to the heart of his pragmatic theory of truth. Ordinary consciousness is not the only consciousness. Other states of consciousness indeed have their "own field of application and adaptation."[87] In addition, even though altered states of consciousness provide us with few "formulas" and explicit directions, they quite clearly influence our "attitudes" and the general orientation of our lives. They constitute a "fringe" or "horizon" to our everyday consciousness. Nevertheless, it is finally the judgments of ordinary consciousness which give us our criteria of lasting value and truth. In the end, James gives higher status to the patterns of ordinary consciousness in his image of the human than he does to altered states. Ordinary consciousness is relational, purposeful, selective, and stretched out upon the world. These qualities of consciousness are central to James's definition of the human. Consciousness can also undergo transitory interludes when its purposeful and selective character is disrupted, when some of the antinomies of everyday life are collapsed, and when a deeper relation with the universe and with God is experienced. These states of consciousness can cast a hue over the processes of our ordinary consciousness and enrich it; but in James's image of man, they never quite take over the center of vision.

James organized this great variety of altered states of consciousness under the title of "subliminal" consciousness. But in reality, the mystical experience is only one of many different unusual states which James discussed in relation to it. The concept was a courageous, if confused, attempt to broaden our understanding of human consciousness. He borrowed it from his old friend F. W. H. Myers and called it the "most important step forward in psychology since I have been a student of that science."[88] James chose not to call it the "unconscious," as Freud and Jung would later do. He already had discarded this term in his refutation of the "mind-dust" and "automaton" theories in *Principles*.[89] James was more inclined to speak of the existence of multiple consciousnesses which were sometimes separated and unaware of one another. In spite of these differences with the two giants of medical psychology, if anything, James's concept of the subliminal is more encompassing than their theories of the unconscious. It contained momentarily "inactive memories," "obscurely motivated passions" and "impulses," all our "non-rational" operations such as intuitions, fancies, and superstitions; our "dreams", our "delusions" and "obsessions"; our posthypnotic suggestions, "supranormal cognitions" and "telepathic" experiences; and finally our mystical experience.[90] Obviously the concept of subliminal consciousness is too general and does little more than give explicit recognition that there are other states besides ordinary consciousness. But in doing this, James performed a great service; he helped break the idea, as Freud and Jung would later, that ordinary consciousness was the only consciousness. Furthermore, the concept saved James from the mistake of seeing the altered states as always and *only* simple regressive states or products of unconscious repression—an error perpetrated by Freud although not by Jung.

In 1910, the year James died, he wrote a little-known article entitled "A Suggestion About Mysticism."[91] It demonstrates how the nature of mysticism was a preoccupation at the very end of his life. There he developed the idea that the mystical experience was a sudden and intense opening up of the normal boundaries of ordinary consciousness. More specifically, this broadening of the boundaries of consciousness is "intuitive or perceptual, not conceptual" and carries with it a "sense of a tremendous *muchness* suddenly revealed."[92] The reason is simple: if the opening of consciousness is "vast enough," a wide range of experience, memories, ideas, and sensations can flow in without any *one* attracting our attention singly. This accounts for the intuitive and perceptual quality of the experience and the feeling that much has been revealed, but in an ineffable way difficult to differentiate and articulate. In this way, one may feel that the "whole of reality" has been uncovered at once.[93] Sometimes this expression of experience can be so radical and rapid that we become afraid of being "swept out to sea" and "getting lost." This undoubtedly is the experience connected with schizophrenic episodes and other experiences of acute identity confusion, and experience James himself may nearly have had with a series of bizarre dreams which occurred during the winter of 1906. In suggesting that mysticism and morbid states of mind, although by no means identical, can be arranged on a continuum, James was anticipating certain contemporary models operative in the quickly growing field of altered states of consciousness.[94]

Towards the end of *Varieties,* James plays with the hypothesis that there is such a thing as a subliminal self, a "more" with which the self of ordinary consciousness can come into union. In religious and mystical experiences, we come into contact with this "more." This "more" comes to us as a subconscious "continuation of our conscious life,"[95] but we also experience it as a power which originates from sources beyond our ordinary selves. Various overbeliefs can be placed on the experience of this "more." Some interpret the experience as consistent with the personal God of popular Judaism and Christianity. Some make monistic, Vedantic, or even pantheistic interpretations of the experience. On philosophical grounds, James would lean toward the Christian and Judaic interpretations. On psychological and phenomenological grounds, James is willing only to say it is a wider power from which saving influence comes.[96]

Freudian psychology might call this "more" the hidden dimensions of the superego which have become expanded, sacralized, and externally projected as only the unconscious can do.[97] There is much in James's writings which would agree with this point of view. In *Principles,* James refers to God as one of the many "social" others whose recognition we seek.[98] Since the subliminal for him can also be a place for forgotten memories and obscurely motivated passions, it would have been only a small step for James to reach the classical Freudian position. James would not have resisted the psychoanalytic position so much as he would have been reluctant to make it the *exclusive* explanation of the meaning of the "more." In addition, he was too much of a phenomenologist and too empathic with the experiences of others to be satisfied with such a drastic and totalistic reduction. Social experiences and more independent experiences of the "more" may indeed intertwine and reinforce each other, but James's pluralistic instincts would lead him to resist any simple reduction in all cases of one to the other.

Recent research into mystical experiences and other altered states of consciousness have refined greatly our explanatory models. Much of the better research gives James credit for opening the field to psychological investigation, moving in the right direction, anticipating more recent advances, and protecting us from premature reductionistic explanations.[99] But James's more lasting contribution was his philosophical evaluation of the truth and value of the mystical state. Since mystical states were considered by James the core of religion, James's general evaluation of religion and specific evaluation of mysticism merge into one another. Of course, for James, truth in the area of ethical and religious phenomena is measured principally by practical consequences; in these matters the "true is what works well, even though the qualification 'on the whole' may always have to be added."[100] This is the center of James's work, but even in religious matters he never left it at that. In order to have credibility, mystical states also had to square with other current states of knowledge and going models of the universe. On this latter score, mystical states have something to say for themselves. The basis of rational beliefs and mystical beliefs is not entirely different; the former are based on "our senses" while the latter are founded on "direct perceptions" which are just as persuasive to the mystic as sensations are to the average person.[101] In addition, if the philosopher grants as much reality to internal psychological events as he does to chemical and physical facts, then mystical states can be seen as compatible with our general view of the cosmos.[102] At this level alone, the claims of mysticism should at least be granted the status of an hypothesis. But it can go no further than this. Mystical states can have no authority over anyone except those who have them. In the public arena, their claims must be verified by their consequences and their fruits.

This is the principle which James believes the mystics themselves use to authenticate the value and truth of their experiences. But even here, the witness is ambiguous. The bizarre and destructive can sometimes flow from the mystical experience. James was no simpleminded celebrant of the inexorable goodness of the contents of the subliminal. He warns us that this region contains

> every kind of matter: "seraph and snake" abide there side by side. To come from thence is no infallible credential. What comes must be sifted and tested, and run the gauntlet of confrontation with the total context of experience, just like what comes from the outer world of sense.[103]

In addition, the "over-abstraction from practical life" and "other-worldliness" of some mystics reduce them to near helplessness. It is clear that practical fruits cannot easily flow forth from individuals in such a state.

But these are examples to the contrary. Mystical experiences do tend to convey a sense of participation and sympathy with a broader range of experience and even with God. They also often convey an abiding sense of peace and security. These states sometimes correlate with the most intense ethical and strenuous activity. They did in Saint Ignatius, who was "one of the most powerfully practical human engines that ever lived."[104] Saint John of the Cross believed his mystical experience gave him an "invincible courage" and unquenchable desire to "suffer" in the service of God.[105] Saint Teresa believed that after such an experience, her soul emerged "full of health and admirably disposed for action."[106]

But the real lesson that James would bequeathe to our present fascination with mysticism comes at another level. Whether mystical experiences enrich the human enterprise depends as much on the cultural and religious overbeliefs associated with them as it does on the unusual states themselves. When mysticism is associated with a broader philosophical monism, it will result in the quietism, indifference, and uncaring attitude which follows from its undynamic, risk-proof, and unrealistically secure vision of the world. When mysticism is associated with the simple theism of the Judeo-Christian tradition with its image of an ethical and personal

God, then it is more likely to constitute a positive support to the strenuous life. This is the image of God which James amplifies in his highly influential *The Pluralistic Universe*. It was an image of God which later received much more explicit philosophical articulation in the writings of A. N. Whitehead and Charles Hartshorne.[107] But we often forget that James gave the outlines of this important vision of God years before Whitehead and his disciple Hartshorne set forth their more refined versions. It was a God both consistent with the major witness of the Judeo-Christian tradition as well as the special contours of James's philosophical anthropology. It was a God which corresponded with the ethical self and the pluralistic and changing universe which James depicts throughout his writings. James first defines this God in contrast to the God of philosophical and mystical monism. It is a God who is *not* equivalent to the whole of the universe, who is *not* the author of everything (both the good and the bad), and who is *not* the immovable, self-caused, omniscient, and omnipotent God of classical philosophical theism.[108] Rather, he is the supreme although finite God of practical religion who is allied with the ideal forces of the universe, who inspires and supports our highest ethical acts, who is not the creator of the world's evil, who is enriched by the contributions and service of finite men, and who, all in all, corresponds to and requires the strenuous life.[109] Mystical communication with *this* God supports the active and ethically heroic life required to survive and flourish in a pluralistic and changing world. And James would add, mystical union with *this* God would be a positive aid to creative life in the context of modernity. James's overbelief about the nature of God includes the data of the mystical state, but it also conforms to the requirements of general experience in an evolving and multifaceted world—a world which demands a moral response from an individual, finite, and evolving self.

James's mysticism stands in the tradition of the West as this tradition has been so successfully illuminated by Rudolph Otto in his *Mysticism East and West*.[110] It is a mysticism placed within the contours of a broader religious tradition with strong ethical and active overtones. It is also a theistic as opposed to a monistic mysticism. James's attack on philosophical monisms of all kinds also can be applied to any variety of monistic mysticism. In this respect, James's view of mysticism should not be considered so much pro-Western and anti-Eastern as pro-theistic and anti-monistic in its biases. The differences between monistic and theistic mysticism cut across the distinctions between East and West. R. C. Zaehner writes in his seminal *Mysticism Sacred and Profane,*

> Here, then, are two distinct and mutually opposed types of mysticism—the monist and the theistic. This is not a question of Christianity and Islam versus Hinduism and Buddhism: it is an unbridgeable gulf between all those who see God as incomparably greater than oneself, though he is, at the same time, the root and ground of one's being, and those who maintain that soul and God are one and the same and that all else is pure illusion.[111]

Hence, James is against any mysticism, East or West, which blurs the distinction between God and man, good and evil, and leads humans to detached, uncommitted, and indifferent attitudes towards life. And he is supportive of any mysticism, East or West, which is encased within a theistic and ethical-type religion. Of course, for James there is little doubt that he drew his major inspiration for his understanding of such a God from the Western tradition.

The main virtue of mysticism is quite similar to the main virtue of monism in any of its forms. Both offer a framework of security which enables humans to relax momentarily from the rigors of the strenuous life. In his essay "The Gospel of Relaxation," James writes that the "sovereign cure" for the worrisome and overanxious life is "religious faith." "The really religious person," he tells us, "is unshakable and full of equanimity, and calmly ready for any duty that the day may bring forth."[112] In his later brief essay "The Absolute and the Strenuous Life," James tells us that human beings living the strenuous life need to grant themselves "moral holidays" and "provisional breathing-spells, intended to refresh us for the morrow's fight."[113] Monism with its all-encompassing and immutable absolute offers this to the strenuous life. Mysticism with its emphasis upon the affirming presence of God offers it as well. In the end, James transmutes these pragmatic values of monism and mysticism by subsuming them under a broader theism which envisions a transcendent, finite, yet highly sympathic God who can enter into our experience without blotting our identities or absorbing our individualities into a static and motionless whole.

Without intending to give a defense of the usefulness of the Western religious tradition for the dynamic character of the modern world, James's overall direction of his psychological and philosophical writings does just this. This tradition and its God could give modern persons the ethical demand needed for the strenuous life; in addition, it can convey the mystical security, relaxation, and sense of oneness required to keep the strenuous life from degenerating into a hypertensive activism which is ultimately both personally and socially destructive. In a day when new forms of mysticism have been discovered, when people all over the Western world are clamoring for the "deep rest" and inner transcendence from the terrors of pervasive historical change which it offers, James's perspective can offer a welcome sense of balance. Mysticism must always be in the service of the strenuous life; it must never become a narcisstic end in itself. Since many commentators are calling the 1970s a decade of "narcissism," the call for the strenuous life which pulls us out of ourselves and leads us to energetic participation in the world is certainly in order. The quietistic and narcissistic impulses of some of our more popular psychologies is now becoming apparent to the general public. Sometimes this takes on quasi-monistic overtones as it does in Maslow's descriptions of peak experiences and his suggestion that these experiences may be a key to reality itself. Sometimes this mystical and monistic impulse appears in the tendency of the culture of joy to collapse the self into the biologically based actualization tendency and to make the tendency into a nearly immanent principle of sacred power. James, however, started in a different direction, and had the modern psychologies been responsive to his leadership, the central cultural impact of these disciplines might have been different.

In the closing lines of his provocative book entitled *The Human Prospect*, Robert Heilbroner argues that modern individuals must move from finding their mythical model in Prometheus to the solitary and overburdened Hercules, who carries the world on his shoulders. This, he believes, is the attitude moderns must take in order to address the great economic, ecological, and social challenges of the next one hundred years. In choosing such an image, Heilbroner is searching for a way to suggest the values of the strenuous life as envisioned by James. Hercules, in all his brute power and lack of sympathy and intelligence, would hardly have been James's candidate for a model. But James is a resource for the kind of image of human beings Heilbroner hopes will emerge in the modern world. We now are beginning to recognize that the slight advantages of modernity come at a high price. For just a small improvement in health care, education, convenience, speed of transport, and protection from the ravages of our environments, we must pay with a high level of active responsibility, adaptive flexibility, and stamina. James understood this in a way few psychologists have before or since his day. And this is because he was not only a psychologist, but a philosopher, ethicist, and student of religion as well. It is the richness of his points of view and the fullness of the synthesis he created which gives his vision such power today.

Notes

1. Paul Ricoeur, *The Symbolism of Evil* (New York: Harpers, 1966).

2. Cushing Strout, "The Pluralistic Identity of William James," *American Quarterly* 23 (May 1971):149.

3. William James, ed., *The Literary Remains of the Late Henry James* (Boston: James R. Osgood and Co., 1885).

4. There are several important anthologies on the scholarly and scientific study of altered states of consciousness. See Bernard Aaronson and Humphry Asmon, eds., *Psychedelics* (New York: Anchor Books, 1970); Charles Tart, ed., *Altered States of Consciousness* (New York: Anchor Books, 1972); John White, ed., *The Highest State of Consciousness* (New York: Anchor Books, 1972).

5. Arthur Danto, *Mysticism and Morality* (New York: Basic Books, 1972), p. 118.

6. Ibid., p. 119.

7. James Edie, "William James and the Phenomenology of Religious Experience," in *American Philosophy and the Future*, ed. Michael Novak (New York: Charles Scribner's Sons, 1968), pp. 247–69.

8. *VRE*, p. 22.

9. Ibid., p. 23.
10. Ibid., p. 28.
11. Ibid., p. 44.
12. Ibid., p. 354.
13. Ibid., p. 40.
14. Ibid., p. 58.
15. *VRE*, p. 61.
16. Ibid., p. 347.
17. Ibid., p. 23.
18. A. J. Ayer, *The Origins of Pragmatism* (London: Macmillan, 1968), p. 218.
19. *VRE*, p. 32.
20. *PU*, p. 269.
21. *P*, p. 177
22. *VRE*, pp. 256–91.
23. Ibid., p. 96.
24. Ibid., p. 115.
25. Ibid., p. 100.
26. Ibid., p. 104–8.
27. Ibid., pp. 76–84.
28. Ibid., p. 92.
29. Ibid., p. 93.
30. Ibid., p. 95.
31. *P*, pp. 180–82; *MT*, p. 227.
32. *MT*, p. 228; *VRE*, p. 99.
33. *TTP*, p. 110.
34. Ibid.
35. *VRE*, pp. 169, 171–72.
36. *MT*, pp. 226–28.
37. *VRE*, p. 117.
38. Ibid., p. 141.
39. Ibid., p. 126.
40. Ibid., p. 135.
41. Allen, *WJ*, p. 17.
42. *VRE*, p. 143.
43. Ibid., p. 144.
44. Ibid., p. 142.
45. Ibid., p. 143.
46. *PP*, 1:288.
47. See above, pp. 79–81.
48. *PP*, 1:139.
49. Ibid., p. 325; see above, pp. 82–83.
50. See above, pp. 157–58.
51. *VRE*, p. 137.
52. John Wild, *The Radical Empiricism of William James* (New York: Anchor Books, 1970), pp. 294–300.
53. *PP*, 1:259–71.
54. *VRE*, pp. 162–65.

55. Ibid., pp. 185–89.
56. Ibid, p. 207.
57. Ibid., p. 207.
58. Ibid., p. 216.
59. Ibid., pp. 216–17.
60. Ibid., pp. 217–18.
61. Ibid., p. 221.
62. Ibid., p. 289.
63. Ibid., p. 288.
64. Ibid., p. 289.
65. Ibid., p. 289.
66. Ibid., p. 289.
67. Ibid.
68. Ibid., p. 275.
69. Ibid., p. 276.
70. Ibid., p. 281.
71. Ibid., p. 282.
72. Ibid., p. 281.
73. Ibid., p. 282.
74. *VRE*, p. 288.
75. Ibid., p. 284.
76. Ibid.
77. Gay Allen tells of what must be considered a mystical experience which James had while camping one night in the Adirondack mountains. See Allen, *William James* (New York: The Viking Press, 1967), pp. 390–91.
78. *VRE*, p. 293.
79. Ibid., p. 298.
80. Ibid.
81. Ibid., p. 306.
82. Ibid., p. 303.
83. Ibid., p. 319.
84. Ibid., p. 385.
85. Ibid., p. 300.
86. Ibid., p. 305.
87. Ibid., p. 298.
88. Ibid.
89. Ibid., p. 188.
90. Ibid., pp. 162–64.
91. *CRE*, pp. 500–13.
92. Ibid., p. 503.
93. Ibid., p. 505.
94. R. Fischer, "A Cartography of the Ecstatic Mind," *Science* 174 (November 1971): 898–905.
95. Ibid., p. 366.
96. Ibid., p. 386.
97. Ibid., p. 388.
98. *PP*, 1:316.

99. Robert Ornstein, *The Psychology of Consciousness* (San Francisco: W. H. Frieman and Co., 1972); Harold H. Bloomfield, et. al., *TM: Discovering Inner Energy and Overcoming Stress* (New York: Dell Publishing Co., 1975), pp. 87–113.

100. *VRE*, p. 348.

101. Ibid., p. 324.

102. Ibid., p. 377.

103. Ibid., p. 326.

104. Ibid., p. 317.

105. Ibid.

106. Ibid., p. 318.

107. A. N. Whitehead, *Process and Reality* (New York: Harper Brothers, 1960), p. 519; Charles Harshorne, *Reality as Social Process* (Boston: Beacon Press, 1953), pp. 110–28, 155–62.

108. *PW*, pp. 265–78.

109. Ibid.

110. Rudolph Otto, *Mysticism East and West* (New York: Meridian Books, 1957).

111. R. C. Zaehner, *Mysticism Sacred and Profane* (Oxford University Press, 1971), p. 204.

112. *TT*, p. 110.

113. *MT*, p. 228.

Bibliography

Ayer, A. J. *The Origins of Pragmatism*. London: Macmillan, 1968.

Becker, Ernest. *The Denial of Death*. New York: The Free Press, 1973.

Berger, Peter, and Luckmann, Thomas. *The Social Construction of Reality*. New York: Anchor Press, 1967.

Browning, Don S. *Generative Man*. New York: Delta Books, 1975.

Campbell, Donald. "Blind Variation and Selective Retention in Creative Thought as in other Knowledge Processes," *Psychological Review* 67 (1960): 380–400.

———. "On the Genetics of Altruism and the Counter-hedonic Components in Human Culture," *Journal of Social Issues* 28 (1972): 21–37.

Clebsch, William. *American Religious Thought: A History*. Chicago: The University of Chicago Press, 1973.

Danto, Arthur. *Mysticism and Morality*. New York: Basic Books, 1972.

Durkheim, Emile. *De la Division Travail Social*. Paris: Felix Alcan, 1893.

Erikson, Erik H. *Childhood and Society*. New York: W. W. Norton, 1963.

———. *Identity: Youth and Crisis*. New York: W. W. Norton, 1968.

———. *Insight and Responsibility*. New York: W. W. Norton, 1964.

Frankena, William. *Ethics*. Englewood Cliffs, N.J.: Prentice-Hall, 1973.

Freud, Sigmund. *Beyond the Pleasure Principle*. New York: Bantam Books, 1963.

———. *Civilization and Its Discontents*. New York: W. W. Norton, 1942.

———. *The Ego and the Id*. London: Hogarth Press, 1957.

———. *The Future of an Illusion*. New York: Anchor Books, 1964.

271

————. *A General Introduction to Psychoanalysis.* New York: Washington Square Press, 1960.

————. *Group Psychology and the Analysis of the Ego.* New York: Bantam Books, 1960.

————. *New Introductory Lectures.* New York: W. W. Norton, 1960.

Fromm, Erich. *The Art of Loving.* New York: Harper and Brothers, 1956.

————. *Man for Himself.* New York: Rinehart and Company, 1960.

————. *The Revolution of Hope.* New York: Bantam Books, 1968.

Geertz, Clifford. *The Interpretation of Cultures.* New York: Basic Books, 1973.

Goldstein, Kurt. *The Organism.* Boston: Beacon Press, 1963.

Gurwitsch, Aron. *The Field of Consciousness.* Pittsburgh: Duquesne University Press, 1964.

————. *Studies in Phenomenology and Psychology.* Evanston, Ill.: Northwestern University Press, 1966.

Hancock, Roger, *Twentieth Century Ethics.* New York: Columbia University Press, 1974.

Hartmann, Heinz. *Essays on Ego-Psychology.* New York: International Universities Press, 1964.

Hartshorne, Charles. *Reality as Social Process.* Boston: Beacon Press, 1953.

Hofstadter, Richard. *Social Darwinism in American Thought.* Boston: Beacon Press, 1971.

Hughes, H. Stuart. *Consciousness and Society.* Frogmore: Paladin, 1974.

Husserl, Edmund. *Phenomenology and the Crisis of Philosophy.* New York: Harper and Row, 1965.

James, William. *Collected Essays and Reviews.* New York: Russell and Russell, 1969.

————. *Essays in Radical Empiricism* and *A Pluralistic Universe.* New York: E. P. Dutton and Co., 1971.

————. *The Letters of William James* 2 vols. Ed. by Henry James. Boston: The Atlantic Monthly Press, 1920.

————. *The Meaning of Truth.* Ann Arbor, Mich.: University of Michigan Press, 1970.

————. *The Moral Equivalent of War and Other Essays.* New York: Harper and Row, 1971.

———. *Pragmatism*. New York: The World Publishing Co., 1970.

———. *The Principles of Psychology*. 2 vols. New York: Dover Publications, 1950.

———. *Psychology: The Briefer Course*. New York: Harper Torchbooks, 1961.

———. "Some Problems of Philosophy," in *The Moral Equivalent of War and Other Essays*. New York: Harper and Row, 1971.

———. *Talks to Teachers on Psychology*. New York: Dover Publications, 1962.

———. *Varieties of Religious Experience*. New York: Bantam Books, 1950.

———. *The Will to Believe*. New York: Dover Publications, 1956.

Lifton, Robert. *Boundaries: Psychological Man in Revolution*. New York: Random House, 1970.

Linschoten, Hans. *On the Way Towards a Phenomenological Psychology*. Pittsburgh: Duquesne University Press, 1968.

Lorenz, Konrad. *On Aggression*. New York: Bantam Books, 1969.

MacLeod, Robert, *William James: Unfinished Business*. Washington, D.C.: American Psychological Association, 1969.

MacMurry, John. *The Self as Agent*. London: Faber and Faber, 1957.

Marcell, David. *Progress and Pragmatism*. Westport, Conn.: Greenwood Press, 1974.

Maslow, Abraham. *Motivation and Personality*. New York: Harper and Brothers, 1954.

———. *Toward a Psychology of Being*. New York: D. Van Nostrand Co., 1962.

Mathieson, O. F. *The James Family*. New York: Alfred A. Knopf, 1948.

May, Rollo. *Love and Will*. London: Fontana Library, 1972.

Mead, George Herbert. *Mind, Self, and Society*. Chicago: University of Chicago Press, 1934.

Morris, Charles. *Paths of Life*. Chicago: University of Chicago Press, 1972.

Offer, Daniel, and Sabshin, Melvin. *Normality*. New York: Basic Books, 1974.

Ornstein, Robert. *The Psychology of Consciousness*. San Francisco: W. H. Frieman and Co., 1972.

274   PLURALISM AND PERSONALITY

Otto, Rudolph. *Mysticism East and West.* New York: Meridian Books, 1957.

Parson, Talcott. *Social Structure and Personality.* New York: The Free Press, 1965.

Peacock, James. *Consciousness and Change.* New York: John Wiley, 1975.

Perls, Frederick; Hefferline, Ralph; and Goodman, Paul. *Gestalt Therapy.* New York: Dell Publishing Co., 1951.

Perry, Ralph Barton. *The Thought and Character of William James.* 2 vols. Boston: Little, Brown, and Co., 1935.

Popper, Karl. *Objective Knowledge.* Oxford: Clarendon Press, 1972.

Ricoeur, Paul. *Freud and Philosophy.* New Haven, Conn.: Yale University Press, 1970.

————. *The Symbolism of Evil.* New York: Harpers, 1966.

————. *The Voluntary and the Involuntary.* Evanston, Ill.: Northwestern University Press, 1966.

Rieff, Philip. *Freud: The Mind of the Moralist.* New York: Doubleday and Co., 1961.

————. *The Triumph of the Therapeutic.* New York: Harper and Row, 1966.

Rogers, Carl. *Client-Centered Therapy.* Boston: Houghton Mifflin Co., 1957.

————. *On Becoming a Person.* Boston: Houghton Mifflin Co., 1961.

Rogers, Carl, and Stevens, Barry. *Person to Person.* New York: Pocket Books, 1975.

Sartre, Jean Paul. *The Transcendence of the Ego.* New York: Farrar, Strauss, and Giroux, 1957.

Schutz, Alfred. *Alfred Schutz: Collected Papers.* 3 vols. The Hague: Martinus Nijhoff, 1966.

Schutz, William. *Joy: Expanding Human Awareness.* New York: Grove Press, 1967.

Skinner, B. F. *About Behaviorism.* London: Jonathan Cape, 1974.

————. *Beyond Freedom and Dignity.* New York: Bantam Books, 1972.

————. *Science and Human Behavior.* New York: The Free Press, 1953.

Smith, Brewster. *Humanizing Social Psychology.* San Francisco: Josey-Bass, 1974.

Spiegelberg, Herbert. *The Phenomenological Movement.* 2 vols. The Hague: Martinus Nijhoff, 1960.

Stevens, Richard. *James and Husserl: The Foundations of Meaning.* The Hague: Martinus Nijhoff, 1974.

Sullivan, Harry Stack. *The Interpersonal Theory of Psychology.* New York: W. W. Norton, 1953.

Turner, Victor. *The Ritual Process.* Chicago: The University of Chicago Press, 1969.

Watson, J. B. *Psychology from the Standpoint of a Behaviorist.* Philadelphia: Lippincott, 1917.

White, Robert. *Ego and Reality in Psychoanalytic Theory.* New York: International Universities Press, 1963.

Whitehead, Alfred North. *Process and Reality.* New York: Harper Brothers, 1960.

Wild, John. *The Radical Empiricism of William James.* New York: Anchor Books, 1970.

Wilshire, Bruce. *William James and Phenomenology.* Bloomington, Ind.: Indiana University Press, 1968.

Zaehner, R. C. *Mysticism Sacred and Profane.* Oxford: Oxford University Press, 1971.

Index

276